VISIONS OF INVASION

RACE, RHETORIC, AND MEDIA SERIES
Davis W. Houck, General Editor

VISIONS OF INVASION

Alien Affects, Cinema, and
Citizenship in Settler Colonies

MICHAEL LECHUGA

University Press of Mississippi / Jackson

The University Press of Mississippi is the scholarly publishing agency of
the Mississippi Institutions of Higher Learning: Alcorn State University,
Delta State University, Jackson State University, Mississippi State University,
Mississippi University for Women, Mississippi Valley State University,
University of Mississippi, and University of Southern Mississippi.

www.upress.state.ms.us

The University Press of Mississippi is a member of
the Association of University Presses.

Copyright © 2023 by University Press of Mississippi
All rights reserved

First printing 2023

∞

Library of Congress Cataloging-in-Publication Data

Names: Lechuga, Michael, author.
Title: Visions of invasion : alien affects, cinema, and citizenship in settler colonies /
Michael Lechuga.
Other titles: Race, rhetoric, and media series.
Description: Jackson : University Press of Mississippi, 2023. | Series: Race, rhetoric,
and media series | Includes bibliographical references and index.
Identifiers: LCCN 2022043331 (print) | LCCN 2022043332 (ebook) | ISBN
9781496844057 (hardback) | ISBN 9781496844064 (trade paperback) | ISBN
9781496844071 (epub) | ISBN 9781496844088 (epub) | ISBN 9781496844095 (pdf) |
ISBN 9781496844101 (pdf)
Subjects: LCSH: Citizenship in motion pictures. | Immigrants in motion pictures. |
Extraterrestrial beings in motion pictures. | Criticism.
Classification: LCC PN1995.9.C5128 L43 2023 (print) | LCC PN1995.9.C5128 (ebook) |
DDC 791.43/652691—dc23/eng/20221223
LC record available at https://lccn.loc.gov/2022043331
LC ebook record available at https://lccn.loc.gov/2022043332

British Library Cataloging-in-Publication Data available

Dedicated to María del Carmen Carlos-Alarcón, mi abuelita

CONTENTS

Acknowledgments IX

Introduction 3

Chapter One: *The War of the Worlds* and Alien Making 27

Chapter Two: *Predator* Assemblages 47

Chapter Three: *Men in Black* Assemblages 74

Chapter Four: *Sleep Dealer*, Nomadic Assemblages, and
    Deterritorializations 104

Conclusion 129

Notes 138

Bibliography 162

Index 176

ACKNOWLEDGMENTS

I would briefly like to thank a number of people whose support and kindness over the years made it possible to complete this book. Anais Lechuga, my partner, and my daughter, Maia Zen Yaretzi, are my first community; I love you and thank you. I would like to thank my mom, Hilda Alarcon, who despite my most adamant pleas refused to pick me up from my dormitory halfway through my first semester of college after I decided I wanted to drop out. She convinced me to unpack my bags and finish that semester then and has done so all the semesters since. She has always been my champion. My father and brothers—Tony Lechuga, Anthony Lechuga, and Chris Lechuga—thank you for loving and supporting me, even though I am the weird middle child. To the friends whose Zoom calls, texts, and *chisme* kept me going—Oso, Fideo, Perrito, Fernie, El Cartero, Aaron, Elias, Atilla, and Bo—thank you. Your support means the world.

I have had so many teachers in my life who have inspired me, both in school and in community. I cannot possibly thank you all. I do want to thank Darrin Hicks and Thomas Nail for their mentorship and guidance, and also my friends and colleagues Christina Foust and Kate Willink. Also, Paula Martin, thank you so, so much for being a light. Thank you, Guillermo Glenn and Tierra es Vida Community Farm, for showing me how to reconnect with earth. During my time at the University of Texas at El Paso, the University of Minnesota, and now the University of New Mexico, I have had many colleagues, students, and friends who have supported my work. I cannot possibly name all of you, but I am grateful for each of you.

I have been lucky to come alongside two mentors in recent years. Without your support and continued encouragement, I could not have found the strength to get through some of the more challenging parts of this process. Catherine Squires, I want to say thank you in particular for the immense kindness you have shown me and my family and for supporting my work. Your greatness as a scholar is dwarfed by your greatness as a human. Kent Ono, I would also like to say thanks from the softest part of my heart for all your support and mentorship. When someone believes in you, it's transformative.

Finally, thanks to the folks at *Capacious: A Journal for Emerging Affect Inquiry* and especially Greg Seigworth for being a supporter of my work over the years. Portions of this book first appeared in the inaugural issue of the journal, which provides a platform for emerging scholars who speak across cultural studies disciplines. I would also like to thank the Obermann Center for Advanced Studies at the University of Iowa for hosting the 2018 Workshop in Latina/o/x Studies, where portions of this book were developed. And of course, thanks to the editorial team at the University Press of Mississippi for opening an avenue for my scholarship and for the other scholars in this series who work at the intersections of race, cultural studies, media studies, and rhetoric. I am grateful to have my work included.

VISIONS OF INVASION

Figures I.1a, I.1b, I.1c, and I.1d. Series of film stills from Steven Spielberg's 2005 *War of the Worlds*; Ray (Tom Cruise) is covered in the ashes of a woman who was vaporized by one of the aliens' laser beams.

INTRODUCTION

In June 2005, in the wake of the *Final Report of the National Commission on Terrorist Attacks upon the United States* (casually referred to as the *9/11 Report*), director Steven Spielberg's version of *War of the Worlds* made its debut in the United States.[1] The film's protagonists play out H. G. Wells's classic narrative, but this time set in a post-9/11 United States, where terrorism and alienhood have become synonymous. Critics quickly pointed to the ways Spielberg relied on 9/11 iconography to retell Wells's tale, Spielberg himself saying: "I wouldn't have done *War of the Worlds* if it weren't for 9/11."[2] Take one of the film's early scenes, in which Ray (played by Tom Cruise) and hundreds of others encounter a towering CGI tripod armed with heat ray weapons that vaporize nearly everyone to ash. Images of ash raining down on bodies are stunning reminders of the images from the World Trade Center attack (fig. I.1). In a later scene, as Ray's white, suburban family is fleeing New York City, his teenage son, Robbie (Justin Chatwin), asks him: "What is it? Is it terrorists?"[3] Reviving the *War of the Worlds* narrative in the wake of 9/11 gave US audiences a story that aligned the migrant alien figure with the figure of the international terrorist. While this connection was made a year earlier in the *9/11 Report*, Spielberg was able to reproduce popular political attitudes toward migrants and terrorists in a narrative form already familiar to and readily consumed by US audiences: the extraterrestrial invasion film.[4]

The fictional alien, a settler colonial subjectivity that is manufactured and distributed in the US, has evolved over time. From its original invocation in the Alien and Sedition Acts (a set of four laws passed in 1798 by the Federalist government under President John Adams), the US government has tried to curb opportunities for nonwhite migrants to become citizens. These acts largely began as an effort to discourage France and its foreign allies from "interfering in American domestic politics" and allowed for the US to imprison migrants who were considered a threat to early white, settler colonial nationalism—namely those who were not of white, northwestern European ethnicity.[5] Since its separation from Europe, the US settler state has been producing political subjections of certain foreigners as criminal aliens, justifying their imprisonment and removal. This practice of organizing migrants into groups of acceptable and unacceptable peoples based on perceived race and nationality continues to be the primary mode of migrant control in the US. Now, thanks to both Hollywood and the US military-industrial complex, the alien figure today is seen and heard, not just described in text. Alien affects, as I contend throughout this book, are the sensory intensities that are contrived by technologies of visibility to accompany the tales of alien invasion that are built into the architecture of the US settler nation.

While nearly everyone migrates, transnational migrants, who often cross oceans, rivers, and invisible national and state borders, are distinct from those who might move across the country for a better job or even those who move around town to be closer to their work.[6] University students often migrate around the country to seek a better opportunity for economic advancement. Families move to put their children in better schools, again, with the aim seeking a better economic opportunity. Some migrate daily from suburbia to metropolitan centers to work in large office buildings and then return home at the end of the day. Just as migration in nature is an essential part of the ecological sustainability of many species, human migration drives the sustainability of our international communities.[7] So, the localized micromigrations of everyday people are not so different from the transnational migrations of those Central American and Mexican migrants currently entering the US at the border with México. Localized and transnational migrations are both typically bound to economic waves that move jobs from sector to sector and town to town.[8] John Urry describes localized mobility—people moving daily through urban and suburban "transportation and material cultures"—and global mobility of migrant groups as components of the same network of mobilities.[9] He suggests that these networks of mobilities are also composed of "'technologies' of information and communication and the emerging infrastructures of mobility and surveillance" that bring global communities together with local communities in certain urban spaces (think Times Square).[10]

However, the forced migration of many transnational migrants creates a situation in which the US (as well as many other settler nations) dramatically limits the ability of some migrants to freely move into the nation while also making it nearly impossible to find any place to stay within the borders of that state or even on the periphery.

Central to this notion of citizenship is both the nation-state providing a single, stable and exhaustive national identity and a civil society organized around a single nation. These features [of citizenship control] ensure a nation-state that is able to striate the space surrounding it, clearly distinguishing its people and institutions inside its borders from those outside.[11]

This logic is exemplified by the US's 2019 "Remain in Mexico" policy, which was created by President Donald Trump's administration to deny asylum seekers entry at the México/US border, regardless of their nation of origin, and make them wait in privately run holding prisons in Guatemala and México to await asylum decisions.[12] Not only has the US government taken measures to control the movements of migrants inside the United States and at its borders, but now we see attempts to control the movements of migrants while they migrate through other nations.

This book focuses specifically on the extreme measures the US has taken to limit nonwhite migrants, especially those who cross the international border from México. This group of migrants is often subjected to strict surveillance, violence, and exploitation. Migration defined by international boundaries privileges citizens—those who are localized within communities inside of state boundaries, who are not forced to cross national boundaries. The stratification between the privileged citizen living in a modern colonial society and those living in today's control societies as alien figures is precisely a matter of movement: "The dimension along which those 'high up' and 'low down' are plotted in a society ... is their degree of mobility—their freedom to choose where to be."[13] For the settler citizen, borders are erased. For alien migrants, borders manifest constantly. Frequent international travel is a reality for many wealthy US Americans. Daily border crossing is common for many who live along the México/US border for business or family. However:

> For the inhabitant of the second world, the walls built of immigration controls, of residence laws and of "clean streets" and "zero tolerance" policies, grow taller; the moats separating them from the sites of their desire and of dreamed-of redemption grow deeper, while all bridges, at the first attempt to cross them, prove to be drawbridges....
> [They] travel surreptitiously, often illegally, sometimes paying more for the crowded steerage of a stinking unseaworthy boat than others pay for business-class gilded luxuries—and are frowned upon, and, if unlucky, arrested and promptly deported, when they arrive.[14]

In the US, the flow of migrants from Central America and México, those who often enter without authorization, are those from Zygmunt Bauman's second world—those who are seen as an imminent threat to the constitutive citizenship paradigm.[15] In response to that perceived threat, the US assembles and distributes numerous military and industrial technologies on the México/US border and in local communities to grow the moats of division that shape our modern society. For me, this insurmountable barrier is most evident at the México/US boundary, where, currently, the US continues investing law enforcement and military resources to administer strict local, state, and federal immigration laws that designate migrants as alien and channel them into migrant control apparatuses where they become institutionalized in state systems of detention, deportation, and even death. This logic divides children from their parents at the border.[16] It leads to the deaths of countless migrants intentionally diverted to the most treacherous of geographic terrains by US border security forces.[17]

Nonetheless, producing a subjective alien as a political figure defines US domestic and foreign attitudes toward nonwhite, non-English speaking peoples.[18] In this book, I demonstrate how the US focus on immigration control is rooted in a legacy of fabricating and spreading false narratives of invasive aliens to justify the securitization of the settlement. The figural aliens manufactured in today's US, however, are not just literary or legal; they are figures manufactured with what I call technologies of visibility—surveillance, cinema, and other imaging technologies. As such, today's alien is not just a discursive figure but one who has been produced to engage our visual and aural senses.

Therefore, *Visions of Invasion* is a critical examination of both the political logics that imagine alien/noncitizen personae and the technologies that materialize and mediate alienhood as a political subjectivity. US extraterrestrial invasion cinema and US border security mechanisms are akin: they are layering visible alienhood onto expression of articulable belonging with the help of advanced digital surveillance technologies. These expressions (re)tell an old tale of a foreign threat in order to maintain white nationalism and settler wealth accumulation modes in the US. This book is concerned mostly with the US version of colonialism: a hypercapitalist settler colonialism, which has created its own version of the alien figure—one that plays out the anxieties of colonial retribution. I argue throughout the book (1) that this alien subjectivity appears across the spectrum of political and popular communication in the US; and (2) that this is evidence of a more sinister plot: an intentional process of population production to subject settler noncitizens (what I will refer to as antitypes in this book) to the exploitative violence of today's settler situation. Studying the subjections of migrants as aliens in this way provides insight into the logics of contemporary settler governance in the US while uncovering how settler colonial ideologies materialize as ongoing violences against Black, Indigenous, and Mestiza/o/x communities.

In political terms, the production of a seeable, hearable, or feelable (or otherwise sense-able) alienhood on bodies that migrate into and through our communities materializes the fantastical anxieties of invasion that are ubiquitous in US politics and popular culture. This brings me to the concept of "alien affects." Sara Ahmed uses the term (as well as the term "affect aliens") in describing the ways alienation is a felt reality for many. For her, an "affect alien is one who converts good feelings into bad."[19] She continues: "[T]o be an affect alien is to experience alien affects—to be out of line with the public mood, not to feel the way others feel in response to an event."[20] Her use of the term "alien affects" is also embedded in a migration context, where alienhood is a feeling of dissonance one experiences in relation to the national affects of a particular space. Ahmed's definition relies on a conception of affects as a register of feeling, where one feels with or against a particular set of cultural, political, social, and national sentiments. My definition for alien affects differs slightly. For me, alien affects are intensities of alienhood that are projected onto bodies of migrants as they move through occupied national territories; they are the visual articulations of noncitizenship planted on bodies that are produced by surveillance technologies. They are intensive movements, qualitative sensations of noticeable difference.[21] They are material forms of political communication that subject people into dehumanized personae. Alien affects are not intrinsic to the body; they are emergent properties attributed to an individual by a citizenship control system that code them as alien in order to move them into a particular flow of control—a flow that for migrants typically leads toward exploitation, apprehension, detention, deportation, and even death.

My goal in *Visions of Invasion*, then, is to demonstrate why *and* how the figural alien subject is manufactured in the US today. Alien making is a political expression of belonging and nonbelonging. Alien affects—those perceived heightened intensities that are cast onto bodies of migrants, nomads, refugees, and others—recode humans as noncitizens in the eyes of the settler state. For example, this book looks at how extraterrestrial literary, film, and television franchises like *War of the Worlds* are continually recycling themselves to imagine the most contemporary visions of alien invasion in the US (and the United Kingdom, for that matter). This, as the extreme political right in the United States recycles former president Ronald Reagan's anti-immigrant tropes of "law and order" to excuse the genocidal subjection of migrants to inhumane treatment at the México/US border. I account for not only the frequent rebooting of alien film franchises like *Predator* and *Men in Black*, but also the frequent recycling of antimigrant tropes in border politics and in communities throughout the country. In fact, I suggest that they are two expressions of the same settler colonial logic of population economics; alien making is and has always been a mechanism of settler nationalism.

To answer the question of *how* alien affects are manufactured, I describe how today's expressions of alienhood are produced through highly developed digital technologies of visibility. These technologies are components in what I am calling the citizenship control assemblage. They interact with the other material and human components of the assemblage, which are all organized by the logics found in legalistic and juridical expressions of the US's settler colonial constitutive citizenship paradigm. Using an assemblage framework allows me to examine the precarious relationships between the industries creating alien affects in cinema and industries producing alien affects in bordering apparatuses, to get at the underlying logics that link them. The trafficking of alien affects in popular film and in popular politics fits into a larger network of logics, personae, and technologies that keep migrants caught in cycles of exploitive violence in order to prop up a settler economy. Simply put, *Visions of Invasion* explains how alien affects are produced, trafficked, and recycled to protect settler colonial control over occupied lands.

Thus, I look at three arenas where a citizenship control assemblage manufactures alienhood: Hollywood extraterrestrial film, federal antimigration and border security legislation, and various immigration enforcement protocols implemented along the México/US border. The mechanisms from these three sites, including and especially technologies of visibility, are the working parts of the citizenship control assemblage described in this book—mechanisms that have been organized by a communicable ideology of settler colonialism that codes the bodies of migrants as alien, territorializes the México/US borderlands, and then reproduces the dominant modes of citizenship production. This process—an interconnected, material, and ideological assemblage-in-motion—distributes control over the territories now called the United States and the people who live in those territories.

For example, in chapter 2, I describe how the Reagan administration reproduced its version of the alien persona to narrate an imminent threat at the México/US border. In doing so, the administration territorialized the borderland by deploying a flow of alien production technologies—what I call "*Predator* technologies" because of their association with the popular Hollywood film franchise—to the border, where they remain today. Then, the Bill Clinton administration reproduced the figural alien yet again, this time to narrate an imminent threat that was already in cities and towns all over the country. This narration initiated a nationwide deployment of alien production technologies—the "*Men in Black* technologies" discussed in chapter 3—which eventually became the infrastructure for the Department of Homeland Security's management over today's settler citizenship population economy. Then, under the Trump administration, technologies of alien production were again redeployed, but this time in an attempt to also produce alien antitypes out of those protesting police brutality against Black communities—most of whom were US citizens.

As I describe in chapter 1, there is something about that colonial anxiety of becoming colonized that can be found throughout the genre of alien invasion narratives. This book is a deep dive into that dynamic, looking specifically at how the figure of the alien has been manufactured through media technologies as a political subjectivity, one that plays out the anxieties, guilts, and fears of colonialism. Underneath each of the film franchises and antimigrant political expressions described in *Visions of Invasion* lies an anxious logic that drives the settler's obsession to manufacture a false invasion from abroad that may pose an existential threat to the settler way of life. Beyond just describing how the invasion narrative circulates in popular media, though, this book also describes how this anxious logic materializes in technologies of visibility—tools developed and trafficked to surveil migrant movements, rendering them as "alien" threats visible to US settler citizens in films, on battlegrounds, at the border, and throughout the nation. Producing these two dynamics—the seeable and sayable threat—are the components of alien making I describe throughout the book.

ALIENHOOD, MIGRATION RHETORIC, AND MEDIA STUDIES

Visions of Invasion pulls from a number of theories to offer a glimpse of the processes of alien making and how they contribute to an ongoing settler colonial project in the United States. Namely, this work builds on rhetorical studies theories and media studies theories to suggest that scholars in each field take more seriously how popular culture texts—like extraterrestrial invasion films—interact and inform political rhetorics about migrants, "terrorists," felons, and other noncitizen groups that are often vilified in public discourse. The second feature of *Visions of Invasion* is its engagement with settler colonial theory to describe a colonial production model that serves as the cultural backdrop on which alien invasion narratives are produced and circulated. Finally, this book affirms the need for a study of rhetorical materialism, especially in light of the technological methods of subjection I describe throughout. Again, defining citizenship control in terms of assemblages allows me to articulate a materialist rhetorical method that can illuminate the complex relationships between industries that manufacture border security technologies and industries that build cinematic technologies for today's Hollywood films.

RHETORIC, VISIBILITY, AND THE SUBJECTIVE MIGRANT

Throughout *Visions of Invasion*, I articulate the ways US Americans see, describe, and think about aliens. I build on research that questions how representations of aliens in film and television reflect the national(ist) attitudes toward migrants from Central America and México.[22] Ultimately, the goal of this book is to describe how a citizenship control logic assembles technologies to code migrants as aliens, perpetuating a mythic tale of inevitable invasion at the core of settler colonial consciousness. I argue throughout the book that this is a rhetorical practice of casting bodies as political personae, organizing them to "autoproduce" the sets of relationships that cultivate settler colonial modes of exploitation and expulsion.[23] My interest in how citizenship control assemblages use technologies of visibility to code bodies speaks to the first engagement the book makes with rhetorical studies: thinking about how citizenship control in the US materializes subjective alienhood on migrant bodies. Current research in rhetorical studies in the US already focuses on how migrant subjectivities are created and communicated, from public address about migration or social movement rhetorics emerging from within pro-migrant activism.[24] *Visions of Invasion* adds to this dialogue by describing the mechanisms that produce alienhood on migrant bodies. This process is rhetorical in its capacity to imagine and project a figural alien subjectivity, then have the capacity to connect that subjectivity to a migrating body onto which codes of control are attached. In short, this study adds to a body of literature that explains how state power is moved onto migrant bodies through various processes of subjection.

To make the case that power is communicated materially and multidimensionally in the US, I start with assumption that power is productive: "[P]ower produces; it produces reality, it produces domains of objects and rituals of truth. The individual and the knowledge that may be gained of him belong to this production."[25] Knowledge production, in this orientation, is power production.[26] Not only that, but knowledge/power is produced to materially invoke subjectivity. "With disciplinary power, the increase of power and the formation of knowledge reinforce one another in a circular process. As power increases, individuals are increasingly specified, hence allowing greater knowledge of those individuals, which, in turn, reinforces power."[27] A subject is knowable precisely because it has been produced to be known by those in power.

Knowledge/power is composed of two forms: "things and words, from seeing and speaking, from the visible to the sayable, from the bands of visibility and the fields of readability, from contents and expressions."[28] They rely on one another; they prop each other up. The visible aspects of the truth, though, are not primary to statements, nor are they reducible to statements. "Knowledge is a practical assemblage, a 'mechanism' of statements and visibilities."[29] They are two dimensions of the same material. In the case of alien making, this means that for an alien subjectivity to be known, it must be produced as an articulable and a feelable entity. Each layer is part of the other, the affective modulating the discursive and the discursive modulating the affective. Thus, lights and cameras (the technologies of visibility described throughout the book) do not illuminate subjects; they produce subjectivities.

The prison, for example, is a surveillance machine organized by the diagram of state power to produce the subject of the articulable penal code: the criminal.[30] Power is not exercised through simply naming the content of the visible; rather, power is exercised through the illumination of the content. The prison "is the form of content since it is a way of acting on and organizing bodies. It is a system of light that constitutes a new way of displaying crime."[31] It is precisely the illumination of the criminal subject with the subsequent articulation of crime that emboldens this diagram of power; the panoptic institution's technological architecture is the visibility mechanism of this otherwise invisible set of forces. I suggest that this dynamic is also true of the alien subjectivity, produced by the lights of border security apparatuses as invader to fit the settler colonial trope.

Simply put, "[v]isibility is a trap."[32] The architectural apparatuses of discipline function in societies to illuminate, alienate, and isolate individuals while giving them the sense they are under constant surveillance.[33] "Light ... is theorised by Foucault not as a medium of emancipation but explicitly as a medium of entrapment: precisely as it enables one to be seen, it also enables one to be caught."[34] Illumination is projection; it makes things—and especially bodies—perceivable and therefore knowable to the state. Visibility and the technologies of illumination that make visibility possible are vital in theorizing the ways diagrams of state power subject migrant bodies as alien. The process of subjection embedded within the panoptic gaze—the casting of bodies with technologies of visibility to both individualize and spatially organize them—is a carry-over from the practices of surveillance in discipline societies.³⁵

While discourses are symbolic, visibilities are affective. "Visibilities are not forms of objects, nor even forms that would show up under light, but rather forms of luminosity which are created by the light itself and allow a thing or object to exist as a flash, sparkle or shimmer."³⁶ In citizenship control assemblages, the figure of the alien migrant is lit up with forms of luminosity that make its body shimmer with alien affects.³⁷ This affective subjection links with the settler colonial legal codes of constitutive citizenship to subject the migrant as alien. *Visions of Invasion* provides readers with a vocabulary to describe how visible expressions of power are both produced and distributed through a citizenship control system in coordination with citizenship codes that subject migrant (and other) bodies as noncitizen alien in order to organize them into sets of exploitative relationships.

SETTLER PRODUCTION MODES AND TRAFFICKING NARRATIVE TECHNOLOGIES

Throughout *Visions of Invasion*, I suggest that the purpose of organizing citizens and noncitizens into sets of exploitative relationships comes down to the desire of the US government to reproduce settler colonial modes of production. Citizenship control materially stratifies subjects of the constitutive citizenship paradigm into structured organizations that maintain the US's territorial occupation. This notion brings rhetorical studies on migration in conversation with cultural studies scholars who theorize settler colonialism, the second contribution this book offers to the field.

First, settler colonialism is distinct from colonialism and imperial genocide.³⁸ While mass murder and imperial coloniality are inherently tied to the structures of settler colonialism, there are specific differences in the ways coloniality is produced and the ways settler coloniality is produced, namely with regard to the production of settler colonial subjects and a sustained reproduction of territorial sovereignty. For one, research in settler colonial studies pushes scholars "to demonstrate that [settler] invasion is a structure rather than an event; that expropriation continues as a foundational characteristic of settler-colonial society."³⁹ It is not just something that happened to Native peoples on the North American continent; it is the sustained and evolving distribution of "a set of technologies . . . of alienation, separation, [and] conversion of land into property and of people into targets of subjection."⁴⁰ Moreover, these "technologies are trafficked. . . . [W]e can see a transit of empire as involving a commute of technologies *and* a translation of ideologies and logics."[41] So, settler occupation is a technological and ongoing territorializing arrangement that actively subjects bodies to suit the political and economic desires of the settlement. In other words, settler invasion is an assemblage rather than a structure or an event.

Therefore, I contend that scholars in rhetoric must take seriously the mode of settler colonial population production. In arranging a "population economy," the organizers of settler colonies express their "recurring settler anxieties pertaining to the need to biopolitically manage their respective *domestic* domains."[42] Settlers, therefore, are not migrants. They, unlike migrants, bring with them in their relocations the (anxious) desire to produce the sets of relationships between themselves, Indigenous peoples, and other migrants who do not share the same ambitions for unchallenged control over peoples and lands. Settler colonizers are also not imperial colonizers.[43] The colonial and postcolonial dualism that marks the dominant and the subaltern—the colonizer/colonized binary—is replaced in settler colonialism with the triadic dynamic between the settler subject, the Indigenous other, and the exogenous (non-Native, but not settler—this includes Indigenous Africans enslaved by Europeans, labor migrants, and those colonial loyalists with ties to Europe).[44] In order to distinguish themselves from the Indigenous persona while also breaking from the colonial European persona, the settler occupies both personae: nativizing themselves to the occupied territories while also using a racial marker of whiteness and language (and therefore Europeanness) as collectivizing characteristics. This production mode is primarily concerned with manufacturing the settler subject and its "antitypes . . . [,] or what the settler is not."[45] The settler citizen, through this dualism, maintains a perceived subjective superiority over those Indigenous peoples deemed "unassimilable" *and* those exogenous groups deemed "undesirable."[46]

In this case, the relationship between the dominant settler citizen class and the settler colonial "subaltern" is predicated on the potential for transfer. "The settler situation is thus characteristically perceived as a dynamic environment where different groups are routinely imagined as transiting from one section of the population system to the another."[47] In colonial societies, the possibility of transfer for the colonized into a class of equality with the colonizer is always postponed, organizing a permanent stratification between the groups.[48] In settler colonies, on the other hand, the machinery of oscillation between subjective inclusion and exclusion of Indigenous and exogenous groups allows the settler class to maintain its capacity to control both who is Indigenous while also controlling what kind of (other) exogenous bodies will be considered desirable (European) and granted inclusion into the settler class. The implementation of this population economy allows the settlement to organize and reorganize power, again and again, while never quite accomplishing the goal of complete erasure/expulsion of the subaltern nonsettler citizen (both Indigenous and exogenous).[49] "In other words, [simultaneous] Europeanisation and indigenisation respond to the complementary needs of transforming the environment to suit the colonising project and of renewing the settler in order to suit the environment.... [T]he 'changes in the land' inevitably correspond to the making of a 'new man.'"[50] Therefore, the production of settler subjectivities of citizen and noncitizen (Indigenous or exogenous) is inherently entwined with the production of settler territorial sovereignty and necessary to comprehend why the US is so heavily invested in alien making.

Second (as I will discuss in chapter 1), continually reproducing alien antitypes and narratives of their invasion circulates a specific type of colonial anxiety that manifests in defensiveness and violence. This is what Lorenzo Veracini refers to as a "settler consciousness," or a particular tendency of "settler colonialism [that] obscures the conditions of its own production."[51] By concealing its modes of production, settler colonialism can operate in a repeating loop, where its production modes manufacture the conditions to autoproduce settler colonial territorialization and reproduce settler subjects (along with their antitypes) with no real trajectory toward progress.[52] An amnesiac settler consciousness cloaks the preexisting subjectivities of occupation (African Indigenous, North American Indigenous, genocidal European invader, etc.) and imagines a settler subjective binary of settler citizen and noncitizen. Moreover, the settler citizen identity is defined by contrasting itself against what it is not: its antitype. The antitype noncitizen is a subjective floating identifier for those deemed (or with the potential to be deemed) undesirable by the settler citizen because they pose a threat to either the settler's claim to indigeneity (Indigenous bodies that are too Native) or the settler's white supremacy (exogenous bodies that are not white immigrants).

The distribution of technologies of visibility serves multiple purposes: (1) to produce material subjections of alienhood (a settler antitype) that are widely distributed in narratives; (2) to maintain a settler consciousness of disavowal and Native erasure; and (3) to provide the settler state with access to technologies of subjection that allow them to replicate the modes of labor and land exploitation central in the sustained colonization of territories in the US. By reproducing settler subjectivities over and over again, the settler state is able to enact settlement in perpetuity. While settler narrative production—the mode by which subjectivities materialize—imagines and recycles a number of settler antitypes (e.g., "terrorist," "welfare queen," or "antifa"), the persona of the alien figure speaks to a specific anxiety within the settler consciousness: being the colonized instead of the colonizer. The settler is tasked with maintaining their own ethnic superiority over nonwhite bodies (an epistemological hand-me-down from their since disavowed European colonial identity), despite the fact that their arrival in the occupied territories is similar to that of the migrant. Again, settlers and migrants are both exogenous, but only settlers are obsessed with controlling a racial hierarchy over other exogenous bodies.[53]

For rhetorical scholars and those interested in narrative in particular, I suggest that it is imperative that we examine how settler consciousness and narratives of alien invasion are linked: consciousness is the settler logic of disavowal, while narrative is a technology that mobilizes and reproduces that logic throughout the settler system. I argue throughout this book that there is always a self-defensive capacity to settler invasion, meaning that the self-defensive expressions of settler sovereignty and lifestyle are what dominate the settler narrative. Settlers are constantly finding themselves the victims of the circumstances they created. By disavowing the founding violence of settlement and the Indigenous peoples who were removed from their lands, settlers nativize themselves to stolen land and utilize defensive violence when it is necessary to protect the settler sovereign claim to the lands. This contradictory nature of settler consciousness, though, is also disavowed because the settler is constantly producing new sets of relations between Indigenous and exogenous groups in order to maintain a production control over the subaltern, noncitizen subjectivity.

Beyond the irony, however, I argue that when the settler has come under a perceived attack from the subaltern (usually as a result of anger or jealousy for their settler way of life), they get violent, reterritorializing the relations between people and lands.[54] This tendency assists in autoproducing the cycles of settler modes, primarily because it reproduces yet another set of extractive violences that will soon be disavowed. When talking about colonialism, Roxanna Dunbar-Ortiz reminds us that "the opposite of truth is forgetting. ... It's not that the origin myth is a lie, it's the process of forgetting that's the real problem."[55] This form of active forgetting, or productive forgetting, stands in for the truth the violences of settler extraction by subjecting the settler as naturalized to the land and anxious about the threat the subaltern poses to their sovereignty—a subaltern that has been produced again and again as such by the settler situation in order to erase the Native claims to land stewardship and to obscure the violent extraction of labor from enslaved Black and brown exogenous bodies.[56]

This is why settler narratives are important: they can communicate settler consciousness to large audiences because they are easily trafficked throughout the assemblages of settler governance. Hollywood's alien invasion narratives, the subject of this book, exemplify how a fictional narrative of settler victimhood manifests in further acts of settler violence and territorialization. Throughout this project, I make a strong case for why studying an alien invasion film can give readers insight into a larger system of white settler power, which is a contemporary and embedded system of colonial political and economic thought. Its reach extends into the entertainment industries where otherwise innocuous science fiction tales are imbued with colonial logics that prime audiences to adopt political and legal rejections of migrants. Settler narrative production obfuscates this settler situation under the guise of national security and economic freedom, two persistent myths of the settler situation.

In each of the case studies in *Visions of Invasion*, I describe the networked relationships between cinema (namely extraterrestrial arrival cinema), migration control, and constitutive citizenship laws in the US. Narrative technologies, including technologies of visibility and the political logics that develop and deploy them, are assembled in each of these three facets of citizenship control. They add layers of visibility to articulations of state power as they circulate through popular media, public discourse, legislative deliberation, and interactions between border security agents and migrants. Thus, I follow the technologies of visibility from their emergence in a cinematic universe (like *Predator*) to their materialization in today's migrant control tools. The technologies of visibility (like night vision, heat sensors, and other technologies that assist in visualizing body movements) are also organized by legislative and juridical narratives that materialize constitutive citizenship subjectivities in the US. The development of these technologies, largely aided by federal and state funding, are having a material impact on the ways "alien" migrants are perceived and channeled into dangerous basins of citizenship control.

Therefore, in analyzing extraterrestrial invasion cinema in the US, this book looks past the representational ascriptions of alien and native identities in cinematic narratives for a grasp of how extraterrestrial arrival films imagine and implement numerous material technologies to mediate intense alien affects to viewers (like special effects, CGI visualizations, etc.). These technologies are assembled to produce highly consumable Hollywood films that attune viewers to alien affects while invoking subjectivities rooted in settler colonial production modes. Those technologies of visibility are material parts of the settler colonial citizenship assemblage that are mobilized at the México/US border and in communities throughout the US to subject migrants into the alien persona.

The personae of citizen and noncitizen bodies as well as the material components of surveillance and security within the citizenship control assemblage are organized with a rationality that is derived from the settler logic of citizenship—a mode of settler population production that relies on a binary between citizen and noncitizen, subjectively adjudicated by the settler state.[57] Cinema, lights, surveillance, computer-generated images, and many other technologies manufacture alien affects for the purpose of aiding in the effort of the United (Settler) States to subject noncitizens. The relationships between those citizenship control, military, and film interests influence the extent to which the production and detection of alien affects—and thus alien personae—are possible. I seek to demystify the process of alienation and challenge the ways settler narratives are circulated, perhaps making a cut into the settler colonial production process.

RHETORICAL MATERIALISM, ASSEMBLAGES, AND TECHNOLOGIES OF VISIBILITY

Rhetorical materialism frames my methodological approach to the study of various narrative technologies found within disparate industries in the US. To account for alien-making technologies on the border and in film, I connect research on rhetorical materialism with critical studies on assemblages that can describe how political logics are organized, communicated, and materialized in modern national contexts. This vocabulary frames the concept of technologies of visibility that I develop to explain the ways migrants are illuminated, coded, and moved into danger by US legal commitments to a constitutive citizenship paradigm.

A shift from traditional rhetoric (i.e., the public addresses of famous settler colonial figures) to materialist rhetoric in the second half of the twentieth century introduced the field of communication studies to a conception of subjectivity that broke from rigid and outdated notions within the persuasion ontology. A study of materialist rhetoric moves beyond the persuasion paradigm and can conceive of rhetoric as both an influence and a constitutive force over subjects.[58] It is something that acts on people; it interacts with people. So, while "[t]he problem with an attempt to build a rhetorical materialism is that it is unable to break free from the logics of representation," the goal is "to offer a materialism based on how rhetoric traverses a governing apparatus. Instead of focusing on how rhetoric represents, we should focus on how rhetoric distributes different elements in a terrain of governing apparatuses."[59] I argue that citizenship control is one of those governing apparatuses: it materially distributes those elements relative to the state subjectivities of citizenship, cast as either belonging or not belonging by technologies of visibility. In other words, a materialist rhetoric replaces "the logics of representation" with a "logic of articulation as a way to map the multidimensional effectivity of rhetoric."[60]

Moreover, this orientation toward materialism views the rhetorical subject as the point though which rhetorical articulations of power emerge to control populations within governing technologies.[61] This means that power is "transformed, displaced, deployed and/or challenged by a particular governing apparatus . . . for the purpose of policing a population."[62] This concept is central in imagining a rhetorical materialism that draws on multidimensional elements of power—including language, law enforcement personnel, and surveillance technology—that are moved through governing mechanisms in order to control populations of political subjects. In short, rhetoric materially affects bodies, and so assemblage theory is compatible with rhetorical materiality precisely because of the focus on the multidimensional effectivity of power at play in articulating and mobilizing governing ideologies, materials, and subjectivities into relation with one another. Linking rhetorical materialism with assemblage theory can explain how white settler colonial power is communicated through governing mechanisms in the US's citizenship control assemblages by a careful deployment of discursive and affective articulations of alienhood.

Scholars in the field of communication studies and rhetorical studies have frequently adopted a rhetorical materialist model for critiquing structural power.[63] The materiality of rhetoric speaks directly to how the relationship between the signifiers and the signified is embedded in a structure of political, social, and economic knowledge.[64] With regard to the structures of citizenship control, several rhetorical scholars have also taken a rhetorical materialist approach to the study of citizenship, migration, and borders.[65] While much has been written about the ways discursive articulations materially deploy power, *Visions of Invasion* enters this conversation by offering a critical study of power through citizenship control assemblages focusing on articulations of visible subjection.

At its core, *Visions of Invasion* is a study of how the US government mobilizes a number of settler governing logics to distribute and operate various technologies within a multidimensional system for controlling migrants. Assemblage theory offers rhetoricians a way to conceptualize the relationships between territory, bodies, and logics of control that mobilize US state power today.[66] Ultimately, I frame the analysis of the US citizenship control assemblage within the context of settler colonial logics that assembled citizenship legal codes in the first place. To this end, I rely on the notion that "the rhetoric of modernity" is a white supremacist and capitalist settler logic that is responsible for the five-hundred-year exploitation of lands/people on the North American continent.[67] This logic undergirds the organization of people, lands, and resources that have come to be known as the United States.[68]

With regard to materialism, Andrew Culp argues that at its core, Gilles Deleuze's work offers a vocabulary of how this world, the capitalist world of exploitation and state violence, operates. "Deleuze and [Félix] Guattari find their superior materialism by exchanging the theater of representation for the factory of production."[69] *Visions of Invasion* focuses on the materialist production of settler governance in *this world* (an occupied territory under settler colonial control) with a unique focus on alien subjection. This focus defines this book's third contribution to the field of rhetoric: attending to the fact that a study of the materialist rhetoric of modernity is not necessarily interested in the public speeches of settlers and their ancestors or in the counterdiscourses of social movements. Rather, scholars invested in a materialist orientation can study the rhetorical arrangements of personae and materials by settler logics that maintain colonial territorialization.

In order to account for the sets of relationships that forge material territories of unequal power distribution between settler citizens and their antitypes, I consider how the mechanisms of the citizenship control assemblage channel power via carefully modulated articulable and visible expressions of alienhood. Since many cultural, corporate, and military agents cooperate to produce alienhood discursively and affectively through technologies of visibility and antimigrant political discourse, an assemblage framework allows me to articulate the nature of the cooperation in terms of the shared technologies organized between numerous groups. Of those, this book focuses specifically on how the cultural-security-industrial complex produces and controls alienhood through a triadic relationship between cinema technologies, border security systems, and antimigrant legislation. Relying on Thomas Nail's analytic framework, I develop a conceptual framework for assemblage that can explain how settler colonial formations territorialize lands and bodies, organizing subjectivities (personae) with technologies of visibility as citizen or noncitizen and arranging sets of social relations that produce power within settler societies of control.[70]

Therefore, I lean on assemblage theory to explain a rhetorical phenomenon of subjection that is organized materially in the US today. To be exact, I am investigating the ways technologies of visibility are mobilized to code migrants as alien (what I am calling the "production of alien affects") in order to align with layers of discursive formations that are produced by settler colonial constitutive citizenship codes with the purpose of exerting more power over territorialized lands and colonized peoples. Assemblage theory explains how settler colonial citizenship logics are organized by citizenship control assemblages to code migrant bodies as alien, setting material relations that lead to exploitation and expulsion. This return to assemblage theory centers around the notion of visibility to explore how the US is increasingly utilizing technologies of visibility in cinema and national security practices.

In my case, a materialist rhetorical orientation provides the analytic framework for studying the citizenship control assemblage of technologies, alien narratives, and political subjection at the core of US settlement. This citizenship control assemblage, which is the focus of this study, is a cultural-security-industrial assemblage. It comprises multiple components—cameras, infrared surveillance technologies, systems of lights, border patrol vehicles, communication technologies, migrants, border agents, transportation infrastructures, legislative and juridical discourses, and many others. Therefore, when I refer to a citizenship control assemblage in this book, I am referring to this particular set of components and processes of assembling, fully aware that there is an array of assemblages controlling bodies in the US today. Each component of the assemblage described here interacts with and distributes technologies of visibility (including language) to shape a territory of national control. The analytical method derived from the literature on assemblages draws attention to how technologies are used by those in each of the three sites with a focus on the flows of language, capital, people, and material that are moving between them.

CINEMATIC TECHNOLOGIES AND SETTLER COLONIAL CITIZENSHIP CONTROL

Visions of Invasion, thus, pulls together theories from rhetorical materialism and settler colonial studies to closely examine how cinematic technologies—technologies of visualization and sound—illuminate and subject the bodies that encounter them, just like the apparatuses of surveillance and control at border checkpoints. Cinematic technologies are material, and they have the power to capture bodies as subjects within a narrative. With advancements in filmic technologies over the past half century, science fiction cinema has actively participated in and benefited, perhaps, more than other film genres from the technological innovations in visual cinematography.[71] The case studies I present in the following chapters detail just how those who produce alien affects—filmmakers and border security agents alike—use technologies of visibility to create the intensive aspects of alienhood. Technologically enhanced visibilities in cinema provide audiences with a sensation of alienhood at the moments when they are interacting with the narrative. Perhaps more importantly, though, is that the production of alien affects is a process that has been deterritorialized from Hollywood filmmaking practices and reterritorialized into a citizenship border security apparatus elsewhere in the US, namely at the country's southern border. I take the opportunity here to briefly introduce how the techniques of cinematic illumination are coding migrants at interactions with state control via surveillance mechanisms.

CINEMATIC LUMINOUSNESS

Returning briefly to the discussion of articulation and visibility, I consider the technologies that make aliens visible. Many scholars, including contemporary surveillance and governmentality scholars, often attribute the notion of self-discipline through a sense of constant visibility to Michel Foucault's work on the panoptic gaze.[72] With that, I would like to draw attention to two important aspects of panoptic logic that are of importance to the study of alien affects and have bearing on the discussion of cinematic technology. First, panoptic logic encapsulates the subject through illumination—it isolates as it captures. The panoptic subject is the "constitution of finite man ... apprehended in its physical individuality as a knowing subject, duplicated in an object to be known, through the gaze of modernity. The prison separates bodies from one another to be counted and catalogued within the system."[73] The alienation from one another is implicit to the inmate's experiences within the panopticon and allows for the guard to more easily "recognize" the inmate—to know the subject of capture. Capture does not just mean being isolated physically, but it describes the process of subjection-through-illumination that panoptic surveillance imposes. Illuminative subjection is capture. Visibility under the panoptic gaze forges an individual subjectivity of discipline in a sort of symbiotic relationship with the articulations of the law holding a diagram of state power together.

In today's US settler society, alien antitypes are subjected not only in detention facilities but throughout the spaces of the nation. However, the logic of illumination remains to capture bodies in subjectivities and to territorialize the fields of relations between those subjectivities. "All social apparatuses, from sovereignty to discipline and beyond, feature regimes of light, regimes of enunciation, as well as lines of force that cross between the visible and the utterable and constitute their power dimension."[74] So, cinema "comprises, firstly, an optical machine. An optical machine consists of lines or planes (plans) of light which structure fields of visibility and invisibility, illuminating some objects and causing others to disappear."[75] Cinematic optical machines are continuous and material; they flow through citizenship assemblages like any other material. What is luminous and what is not depends on the technologies of light that are structuring perception within them.

Cinema is a mechanism of power that emerges in societies of control; a technology of visibility that subjects personae within fields of relations to organize power.

> Film spaces are opened out by technologies of vision so they are not self-contained.... The watching individual is a mobile, changing, and unstable assemblage of actions. Deleuze is right to define the process through "assemblage" rather than tools. This step allows us to move from a focus on the motion of images swirling around an analytically stationary and embattled subject to a view of the subject in motion and occupying the same terrain as the images.[76]

Consequently, cinema is part of a visual assemblage of power that calls bodies into subjectivity by casting a light of visibility upon their bodies. Like all assemblages, it is political. In drawing only some subjectivities into luminous visibility, the optical assemblage primes its audiences to those with "unwanted" subjectivities, producing a rejectable subject. Again, the narrative elements of alien cinema are not the only important facet in studying alien affects. A materialist orientation asks us to consider how optical machinery of visibility is mobilized in citizenship control assemblages alongside the narrative coding of alienhood such that migrant bodies are illuminated with intense shimmers of alienhood, captured in flows of dominant US state power. The seeable and the sayable work in unison to manufacture the alien. In a settler control society like the US, capture for migrants means being coded as alien and then getting channeled into the cycle of state violence predetermined by the settler colonial schema of population economics.

So, as cinematic narrative technologies get trafficked throughout the US, they circulate modes of subject production that participate in a social forgetting, obfuscating the original violence by Europeans colonizers against the Native lands and Native peoples with a vivid and persistent tale of alien threat. By recoding Native and Mestiza/o/x subjects as alien migrants, reterritorializing land arrangements for the sake of settler value extraction, and then staking defensive claims when under attack from subaltern groups produced as antitypes, the settler society enacts a production mode that replicates colonialism while hiding behind a fictive tale of imminent threat. This narrative mode appears in numerous settings and through ever-evolving media formats, including literature, film, television, gaming, and others.[77] My focus, though, is to demonstrate how the narrative loop of alien making in the US is repeated, time and again, in a number of extraterrestrial invasion film franchises and in the lingering national political discourses of the past four decades. Franchises like *Alien*, *Predator*, *Independence Day*, *Men in Black*, *Star Wars*, and others have, for nearly half a century, recycled their narratives to meet the demand of the alien-making assemblage in the US.

I attribute this cyclical characteristic of today's alien invasion narrative to the fact that settler colonial narratives are palindromic (with a caveat); they are set in a narrative trajectory of interruption and return to the beginning.[78] When read forward to end, the settler narrative: begins with a peacefully settled settler, normalized in their previously unoccupied home space; then the invasion by the subaltern other occurs, and the settler must resort to self-defensive violence in order to protect both their settler home *and* their lifestyle; and finally, the subaltern invader is eliminated and the settler returns to a world in decline where it is obvious that they must rely on their heroic individualism and capacity for rebuilding after the invasion. When read backward: a rugged, self-reliant settler in a declining colonial/imperial world must rely on the violent occupation of Native stewarded lands to assert settler sovereignty, then begin a process to disavow violence that imagines terra nullius ready for the settling. The caveat is that when read forward, this narrative reads like the imagined settler condition undergirding settler consciousness and most of today's alien invasion narratives. When read backward, though, it reads like the actual settler condition of unchecked, individual violence and larceny inherent in the modes of population and sovereignty production—followed by a process of active forgetting. Perhaps then, less like a palindrome, the settler narrative is more akin to a Led Zeppelin record when played backward, revealing a more sinister, truer message that what is obviously communicated at first.[79]

The us/them, settler citizen/noncitizen binary that is manufactured by settler colonialism, thus, replaces the colonizer/colonized binary to produce a settler consciousness that nativizes the settler and normalizes the settler's claim to Indigenous stewarded lands while justifying the violent enslavement of exogenous, Black, and Mestiza/o/x bodies.[80] The settler narrative arc locates the ideal spatiotemporal setting for the reproduction of settlement at the time/place just after the establishment of settler population economies: before the complete erasure of Native peoples, and at the height of the enslavement of nonwhite exogenous populations. And in order to produce an us/them binary in settler narratives that continually relocates to this moment, there must be a manufactured subjective *them* to contrast with the figure of the settler at the imagined moment in history when the settler is peacefully settled on terra nullius. The settler will always desire to return to that point. Not surprisingly, this is the point in the settler timeline that most of the films studied in this book take place—in an imagined time when settler heroes are (re)taking control over the uncertain terrains of a world in upheaval following a deadly alien invasion.

Technologies of narrative production—like the technologies of visibility that are the subject of this book—are the machinery mobilized throughout the assemblage of citizenship control to both produce subaltern alien noncitizens and to recycle settler anxieties of invasion—a process of disavowal that keeps settler citizens organized atop the sets of material political structures in the US. This is why technologies of visibility are important to study: they are produced and trafficked to create alien affects, materializing the settler narrative into sets of societal relationships. This process realizes the settler imaginary to manufacture a subjective population of aliens that are always a threat to settler sovereignty.

LOOKING AHEAD

In the first chapter of *Visions of Invasion*, I describe the recent film and television reboots of *The War of the Worlds* to frame how colonial anxieties manifest in narratives of alien invasion. Using H. G. Wells's own accounts of the relationship between extraterrestrial fiction and coloniality, the chapter describes the origins of the alien invasion genre and its influence in the US film genre. I then speak to cinematic alienation and settler logics of narrative production, which require a concomitant erasure of the Indigenous and control of Indigenous stewarded lands paired with the "nativizing" of the settler persona. A study of the development of alien cinema technologies uncovers how they materially mobilize settler colonial ideology through a narrative reproduction of settler logic that assembles the ever-evolving technologies, images, and discourses of settler nationalism. By connecting various examples that intersect extraterrestrial and settler colonial narratives—including the *Alien* and *Star Wars* franchises—I articulate how the production of an alien subject reorganizes the narratives of settlement and invasion to reterritorialize Indigenous-stewarded lands and code subjects as outsiders to the settlement. This is a material process because of how technologies are mobilized to manufacture alien subjectivity.

Chapter 2 begins with a description of the alien affects used to create and grow the *Predator* film franchise for more than three decades. Numerous technologies are employed to manufacture the Predator alien in the filmic imaginations of US Americans, and that has led to the (fictional) alliance between humans and Yautja Predator aliens in hunting Xenomorphs (those slimy, black creatures from the *Alien* film franchise). The chapter describes how the cinematic production of the Predator relies on the visualization of the alien's cloaking ability and its superperception—like amplified hearing, infrared sense perception, and night vision. As these technologies have quickly evolved over the past three decades in the films, they have also been more actively mobilized to subject migrants as aliens along the México/US border. On a large scale, many states in the US and the federal government are territorializing the borderland to drive migrants through certain channels with the hope of apprehending most of them; *Predator* technologies are aiding in this effort. I end the chapter by describing how legal and juridical apparatuses in the US organize these technological distributions to align with the constitutive citizenship paradigm that is at the heart of US settler governance.

In chapter 3, I consider *Men in Black* (*MiB*) technologies. The extraterrestrial film franchise *Men in Black* develops a number of technologies to produce alien affects. These technologies include biometric surveillance and virtual walls; like the technologies described in chapter 2, they are also being adopted by US citizenship control agencies to police migrants. In the films, agents surveil small differences in alien affects in order to pursue and apprehend aliens who are on the planet without authorization. They also use "neuralyzer" technology to mediate narratives of alienhood that obscure the ways the government controls aliens. The chapter also examines how the citizenship control assemblage in the US adopts *MiB* technologies in the surveillance of migrants in places like border checkpoints and airports and in immigration raids, while the national media redirects the attention of citizens to hide the violent and exploitative nature of citizenship control. I return to a discussion of the US legal and juridical apparatuses to demonstrate how they also mobilize *MiB* technologies that produce alien affects to limit unwanted migrants and obscure the government's role in controlling migrants to autoproduce settler ideology.

Then, chapter 4 imagines a new set of possibilities for technologies of visibility. In the first two cases, the manufacturing of alien affects in film coincides with those used in the surveillance and control of migrant movement—a territorial-state control assemblage. In this chapter, though, we see how some are engaging in a nomadic resistance by embracing film and surveillance technologies often seen in and used to make Hollywood's alien films and to surveil the México/US border. I argue that these artist/activists are mobilizing nomadic assemblages. This chapter includes a discussion of nomad thought, a concept that guides my study of nomadic assemblage, and considers the affirmative aspects of rearranging technologies of visibility for the purposes of resisting the techniques of migration control. I incorporate a study of nomadic assemblages into an analysis of the film *Sleep Dealer* (2008), an activist film that challenges the US's depiction of alienhood.[81] I then explore how those employing nomad thought in their ability to make sense of the territorializations of citizenship challenge the dominant codes operating in those terrains by reorganizing the technologies of visibility to narrate the "end of the settler colonial story."[82]

Finally, the closing chapter confronts readers with the grim reality of what alien making can do in our country today. I start by describing a common trope from alien invasion—the destruction of the US Capitol—and what it means in terms of settler consciousness. I use scenes from the 1996 film *Mars Attacks!* to frame the conversation about alien making around the ongoing settler violences in the US, including the January 6, 2021, attack on the US Capitol by a mob of angry settler citizens and the ongoing aggression toward migrant communities at the US/México border. Each of these phenomena, I suggest, is demonstrative of the settler project's focus on producing and organizing the relationships between settlers and their antitypes as a rejection of a society that values equality. Finally, after revisiting other major implications of the book, I end by calling on coconspirators in the anticolonial project to narrate the end of settler colonialism—to abolish the assemblages of hate and authoritarianism embedded in our entertainment media and to reassemble a consciousness outside of settler logic by rejecting settler subjectivities, settler claims to sovereignty, and the circulation of settler narratives.

Chapter One

THE WAR OF THE WORLDS AND ALIEN MAKING

> [W]e cannot simply say that settler colonialism or genocide have been targeted at particular races, since a race cannot be taken as given. It is made in the targeting. Black people were racialized as slaves; slavery constituted their blackness. Correspondingly, Indigenous North Americans were not killed, driven away, romanticized, assimilated, fenced in, bred White, and otherwise eliminated as the original owners of the land but *as Indians*.
> —PATRICK WOLFE, "Settler Colonialism and the Elimination of the Native"

Subjection—communicating the terms of one's humanity—is a primary facet of colonial encounter.[1] In order to sustain a long-term colonial project (like the settler situation in the United States), I contend that the settler state must deploy the narrative machinery of subject making that can sustain colonial subjections over the span of the colonial project.

Today's extraterrestrial invasion cinema, like H. G. Wells's alien invasion novel of a century ago, has a material component. It organizes the personae of colonial logics into relationships with the technologies that autoproduce more colonial power. Alien subjects are *made* to fit into a narrative form that for more than a century now has materialized as a political myth justifying colonial violence against Black peoples, Indigenous peoples, and Mestiza/o/x peoples, as well as the lands on which the settler colony is built. This chapter describes the specific trajectory of settler narratives unique to US alien cinema and the production of a settler consciousness that emerges out of the manufacturing of alienhood in film. Today, the production of settler narratives has become a visual mode, especially those involving alien invasion. And as a visual mode, alien film industries participate in an alien film-border security-settler nationalist assemblage that mobilizes settler narratives for the purposes of population control. The visual mode of alien making fits with and updates the US's history of making migrants into aliens.

So, extraterrestrial invasion film can be a rich genre for studying settler subject production. Not only can we see how the narrative of the invasive alien appears again and again as a popular culture trope, but studying science fiction can shed light on how the film industry participates in manufacturing and distributing technologies of settler subjection.[2] While alien invasion narratives (and their intertwined histories with colonialism) have long existed in prose, filmic colonial sci-fi for the past half century relies on a visible production mode to pair with the articulable narratives of the films. Simply put, filmic subjection is a process of simultaneously organizing both the visible *and* the sayable expressions of subjectivity. Like the machinery of Foucault's panopticon, film is a technology that produces visibility in order to subject bodies as personae. In alien invasion cinema in the US, articulable layers of noncitizenship are constructed around visual layers of alienhood to materialize a subjective subaltern, which is cast as an antitype to the rugged settler protagonists. These expressions are recycled through generations of settler narratives that reproduce a settler consciousness of disavowal and settler-nativizing in the US. In fact, we cannot think about narrative production of alienhood in the US settler state without thinking about the numerous technologies of visibility that have been materially arranged to produce alien affects on bodies.

So, alien making in US American science fiction narratives has been a key component in the distribution of a colonial consciousness for more than a century, materializing and mobilizing anxieties over the foreign Other—from Wells's 1898 *The War of the Worlds* through today. Then, Hollywood became involved in alien making, producing the visibilities of aliens for US American audiences for more than seventy-five years. The earliest alien affects were generated using camera tricks and lighting, but more recently, computer-generated imagery (CGI) technologies have been tasked with making aliens more intense than ever. Both techniques of producing alien affects rely on technologies of visibility, and I explain briefly how each is still used in the production of settler colonial subjectivities—a part of a citizenship control assemblage in the US responsible for maintaining divisions among groups of settler colonial subjects. This chapter ends with a discussion of how alien making, and the technologies used in the process, manifest in moments of colonial political division. I focus on how alien-making technology was mobilized by the Donald Trump administration to produce #BLM protesters as alien threats in the wake of the violent murder of George Floyd by Minneapolis police officers.

Figure 1.1. Screenshot from the BBC's 2019 miniseries *The War of the Worlds*; an alien tripod equipped with a heat laser encroaches on the city.

THE WAR OF THE WORLDS

Two separate televised adaptations of H. G. Wells's 1898 novel *The War of the Worlds* premiered in the fall of 2019 to international (English-speaking) audiences.[3] Both adaptations (the BBC's *The War of the Worlds* and Fox/Canal's *War of the Worlds*) retold Wells's classic tale from the perspective of (mostly) white protagonists whose seemingly mundane lives had been destroyed by an unexpected invasion from outer space. *The War of the Worlds* (from the BBC) is a three-part miniseries set in England at the turn of the twentieth century.[4] This version showcased CGI tripod destroyers along with heat rays from the sky and a number of other highly intensive alien affects that made the lowly earthling technology of Edwardian England seem primitive (fig. 1.1). Of the two versions of the story released in 2019, the BBC version most closely re-creates Wells's narrative of the shock of seeing a technologically advanced species commit genocide on a pre–World War I European society.

The other 2019 version, *War of the Worlds* from Fox/Canal, however, is set in present-day France and England.[5] This series follows a dozen or so characters who are trying to survive after alien invaders use electromagnetic pulses to "scan" Earth for human DNA. Very quickly, the alien invaders eliminate (nearly) all humans with an intense, subretinal pulse that is broadcast around the globe; everyone who is aboveground or not sheltered in a bunker is killed by the electromagnetic pulse (EMP) (fig. 1.2). This updated adaptation of *War of the Worlds* features an alien technology of visibility that can both scan for human biometric data and project highly intensive

Figure 1.2. Screenshot from Fox/Canal's 2019 series *War of the Worlds*; Kariem (Bayo Gbadamosi) climbs from a tanker truck to see an abandoned city.

Figure 1.3. Screenshot from Fox/Canal's 2019 series *War of the Worlds*; Emily (Daisy Edgar-Jones) narrowly escapes from a robotic doglike alien that uses DNA scanners to track and eliminate humans.

waves onto humans—allowing alien invaders to see human subjects and then destroy them.

The first season of Fox/Canal's *War of the Worlds* also features several frightening doglike biomechanical drones that are hardwired to "see" human DNA and kill on sight. They wreak havoc on the survivors of the initial attack, slaying terrified humans. These robot-dogs are equipped with DNA scanners that help them identify humans, making the alien invaders' task of seeking and eliminating people much easier (fig. 1.3). The Fox/Canal adaptation breaks from the novel considerably in that regard; it relies on visualizations of technologies that are more widely seen in today's science and technology trade magazines than those described by Wells in 1898. In fact, the same year this series was released, Boston Dynamics announced the release of Spot—the consumer-grade robot-dog that can aid in search and rescue, light construction, and handling hazardous materials.[6] Spot is part of a long line of the company's commercial- and military-grade robot-dogs but the first to be released to the public in the twenty-six-year history of the company.⁷ So, just as the updated *War of the Worlds* series is visually producing technologies that will eradicate humans, the very same technologies are being built by companies like Boston Dynamics to aid in waging war, policing communities of color, and streamlining multiple arenas of consumer life for their First World citizens.

That is to say, the Fox/Canal adaptation of the novel arranges the 120-year-old narrative of alien invasion and genocide adjacent to contemporary visions of modern technological control within contemporary geopolitical frameworks. With weapons like the robot-dog and EMPs, the Fox/Canal series assembles a visually/aurally stunning narrative in which the world's weapons of colonization—already being wielded by the colonial elite against Black peoples, Indigenous peoples, and Mestiza/o/x peoples throughout the world—are turned against the colonizer class. We can see this also in Steven Spielberg's 2005 *War of the Worlds* film, in which several scenes show the protagonist, Ray (Tom Cruise), walking about in the wreckage of a downed aircraft or passing walls filled with photographs of the missing (figs. 1.4 and 1.5). Again, for Spielberg, situating the film in the imagery of 9/11 was his way of manifesting the geopolitics of the moment into his retelling of the story. In both Spielberg's and Fox/Canal's versions of *War of the Worlds*, the activation of the collective anxiety, as I will note throughout this book, concurrently manufactures the subjective alien and the settler citizen subjectivity

Figure 1.4. Film still from Steven Spielberg's 2005 *War of the Worlds*; Ray (Tom Cruise) walks through plane wreckage in a suburban town.

Figure 1.5. Film still from Steven Spielberg's 2005 *War of the Worlds*; Ray (Tom Cruise) walks next to a wall of memorials and photos of missing victims of the alien invasion.

by situating the white, heteronormative protagonist among the visual expressions of disaster enacted by aliens.

This matters for a couple of reasons. For one, Wells's criticism of British imperial colonialism embedded in the narrative of his novel is no mystery to critics. Many scholars contend that the genre of Anglophonic science fiction literature as a whole emerges out of the colonial backdrop of a diminishing British Empire, and Wells's *The War of the Worlds* is perhaps the exemplar of those works, most explicitly drawing the analogy between alien invasion and colonial violence.[8] To say the least, the genre of extraterrestrial invasion fiction already has an intrinsic link with the colonial consciousnesses that thrives in the societies from where those narratives emerge.

However, the novel, its recent film and television adaptations, and countless other narratives of alien invasion erase the Indigenous victims of imperial colonial violence and replaced that figure with a white, Western victim. While "sci-fi is often obsessed with colonialism and imperial adventure ... the Martian conquest is presented as analogous to, and even as just retribution for, Britain's colonial genocide. As has been visited on *them*, so shall it be visited on *us*."[9] This is a problem primarily because it normalizes genocidal colonialism as a natural inevitability. Renowned astrophysicist Stephen Hawking even suggested, for example, that "[i]f aliens visit us, the outcome would be much as when Columbus landed in America, which didn't turn out well for the Native Americans.... We only have to look at ourselves to see how intelligent life might develop into something we wouldn't want to meet."[10] Or in Wells's own words:

> [B]efore we judge of [the Martians] too harshly we must remember what ruthless and utter destruction our own species has wrought, not only upon animals, such as the vanished bison and the dodo, but upon its inferior races. The Tasmanians, in spite of their human likeness, were entirely swept out of existence in a war of extermination waged by European immigrants, in the space of fifty years. Are we such apostles of mercy as to complain if the Martians warred in the same spirit?[11]

Yet, despite the critique of British imperial colonialism underlying this message, Wells's inherent colonial logic prevails in normalizing the imagined violence of alien invasion. This logic, as Hawking's comment suggests, still prevails. A colonial logic that views incursion as a natural tendency is not only expressed in *The War of the Worlds* and its various adaptations, but also undergirds the US American settler colonial narratives of alien invasion that are the subject of this book.

The second reason the Fox/Canal adaptation of *War of the Worlds* matters in the context of citizenship control is because it arranges the colonial narrative of genocide with the technologies of war that are currently materializing on streets and in battlefields. In fact, *War of the Worlds* is just one of dozens of alien invasion franchises that have been released in the US in the past half century that continually reproduce colonial (or settler colonial) narratives while also featuring new casts of characters armed with new technologies. *Star Wars, Star Trek*, the *Alien* franchise, and even Roland Emmerich's film *Independence Day* span decades in US cinema and television and are updated in each iteration with more advanced war-waging technology (the two major film franchises I will study in this book are the *Predator* franchise and the *Men in Black* franchise). Which begs the question: what is the value of reproducing colonial narratives of alien invasion that develop and deploy highly technological warfare on white victims?

H. G. Wells has an answer for that, too. In *Anticipations*, Wells writes about the symbolism in his 1898 novel, describing *The War of the Worlds* as a cautionary tale for societies to invest in superior war technology.[12] As David Seed explains:

> Wells takes as his premise rapid technological change, which was already revolutionizing warfare, and he speculates on the imminent development of flying machines, which will further transform the conduct of war.... Wells is suggesting a paradigm shift in which the wars of the future will be sudden, rapid, and virtually irresistible. In

other words, they will have all the characteristics of the Martian invasion, which brings with it confusion and panic.[13]

In short, repeatedly deploying narratives like *The War of the Worlds* imagines what a more swift and violent invasion might look like for a colonial society who only has to imagine their own fantastical demise to be spurred into further developing better and faster technologies of war. It's the ultimate colonial "cry foul," in which the colonizing culture fabricates a wild narrative of invasion to justify the defensive violences that are perpetuated to protect the colonizer and/or settler from an attack that never happens. This is how settler consciousness manifests as narrative; colonial anxiety is turned into a tale of future potential victimization that organizes us/them subjectivities. As I describe throughout this book, reproducing and circulating settler colonial narratives is a mode of production linked to the materialization of settler colonial ideology in mechanisms of state control in the US today.

So, while *The War of the Worlds* might be read as a critique of colonialism by some, it actually participates in erasing the Native victim of colonial violence by centralizing the white victim of extraterrestrial coloniality. It is narrative disavowal. Beyond this, though, its retelling circulates settler narratives that also feature the latest in war-waging technology only to see that technology adopted in the service of further coloniality. Wells's *The War of the Worlds* and recent adaptations are cautionary tales to colonizing nations that more technology is needed to maintain colonial control. The tendency to arrange the narrative of alien invasion produces a "better get them before they get us" logic that, I argue, undergirds settler colonial logic (and, by consequence, most settler colonial narrative). But first, we need to know who *them* is—or, more accurately, we need to understand how a *them* is produced in order to have a target on which to unleash a sudden and irresistible war.

ALIEN MAKING IN HOLLYWOOD

Technologies of visibility layer the affective indicators of rejection—alien affects—onto those bodies deemed undesirable by the US settler state. Technologies of visibility materially change the ways personae are perceived, and with this facility to alter the affective layer of one's being, the capacity of the settler to produce subjects of noncitizenship greatly increases. Given the quickly developing technologies in surveillance and cinema, some now have the capacity to manufacture subjects in real time: subject making does not rely solely on verbal technologies but on an amalgamation of verbal technologies and technologies of visibility that immediately activate the affective archive of undesirability attached to the exogenous body the settler desires to be rejected. As I demonstrate in this section, as well as in the case studies in the following chapters, numerous narrative technologies, verbal and visible, combine to manufacture the alien antitype, which is cast as subaltern to the settler persona.

ILLUMINATING ALIEN AFFECTS

For more than half a century in US American cinema, extraterrestrials have made a visible transition from benevolent visitors to monstrous attackers.[14] Although films depicting extraterrestrials have been produced since the turn of the twentieth century, only a few were made and largely distributed in the US and Europe before the 1950s.[15] We see in films like *The Day the Earth Stood Still* and *The Thing from Another World* alien others who are very much like the humans they are visiting.[16] The bodies of those aliens don't shimmer with alienhood quite to the extent that today's do, but through cinematic cueing, we are able to recognize the flashes of alienhood that are attached to their bodies. During this early period of alien cinema, visual and aural effects were basic. Filmmakers relied on camera tricks like stop-motion and double exposure to make aliens appear on and disappear from the screen.[17] Given the under-evolved film technologies used to make these early alien invasion films, human actors in costume usually played as alien characters. In the case of *The Thing from Another World*, the large alien creature is an actor in a shiny suit. In the few scenes in which the alien is actually seen, for example, the foreground is darkened and the alien is backlit, making the figure appear taller—a basic alien affect but one that attaches ominousness to the creature. At another point in the film, the protagonists use electric bolts to fight off the alien figure. In this action-packed scene, the "thing from another world" is set ablaze, casting a sharp contrast against an otherwise dark set (fig. 1.6). This literal illumination of the alien figure marks the beginning of a trend in film, using technologies of visibility to make aliens visible *and* to bring harm to them. Thus, just as much as the narrative of invasion made audiences feel anxious about the creature, the techniques of lighting and camera effects contributed to the ways the alien subject was felt by audiences.[18]

This trend continued through the middle of the twentieth century; alien visual effects techniques in films and television programming remained relatively basic and usually involved a human actor portraying the alien figure. To manufacture subjective alienhood in early cinema, actors were arranged in relation to cameras, lights, backdrops, and props to code the alien persona

Figure 1.6. Film still from Christian Nyby's 1951 *The Thing from Another World*; the alien invader (James Arness) is killed when a team of scientists lures it into a trap, then electrifies it.

on the visual screen. When color was added to the cinematic landscape, visual effects techniques evolved into the more traditional special effects popular during the 1970s.[19] The visual effects used to create alien affects at this time were a bit more believable than a generation before: filmmakers at this time were using robots and human-operated puppets, small-scale replicas, basic holographic superimposing, and elaborately choreographed lighting that illuminated shimmers of alienhood for audiences. Two of the most popular films of this period, which also happened to eventually spawn extensive film franchises—*Alien* and *Star Wars*—utilize each of these techniques in some capacity to produces alien affects.[20]

If anything, the *Alien* and *Star Wars* franchises (each spanning more than five decades) teach us that films can participate in political assemblages. Filmmakers arrange a number of materials, technologies, geographies, personae, and myriad other elements in achieving the goal of telling a linear visual narrative. These material components include the various technologies of alien visibility already described and many that had yet to be invented by the time the films had been released. This is also true then of the citizenship control assemblage in the US, where border security agents and politicians compile a variety of technologies and people in prescribed roles to narrate a tale of alien invasion. Like Rube Goldberg machines, the narrative assemblage draws together heterogeneous technologies in relation to actors in order to narrate a qualitative set of relations that code characters as subjective Others.[21] This is especially true of technologies of visibility—the machinery of alien subjection. For example, what is most memorable from

Figure 1.7. Film still from Ridley Scott's 1979 *Alien*; Kane (John Hurt) examines alien egg pouches. Scott used lasers borrowed from the British rock band the Who to light the scene.

Ridley Scott's *Alien* is the terrifying, tall, black, slimy Xenomorph alien figure that hunts the crew of the *Nostromo*. An actor (Bolaji Badejo) in a slimy alien suit became Scott's alien figure through cinematic magic. Critic Roger Ebert suggests that it was Scott's use of lighting, and perhaps more importantly shadowing, that kept the creature obscured from audiences, making the alien figure especially frightening.[22] Moviegoers never quite get a glimpse of the alien until it is jumping out and attacking someone. This is exemplified in perhaps the film's most famous scene in which a newborn alien hatches out of the chest of one of the crew members and scurries away. Scott carefully orchestrated the lighting and shadowing of the most intense parts of the film in relation to numerous actors to show shimmers of alienhood without ever fully shedding light on exactly what the alien is.

So, thinking of *Alien* as part of an assemblage can demonstrate how a multitude of technologies of visibility, actors, creators, and a colonial narrative story line of alien danger come together to code alien personae in a material narrative that gets commercially distributed. *Alien* uses lighting, scale, and holographic techniques to achieve a believable rendering of horrific alien infestation.[23] For example, the first encounter in the film with an alien egg is enhanced by a set of glowing lasers used to backlight the leathery, slimy texture of the egg sack (fig. 1.7). Scott is said to have borrowed the lasers from the British rock band the Who, who were preparing them for a light show in a studio nearby.[24] For other scenes, including those depicting the crew of the USCSS *Nostromo* traversing the terrain of an alien planet, Scott used scale modeling, intricate blue and gray lighting that rendered scenes partially invisible at times, and smoke fans to create a highly intense alien atmosphere.[25] So, while Scott's *Alien* appears as a linear narrative for audiences, the processes of alien subject production at the heart of the film's narrative are arranged using technologies of visibility that interact with a number of actors, creators, prop designers, costume designers, and others, manufacturing a colonial narrative of alien danger.

The *Alien* franchise (with eight films in total, including the two *Alien vs. Predator* films) has become a quintessential presence on the US cinematic landscape.[26] Each film in the franchise builds on the narrative linearity of the others but assembles different actors and more advanced renderings of the Xenomorph alien, made possible by continuously developing technologies of visibility. As the franchise reproduces and redistributes its colonial narrative, it showcases the latest in cinematic technologies, like the eventual incorporation of CGI into the franchise. In *Alien: Resurrection* (the fourth film in the franchise), director Jean-Pierre Jeunet collaborated with Blue Sky Studios to incorporate the first CGI renderings of the franchise's alien figure, marking a shift in the way the alien persona was produced.[27] From this point on, CGI became standard for producing alien affects in the franchise's films. To me, this demonstrates that assemblages work on multiple levels, what Manuel DeLanda calls "assemblages of assemblages," or "sets of sets."[28] While *Alien* the film is one assemblage in the set of *Alien* franchise films, the films in the franchise are also connected to other assemblages (like special effects companies, film studios, distributors, trade unions, theaters, etc.). They represent a part of the networked machinery of settler narrative production modes, and thus they are also part of a broader citizenship control assemblage in the US.

Another film franchise that exemplifies this networked machinery of settler narratives is the *Star Wars* franchise. George Lucas (director and writer) creates aliens, alien landscapes, and battles between the Jedi and the Empire using many of the same visual effects techniques seen in *Alien*—costumed actors, superimposed flashes of light (for lasers and lightsabers), scaling, animatronics, and eventually CGI aliens (think Jar Jar Binks) (fig. 1.8).[29] Although his aliens are usually more benevolent that Scott's aliens, Lucas relies on essentially the same technologies of visibility that Scott does. Despite the global success of the *Star Wars* franchise, though, perhaps Lucas's most widespread impact on today's Hollywood alien cinema is his contribution to the development of what is now one of the largest cinematic visual effects studios in the world: Industrial Light and Magic (ILM). Founded by Lucas in 1975, the studio is a division of Lucasfilm (now a part of the Disney conglomerate) and has been at the forefront of rapidly developing technologies of visibility in alien films for four decades. ILM was born alongside the *Star Wars* franchise, initially relying on puppets and lighting to create Lucas's aliens, but it is now leading the industry in CGI technology. ILM has worked

Figure 1.8. Film still from George Lucas's 1979 *Star Wars*; extras cast as aliens in a cantina.

on *E.T. the Extraterrestrial*, the *Star Trek* film franchise, the *Transformers* film franchise, the *Men in Black* film franchise, and countless other productions of cinematic alienhood in the US.[30] That is to say, Lucas and *Star Wars* are intertwined with countless other alien film franchises in the US, assembled together to mobilize a vast array of technologies of visibility.

CODING ALIEN SUBJECTS

As technologies of visibility are becoming more advanced, their capacity for producing more intense alien affects grows. So even though the transition from puppets and lighting to CGI was slow, by the mid-1990s, CGI had given filmmakers to the capacity to depict alien affects without having to rely on many of the analog technologies of generations past. So while the narrative structures of *Alien* and *Star Wars* can be read as somewhere between colonial and settler colonial (given their narrative arcs of progress, the exploratory and expansive desires of the characters, and the mobility of the protagonists), I contend that both of these film franchises participate in a national citizenship assemblage mainly because they were at the forefront of this shift from lighting up alien affects to now coding aliens with the latest computer imaging technologies.[31]

Two films released during this time period gave audiences their first glimpses of aliens rendered entirely with CGI technology. *Starship Troopers* is an extraterrestrial battle film that uses aliens rendered almost entirely using CGI technology (some battle scenes required large-scale robotic puppets that interacted with actors).[32] Director Tim Burton's *Mars Attacks!*, however, is the first major Hollywood film in which the alien invaders were rendered exclusively by CGI technology (fig. 1.9).[33] In parodying Wells's *The War of the Worlds*, it comically recycles the tropes of unprovoked invasion,

Figure 1.9. Film still from Tim Burton's 1996 *Mars Attacks!*; invading aliens disembark from their ship.

self-defensive attack, and return to a chaotic, unsettled world (in the conclusion of this volume, I speak more about *Mars Attacks!* and settler consciousness). The CGI alien affects in *Mars Attacks!* mark a dramatic shift in the ways alien affects are visualized in US cinema and serve as a prototype for today's experience of alienhood in film (for example, the aliens in *Avatar* and those in the *Transformers* franchise).[34] It is no coincidence that in both films, ILM was the primary visual effects company hired to render alienhood.[35] ILM—along with other companies like Amalgamated Dynamics, Autumn Light Entertainment, Hunter/Gratzner Industries, Vision Art, and Digiscope—is actively producing increasingly intense alien affects with computer-generated images in wider varieties of alien invasion film.[36]

In thinking about the *Alien*, *Star Wars*, and other film franchises, one must consider how complex networks of assemblages begin to connect to one another through distribution networks that circulate technologies of visibility. This discussion of cinematic alienhood is meant to draw attention to both the shift from lighting technologies to coding technologies and also how, as this shift occurs, an intricate system of industrial, technological, and cinematic agents emerges. These agents—like Lucas, Spielberg, and ILM—collaborate to produce and reproduce alien subjects as a settler colonial antitype throughout the US citizenship control assemblage and, not to mention, earn tremendous revenue from the narratives they produce.

Thus, the growth of technologies of visibility to include both lighting and coding also increases the capacity of the broader US citizenship control assemblage by trafficking the optical technologies of visibility through military and law enforcement networks to render alienhood onto human bodies the settler class wishes to cast as noncitizen. Just as cinematic assemblages become interwoven with one another through the distribution of industrial technologies of visibility, they have also woven themselves into the territorial-state assemblages of US border security apparatuses. Describing this phenomenon—technologies of alien making trafficked through multiple arenas of the US citizenship control assemblage—is the focus *Visions of Invasion*. My goal is to demonstrate that the distribution of these technologies is productive: it serves to perpetuate modes of settler colonial production that manufacture populations to actively sustain a settler consciousness rooted in a cycle of anxiety, defensiveness, violence, disavowal, then return to anxiety.

ALIEN MAKING AS AN ONGOING SETTLER POLITICS

In the midnight hours between May 28 and May 29, 2020, the US Customs and Border Protection agency (CBP) launched an MQ-9 Reaper drone—more commonly referred to as the Predator B drone—from Grand Forks, North Dakota. This particular drone, CBP-104, left Grand Forks Air Force Base after a request from an Immigration and Customs Enforcement (ICE) agent who had been deployed to Minneapolis to monitor anti–police brutality demonstrations "after reports of arson and violence in the area."[37] Three days prior, on May 25, 2020, four Minneapolis police officers had murdered George Floyd, an unarmed Black man. A store clerk had accused Floyd of using counterfeit money and called the police. Surveillance video and cell phone video taken by witnesses at the scene portrayed his brutal murder for millions around the world, sparking international demonstrations to end police brutality against Black communities in the US. After three nights of demonstrating in Minneapolis, which culminated in the burning of the Third Precinct's police station (the place where the four police officers worked), the ICE agent made their request to CBP to fly the predator drone around the city for added "situational awareness."[38]

That night, CBP-104 maintained a hexagonal-shaped holding pattern over Minneapolis for several hours, coordinating with law enforcement teams on the ground. Live video from the protests was "sent to a mobile operations center where a group of agents monitor[ed] television screens while moving the drone with joysticks. Other federal agents that request[ed] a view from the sky [could] also see the footage on their phones."[39] Thus, with the MQ-9 Reaper drone at their disposal, ICE agents—federal law enforcement personnel with a mission to "protect America from cross-border crime and illegal immigration that threaten national security and public safety"—were turned on US citizens who were protesting police violence.[40] It turns out that the protesters in Minneapolis were not alone; over the span of about two weeks in June 2020, CBP operated both crewed and uncrewed aircraft in fifteen cities—including Buffalo, New York City, Philadelphia, Detroit, San Francisco, and Los Angeles—to provide increased surveillance capacity to law enforcement agencies suppressing protests.

This begs the question: what are ICE and CBP doing in major US cities surveilling civilian protesters? K. Campbell, former US Air Force intelligence officer, believes that "psychological warfare shouldn't be used against U.S. citizens. That's something we use against our adversaries and enemies overseas."[41] So, while the retired intelligence officer is correct in calling out the unconventional practice of turning military surveillance technology against people in the US, I disagree with the premise that intrusive surveillance is somehow only used to monitor foreign "enemies" who already pose a threat to the US. In fact, throughout *Visions of Invasion*, I make the case that the primary purpose of technologies of visibility, like drone surveillance, is strictly to manufacture a visible adversary that can be cast as a threat to the nation. This process of subjecting people as noncitizen terrorists is an effort the US government had been practicing for nearly twenty years before the 2020 protests.[42] It also makes sense that the US would be employing CBP-104 to aid in this process; the MQ-9 Reaper drone has been in operation for nearly fifteen years. Since 2007, CBP-104 spends its time "collecting synthetic-aperture radar imagery (topographic imaging) and full-motion video to aid in actions such as surveilling" both the México/US and Canada/US borders.[43]

Despite efforts to subject #BLM protesters and others as noncitizens, though, the overwhelming majority of the aerial surveillance by Air and Marine Operations (the branch of CBP responsible for crewed and uncrewed aerial surveillance, such as drones) continues to be at the México/US border. Of the more than ninety-two thousand hours of aerial surveillance logged by Air and Marine Operations in fiscal year 2019 (October 1, 2018, to September 30, 2019), more than eight-four thousand hours (roughly 91 percent) were spent monitoring the southern border.[44] The combined operating budget of ICE and CBP for fiscal year 2019 is more than $20 billion, with nearly $3 billion earmarked for detention beds, $1.8 billion set aside for border wall infrastructure, and more than $1.6 billion allocated for aerial and ground surveillance technologies, making technologies of visibility the third-largest infrastructure expense for the agency.[45] This overwhelming mobilization of technologies of visibility to national borders, it would seem, means that migrants at US borders and in communities throughout the US are targeted to be cast as adversaries in the US.

So, while national boundaries control movement, they are only a part of the political apparatuses constructed to keep populations of Native and Mestiza/o/x, Black, and European settlers stratified in castes of settler citizenship. Although bordering mechanisms are the material parts of a citizenship control assemblage that maintain divisions between colonial subjects, the subjection of nonwhite bodies is manufactured long before the erection of physical barriers. For example, at the México/US border, CBP relies on drones like the CBP-104 to surveil territorial boundaries, already assuming that the migrant bodies being monitored do not belong and threaten the constitutive citizenship paradigm established by settler governments centuries ago—or more simply put, that they are aliens. As a result of the visualizations from technologies of visibility, migrant bodies are literally alienated from others based on certain attributes—like skin color, vocal inflection, and other factors. In short, citizenship control policies rooted in a defense of a subjugated US American "identity . . . demonstrate that [by] using the institutional apparatuses of alienhood, the nation has been 'cleansing' itself by keeping out those who are deemed threatening or undesirable, and disciplining those considered admissible."[46] The process of alien making is about managing those populations of manufactured subjectivities as if they were naturally occurring identities.

I return to the days after the Minneapolis police murdered George Floyd, a murder that was captured by handheld surveillance technologies and shared widely around the globe. By the first week of June 2020, anti–police brutality protests began to grow beyond Minneapolis to Atlanta, Buffalo, Louisville, Los Angeles, New York City, and St. Louis.[47] During these protests, ICE agents were on the ground to monitor the protests, and at least one MQ-9 Reaper drone (along with a number of other aerial surveillance aircraft) was in the air to provide situational awareness to the ICE agents who had been mobilized by then President Trump and his attorney general, William Barr.[48] In the wake of Floyd's murder, Trump and Barr responded by trafficking their alien-making technologies to cities around the nation in order to make aliens out of citizens who were protesting violence against Black communities at the hands of local law enforcement agents.

It turns out that in addition to the ICE agents and MQ-9 Reaper surveillance that the Department of Homeland Security (DHS) turned against protesters, Trump and Barr considered mobilizing another technology once only imagined by extraterrestrial invasion science fiction. On the morning of June 1, 2020, after days of protests in Washington, DC, Trump made an appearance for a photograph in front Saint John's Episcopal Church near the White House. That morning, military police officers charged with securing the site of the photo-op made an inquiry to a local military base about the availably of the Active Denial System (ADS)—a heat wave weapon that would burn protesters gathered in Lafayette Square (adjacent to Saint John's) in hopes of dispersing them. Instead, military police settled for tear gas.⁴⁹ This begs the question, why does the US military have this weapon in the first place?

Two years before, the administration considered turning the weapon against migrants. In response to the "migrant caravans" that President Trump fabricated ahead of the US midterm election of 2018 as a way to mobilize antimigrant sentiment,

> Department of Homeland Security, Customs and Border Protection officials [also] suggested deploying a microwave weapon—a "heat ray" designed by the military to make people's skin feel like it is burning when they get within range of its invisible beams.... Developed by the military as a crowd dispersal tool two decades ago, the Active Denial System had been largely abandoned amid doubts over its effectiveness and morality.⁵⁰

While the US military's heat ray was not designed to vaporize humans like Wells's or Spielberg's, its mobilization demonstrates that the US is willing to inflict pain on those it sees as alien antitypes in order to maintain control of settler population production modes. This proves the lengths the settler state will go to in order to perpetuate the more than five-century encroachment by settler colonizers onto what is now North America, including trafficking anti-alien technologies from battlefields, to the border, and into local communities.

So when Trump announced on May 30, 2020, that the US would be invoking the terrorist group designation for "the far-left anti-fascism activists" known to him and many others as antifa, he was signaling a desire to have groups of protesters in many cities who opposed his "law-and-order" policies transferred out of the citizenry *as if they were* alien antitypes.⁵¹ In fact, by June 1, when the Capitol military police cleared protesters with tear gas near Lafayette Square, the administration had already decided that protesters were antitypes. There is no legal basis for the US to designate a group of domestic agitators as "terrorists," given that currently this designation is only reserved for foreign nationals who meet DHS's criteria for a terrorist.⁵² In some cases, the US can prove in court that a person committed violent crimes and was motivated by an ideology that originated outside of the United States, but that is rare.⁵³ This didn't stop Trump and Barr, though, from referring to the protesters as "domestic terrorists," and considering the use of a heat ray on them.⁵⁴

By mid-June 2020, reports emerged of ICE agents at protests in Oregon; they arrived in unmarked vehicles to haul away protesters and protest organizers, in many cases denying them their constitutional rights to free speech and against unlawful detention.⁵⁵ So, while the Trump administration was not directly invoking the figural alien, it mobilized alien-making technologies in order to manufacture a seeable and sayable subject that is transferable out of the citizenry: the far-left *domestic terrorist*. The Trump administration relied on language from the Real ID Act of 2005, which was passed by the US Congress and signed into law by the George W. Bush administration in the aftermath of 9/11 and the *9/11 Commission Report*.⁵⁶ The bill gives the authority to DHS, with consultation of the attorney general, to designate a group of "two or more individuals, whether organized or not, which engages in, or has a subgroup which engages in," terrorist activity.⁵⁷ Therefore, aligning the definition of a terrorist organization with a set of legal codes that are intended to document US citizens' IDs demonstrates that the Real ID Act's effort to define terrorism is a process aligned with controlling removable alien antitype populations. In fact, most of the act outlines the "inadmissibility" of those who might be vaguely defined as "terrorist" or someone who might engage in "terrorist activity."⁵⁸ Like Spielberg's *War of the Worlds* and the *9/11 Report*, The Real ID Act of 2005 affiliates the figure of the terrorist (foreign or domestic) with the figure of the alien by giving DHS the authority to detain and remove the terrorist antitype just as if they were an alien antitype. Making it easier to transfer antitypes between the alien and terrorist personae makes those in either subjectivity more susceptible to removal. In other words, anyone is at risk of becoming an antitype to the settler state once the settler state deems that individual a threat. Alienhood—one of many antitypes—can be produced almost anywhere, with the mobilization of the right technologies of visibility in the hands of agents of the state.

How did things get to this point? In the next two chapters, I will detail just how US migration policy over the past four decades has adopted alien-making technologies to weave a narrative of invasion. I approach the study of technologies of visibility from a material rhetorical orientation, meaning that I am concerned with how power is organized, on occupied land, onto bodies through structural manifestations and how these manifestations materially arrange the relationships between those deemed citizens and those not. Technologies of visibility are both *produced* and *productive*. To develop them requires financial and technological resources, which are materials that are distributed according to the settler citizen/noncitizen binary. Those with these resources are typically those who are able to leverage technologies of visibility in their favor. Once they are produced, like any commodity, they are trafficked, traded, and sold to those with a desire to produce settler subjectivities. In the next two chapters, then, I will describe how filmmakers and the US government both have leveraged financial and political resources to traffic technologies that appear in the *Predator* and *Men in Black* film franchises. The cases will demonstrate just how technologies of visibility are made, moved, then redeveloped and redeployed in citizenship control assemblages.

Chapter Two

PREDATOR ASSEMBLAGES

Before Ronald Reagan became the governor of California and eventually the US president, he was an actor. Reagan acted in dozens of Hollywood films, both before and after his army service from 1942 to 1946.[1] At the end of his acting career, it seems that he was committed to the settler narrative genre, starring in films such as *Law and Order*, *Cattle Queen of Montana*, and *Tennessee's Partner* and in television series like *Wagon Train* and *Death Valley Days*.[2] While Reagan was a regular on television screens in the 1960s, perhaps his most memorable onscreen performance in the role of a settler citizen was when he appeared on national television to deliver a speech in support of Barry Goldwater, who was running for the presidency in 1964. In his "A Time for Choosing" speech, Reagan conjured up a settler narrative in which the federal government had become too big and was unfairly repressing the freedoms of individual citizens. For Reagan, the vision of a settler state was unambiguous:

> [T]his idea that government is beholden to the people, that it has no other source of power except the sovereign people, is still the newest and the most unique idea in all the long history of man's relation to man. . . . This is the issue of this election: whether we believe in our capacity for self-government or whether we abandon the American revolution and confess that a little intellectual elite in a far-distant capitol can plan our lives for us better than we can plan them ourselves.[3]

Reagan's claim that the elite metropole cannot represent the sovereign citizen out west, whether a carry-over from his acting career or not, directly expresses a settler consciousness interpolated through a framing of political sovereignty and now adopted as conservatism. The individual settler citizen, for Reagan, is the ultimate bearer of freedom, who therefore must be defended by the government while not limited in their capacity to express that freedom. And while one may read this speech as a rejection of socialism, it can also be said that Reagan is simply recasting his own settler film persona in a national political theater. I contend that this transition from the film industry to national politics was easy for Reagan, because the settler persona in narrative is precisely a political one, produced in order to fortify a settler colonial consciousness. So, with regard to settler subjectivity production in the US, I agree with Reagan when he suggested that "there is no such thing as a left or right. There's only an up or down."[4] Like Lorenzo Veracini's assertion that a subject population economy in a settler situation is about elevation into the settler class or descension into a subaltern antitype, Reagan affirms that in his political vision, the US citizen can either rise up to their "old-aged dream, the ultimate in individual freedom consistent with law and order, or [fall] down to the ant heap of totalitarianism."[5] This was the beginning of the Reagan "law-and-order" mystique—a mystique rooted in settler consciousness that eventually characterized his governorship, his presidency, and in reality the majority of conservative politics in the US since.[6] If anything, this settler political persona that Reagan develops in the narration of the speech is a demonstration of the capacity for colonial population production mechanisms to produce antitypes through dispossession and violence, but in the process, simultaneously produce the settler citizen–type. After all, for every alien invasion (at least those described in this book), there is always the settler citizen ready to save the day and usher in a new world order.

It shoud come as no surprise, then, that in 1981, a newly inaugurated President Reagan offered his remarks at the annual meeting of the International Association of Chiefs of Police, where he again laid out a vision for his law-and-order agenda that was based on the protection of individual sovereignty against violent drug-trafficking criminals, foreign threats, and the failures of a government that had overreached its powers. In these remarks, he describes the ways drugs have created an exceptional criminal figure: "[A] portrait emerges. The portrait is that of a stark, staring face, a face that belongs to a frightening reality of our time—the face of a *human predator*, the face of the habitual criminal. Nothing in nature is more cruel and more dangerous."[7] The soon-to-be-declared "war on drugs" became a way for the Reagan administration to push its anti-Black/antimigrant agenda under the veil of national security.[8] Therefore, the violent drug dealer—the human predator of Reagan's imagination—became code for the settler antitype that was conjured in the image of the violent migrant invader and/or Black criminal antitype (both exogenous threats to the settler persona).

Then in 1986, President Reagan signed National Security Decision Directive no. 221, which declared that the narcotics trade posed a serious threat to US national security and authorized the US military to aid in securing the borderlands against narcotics traffickers.[9] This directive made the US borderlands a militarized zone where surveillance technologies would be employed to assist border agents both in finding narcotics and in halting unauthorized migration.[10] In 1991, the senate passed the National Defense Authorization Act, authorizing the use of National Guard troops as technical support for local communities and states to secure the southwestern US border.[11] While the goal of these executive and legislative acts was to target drug smugglers, they also arranged the relationship between the military and border security agencies. This relationship laid the foundation for the adoption of technological surveillance systems that would eventually be used to track and capture unauthorized entry of all migrants crossing the border.

Incidentally, not long after Reagan's declaration of war on drugs and the subsequent militarization of the México/US border, a cruel and dangerous predator with a stark face materialized in US cinema. *Predator* was released in 1987 and was the first of seven films in the *Predator* franchise, subsequent films being *Predator 2, Alien vs. Predator, Alien vs. Predator: Requiem, Predators, The Predator*, and the most recent installation called *Prey*.[12] The franchise is recognizable for its depiction of a large predator alien species—the Yautja—who are ritualistic hunters that have come to Earth to pursue and kill Earth's most skilled human hunters (except in *Predators*, where human protagonists find themselves being hunted on an alien planet). The Yautja are a technological species, relying on myriad devices, tools, and instruments to assist them in hunting humans as a rite of passage (and eventually Xenomorph aliens from the *Aliens* franchise when the two franchises merged in 1997). Throughout the *Predator* franchise, Yautja Predators employ their arsenal of technologies to hunt and kill a more grotesque alien species in a sort of sport, narrating an invasion story that depicts the human victim of the predator as unassuming yet capable of violence. In any case, from its advanced weaponry, like a laser-guided shoulder cannon and small nuclear explosives, the Predator alien is defined by its relationship to technologies of capture.

This chapter analyzes the technologies used to create alien affects in the *Predator* film franchise—namely thermal sense imaging and cloaking (what I am calling *Predator* technologies)—and how they have been distributed throughout the settler citizenship control assemblage in the US. After all, the entire *Predator* franchise—from the visual effects strategy to the plotline of the films in the series—is about the relationship between visibility and invisibility.[13] In this case study, I rely on a materialist assemblage method to analyze the films' technologies of visibility and invisibility (thermal sensing, cloaking, and others). I explain how these technologies are organized in relation to militarized border security mechanisms and describe how these technologies have been mobilized throughout the US by state legal and juridical mechanisms, all to autoproduce the conditions for sustained settler sovereignty.

PREDATOR

In John McTiernan's *Predator*, a group of elite ex–special forces mercenaries led by "Dutch" (played by Arnold Schwarzenegger, who, like Reagan, served as the governor of California after a successful acting career) are called in by the US Central Intelligence Agency to rescue a group of prisoners believed to be held hostage in the jungles of a fictional Central American rogue nation named Val Verde.[14] One by one, these elite soldiers are hunted down and killed in cold blood by the Predator—a camouflaged trophy hunter from another planet that adorns tribal imagery and participates in ritual killings. The Predator is able to evade capture and hunt the mercenaries primarily because it uses light-bending cloaking technology to blend into the jungle scenery and thermal sensing vision that allows it to track the commandos. The technology used to achieve this effect is a combination of camera techniques and postproduction special effects that were edited into the final scenes.[15] Stan Winston Studios (which also designed and produced creatures in the *Alien, Jurassic Park,* and *Terminator* franchises, to name a few) created the alien figure in *Predator* after the first version of the alien was sent back by McTiernan and the studio for not being realistic enough.[16] The final version of the alien figure was a combination of an actor in a suit (played by seven-foot-tall Kevin Peter Hall), a remote-controlled mechanical Predator head that was used for close-ups, and a series of lighting and special effects techniques (fig. 2.1). Like earlier alien franchises, *Predator* relied largely on absence (or invisibility) to create anxiety about the potential of an alien. There are very few scenes in the first hour of the ninety-minute film that depict the alien, only shimmers. To provide these shimmers, as well as to show how their alien sees, McTiernan and the visual effects crew relied on computer-generated images to produce the two visualizations of alien affects shimmering from the Predator: light-bending camouflage and first-person thermal vision.

Figure 2.1. Film still from John McTiernan's 1987 *Predator*; a shot of the Predator alien's face after removing its mask.

For Joel Hynek, the film's visual effects supervisor, creating the Predator's cloaking device and displaying its first-person thermal perspective were the two primary functions of the visual effects team.[17] R/Greenberg Associates created these two alien effects for the film, as well as the iridescent yellow blood left on the jungle floor from an injured Predator.[18] First, to create the appearance of a camouflaged Predator, the visual effects team filmed a stunt actor in a red suit who would be shot with the other actors as they moved through the jungle. The stunt suit needed to be red so that in postproduction, the figure of the alien in the suit could be removed from the dense green background and replaced with a second layered image of a body bending light around it. Film critic Les Paul Robley describes this process in more detail:

> At the first stage in the filming, the actor who played the creature was photographed wearing the red suit in the jungle exterior. Next, the actor left the frame and an identical take was repeated, this time recording only the background. Finally, a third take was made using a 30% wider lens on the camera. These three negatives were later optically combined, resulting in a composite which revealed a vague outline of the creature moving through the greenery as the background bent around its shape. When it stopped, it vanished completely.... "It was as if you were taking a Fresnel lens and moving across the environment," said [Hynek]. "As soon as he moved, we'd get all these weirdly distorting shapes and textures of the jungle."[19]

Figure 2.2. Film still from John McTiernan's 1987 *Predator*; the Predator alien activates its cloaking device, making it barely visible against the jungle background.

The shimmer of the Predator's cloaking is a product of its movement. It shines as it moves across the cinematic surface (fig. 2.2). Also, this visual effect is one of the first encounters audiences have with the Predator's alien affects. Despite the fact that to the characters in the film, cloaking might be a technology of invisibility, for audiences, this effect provides a visibility of alienhood.

Second, the Predator's vision is aided by thermal sensing technology that is embedded within the battle mask worn by the Predator while on a hunt (fig. 2.3). Initially, McTiernan and Hynek wanted to film the scenes from the Predator's perspective using only an infrared camera. However, Hynek thought that the images generated by thermal imaging cameras alone were not dynamic enough—commercial and military thermal cameras at the time used only a gray-scale visualization to signify temperature variance. They didn't have the bright colors representing the contrast they were hoping to visualize and what we eventually see in the film.[20] To complicate matters, the rugged and hilly jungles of southern México, where *Predator* was filmed, were quite warm. This meant that the body temperatures of the actors were nearly identical to the jungle backdrop through which they were trekking, making them virtually undetectable by the infrared camera.[21] The final images of the Predator's thermal vision in the film are composites of standard film images and thermal film images layered on top of one another. The visual effects studio then colored in the composite footage with a visual light scale from red to violet in order to accentuate the bodies of the commandos moving across the cinematic screen.[22] This first-person thermal image perspective, like the Predator's cloaking, was a technology of visibility that lit up bodies'

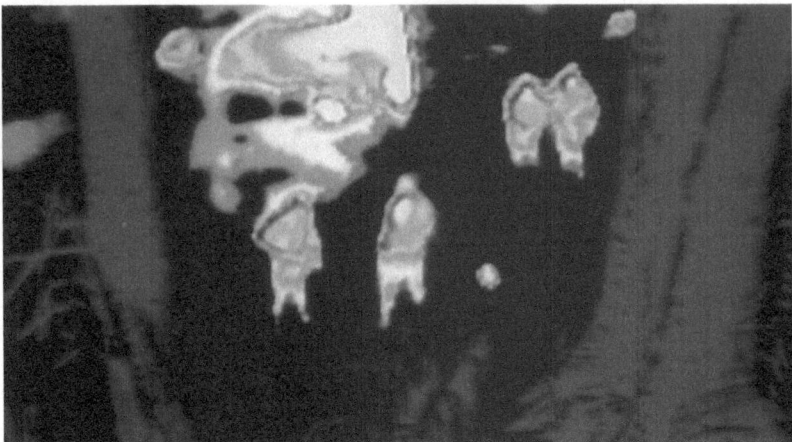

Figure 2.3. Film still from John McTiernan's 1987 *Predator*; a view from the perspective of the Predator alien's thermal vision filter against a jungle background.

intensive movements—or affects—as the characters moved through the jungle. By using a combination of the two technologies, the Yautja Predator easily captures (and eventually kills) most of the commandos. These two technologies of visibility—cloaking and infrared sight—continue as staples throughout the *Predator* franchise.

Predator 2 was released in 1990, and in it, a new Yautja Predator is hunting in the streets of Los Angeles in the midst of both a heat wave and a violent gang war. The Predator in this film is no longer hunting well-trained commandos but rather killing rival drug gang members.[23] Like McTiernan in the first film, director Stephen Hopkins illuminated the alien's affects in *Predator 2* using composite imagine techniques that included thermal imaging and light-bending camouflage.[24] The premise of the second film is similar to that of the first—Yautja hunters find violent humans to hunt as trophies. For the most part, the technologies also carry over from the first film. The two *Predator* technologies of visibility are still the primary ways in which the Yautja can be seen moving across the cinematic screen in *Predator 2* to capture their prey—they mostly remain invisible (fig. 2.4). For the sequel, Stan Winston Studios again created the physical Yautja alien costume for the Predator (again played by Hall), and R/Greenberg Associates produced the alien effects of cloaking and thermal imaging.

The impetus for the second film was that Hynek (the visual effects supervisor on both films) and writers Jim and John Thomas wanted to get a sense of what the *Predator* technologies would look like set against the landscape of the crime-ridden streets of a major US city.[25] This portrayal seems to invite

Figure 2.4. Film still from Stephen Hopkins's 1990 *Predator 2*; a view from the perspective of the Predator alien's thermal vision filter against a city background.

the *Predator* franchise into the realm of settler narrative: the rugged protagonist, LAPD officer Lieutenant Mike Harrigan (played by Danny Glover), has to take matters into his own hands to eliminate the Predator threat and bring order to the chaos left in the aftermath of alien invasion. The film also shows Harrigan reject the authority of the US government while also positioning himself on the defensive (even though he eventually tracks down and kills the Predator at the end of the film). In one key scene about an hour into the film, for example, Harrigan stumbles into a stakeout conducted by the federal government to capture the Predator. Special Agent Peter Keyes (played by Gary Busey) explains to Harrigan the new ways the US government is tracking the Yautja after an attack on a group of special forces in the Central American jungles a few years earlier (the plot from *Predator*). Keyes gives a brief description of the technological capabilities of the Yautja (as much for the film audience as for Officer Harrigan), including their ability to cloak by bending light and their reliance on thermal sensing vision. When Harrigan asks whether Keyes and his group of agents admire the alien, Keyes replies by saying, "Not for what he does, lieutenant; for what he is—for what he can give us . . . A new era in scientific technology." In this film, the government does not want to kill the alien as much as capture it to adapt its technology. This nod to the US security apparatus in the narrative of the film is slight, but it momentarily offers a glimpse of assemblage logic: take what technologies work in one area and apply them to another.

The final scene of *Predator 2* takes place inside a Yautja space vessel that temporarily houses the Predator aliens when they hunt.[26] In the end,

Harrigan injures the film's antagonist, translucent yellow blood squirts everywhere, and the alien dies. Perhaps the most important part of this scene, though, is not the killing of the alien but a five-second shot of the trophy case the Predator alien has kept. In the case, along with human skulls and those of extraterrestrials never before seen, there is a long, slender skull of a Xenomorph (from *Alien*)—an artifact from another alien film franchise. Set designers and visual effects teams who worked on both films decided that it was a way to pay homage to the popular graphic novels *Alien vs. Predator* and set the stage for the next act in the *Predator* franchise. Given the Yautja's capacity to see a body's micromovements using advanced technologies while remaining unseen, it makes sense that the US government would come to regard them (and their technology) so highly. By the second *Predator* film, humans have grown to respect and even admire the Yautja for "what they can give us": a way to hunt the slimy, invasive Xenomorph aliens. In fact, in the next two *Predator* films, the Yautja Predator becomes recoded as a protagonist alongside humans in the hunt for Xenomorph aliens.

In the first *Alien vs. Predator* (*AVP*) film, three Yautja Predators come to Earth to do combat with Xenomorph aliens as a rite of passage. During a mining expedition to the Antarctic, a group of archaeologists and scientists and a security team are caught in the middle of this ritual, triggering a series of events that lead to the eventual collaboration between human and predator to kill Xenomorphs and save humanity (leaving all but one human protagonist dead, which is a common narrative in the *Predator* franchise). One aspect of the story line that is particularly indicative of a settler narrative is the way the mythology of the Yautja Predator species is tied to the construction of pyramids throughout the world. One researcher on the expedition, Sebastian de Rosa (Raoul Bova), who was in the middle of conducting field research at Teotihuacan, México, describes later in the film how the Yautja species uses pyramids to perpetuate human sacrifices for their own ritualistic practices. This sets up the alliance later, when the Predator and Alexa (Sanaa Lathan), the last human standing, share a mutual respect (fig. 2.5). The theme of Yautja/human alliance reemerges in *Alien vs. Predator: Requiem*, in which the hybrid Yautja/Xenomorph that was born at the end of the *Alien vs. Predator* (referred to as the "Pred-alien" on some fan discussion boards) returns to Earth in a hijacked space vessel, along with several facehuggers (the scorpion-like creatures that implant a host with a Xenomorph larva). They eventually infest a small Colorado town with Xenomorphs, and a Yautja bounty hunter is called in to eradicate the Xenomorph/Pred-alien invasion. The film again ends with both the Yautja Predator and rugged white humans collaborating to fight off the Xenomorph invasion, while the US government

Figure 2.5. Film still from Paul W. S. Anderson's 2004 *Alien vs. Predator*; Alexa Woods (Sanaa Lathan) allies with a Predator alien to defeat the Xenomorph alien queen.

fails to contain the disaster (another common theme throughout the *Predator* franchise).

In many ways, positioning the Predator against the Xenomorph in the two films allows audiences to see the Yautja Predators go through a process of elevation whereby their exogenous nature is rendered desirable in contrast to the Xenomorphs, who must be eliminated at all costs. This population economy, in which one exogenous group can transfer into the settler class while another will always be seen as subaltern, is at the heart of settler population production. The settlers did it to themselves and other exogenous groups who entered the settlement. As is the case here, acceptance into the settler citizen class might depend on one's willingness to share weapons of subjection along with the willingness to use them against the antitypes the settlers deem most threatening. Another common trend in this process is seeing the human protagonists reject the US government for an alliance with the Predator alien, evoking the rejection of the colonial metropole that is characteristic of settler sovereignty production.

Along with a major narrative shift in the *Predator* franchise, the two technologies of Predator visibility found in the original films are updated for the *AVP* films to make more visually stunning alien affects. According to John Bruno, visual effects supervisor for the first *AVP* film, whereas the first two *Predator* films required a layering of image and coloring techniques to achieve the Predator's cloaking and thermal vision renderings, computer-generated images were used in the *AVP* films to enhance those technologies. For the cloaking effect, Bruno worked with the Double Negative visual effects studio to replace the alien cloaking with a CGI effect that accomplished the same image: "light-bending" camouflage.[27] For the thermal vision renderings of the Predators' perspective, Bruno relied on both the technique of using a "military" thermal imaging camera to shoot human actors and CGI to add color and alien figures seen by predators.[28] He hired Double Negative and Cinesite to create these effects.[29] In *Alien vs. Predator: Requiem*, Colin and Greg Strause (directors and visual effects supervisors) used a CGI cloaking effect for the Predator as well. They also added more layers to the Predator's thermal vision, including electromagnetic imaging and X-ray vision.[30] In 2010's *Predators* (directed by Nimród Antal), the Predator's cloaking is still CGI, and the thermal imaging, unlike in the previous film, is now all CGI.[31] Another difference is that *Predators* takes audiences to a distant "game reserve" planet where the Yautja hunt humans who have been abducted and brought to the planet. The film still features alien cloaking and thermal/electromagnetic/X-ray imaging. The film also further serves to nativize the Predator aliens alongside the white protagonists—an Israeli Defense Forces sniper named Isabelle (Alice Braga) and Royce (Adrien Brody), a former member of US Special Operations Forces and now a black ops mercenary—who in the end survive the ritual hunt, earn the respect of the Predators, and escape from the planet. Here, we have a direct alliance between the contemporary settler persona—as depicted by an IDF sniper and a US private security mercenary—and the Predator alien persona, and along with it an adoption of the *Predator* technologies.

The Predator (2018) picks up the franchise with a narrative that takes audiences to a mysterious UFO crash in México.[32] A group of US soldiers on a secret antidrug mission are interrupted by a Predator ship that crash-lands. The soldiers engage the Predator and all but one are killed; the surviving soldier is captured by army reinforcements. Before the survivor, Quinn McKenna (Boyd Holbrook), can be interrogated by the US government, though, he mails a predator battle mask to his son, who lives in an unidentified US suburb.[33] The battle mask becomes a central artifact in the film, leading an upgraded, ten-foot-tall Super-Predator bounty hunter (called an Upgrade Predator in the film) to try to recover the missing technology and also kill the Predator who had let the technology fall into the hands of humans in the first place. Later in the film, a group of protagonists who have escaped from a military psychiatric hospital (many of whom were there because they believe in aliens; again, a nod to conspiracy theory production and a rejection of the US colonial metropole, both characteristic of settler consciousness) team up with a group of scientists trying to weaponize Yautja technologies and eventually kill the Upgrade Predator (fig. 2.6). The film ends with McKenna and his son (the settler types) collaborating with scientists to decipher the Yautja language. Again, this film frames the alliance between Predator and human as natural, nativizing both. However, the antagonist

Figure 2.6. Film still from Shane Black's 2018 *The Predator*; a showdown between a typical Predator alien and a much larger Upgrade Predator alien.

of the film is an upgraded, bounty hunter Predator, not a Xenomorph. This makes explicit the value of *Predator* technologies to the settler subject and recasts the Yautja as rejectable aliens.

As the films in the franchise evolved, so did the visual effects teams' capacity for developing technologically advanced illumination techniques and computer-assisted visibility to intensify alien affects onscreen. Those technologies were assembled and reassembled over time to materialize a particular type of subjective production process that nativizes both humans and Yautja aliens to reject the undesirable Xenomorph. Although the *Predator* film franchise relies almost entirely on actors in alien suits to act out the narratives of these Hollywood thrillers, its visual effects capacity for rendering *Predator* technologies on screen has evolved tremendously as well. The franchise's relative financial success and large cult following can primarily be attributed to these technological contributions that various directors and visual effects crews incorporated in the cinematic illumination of alienhood, which eventually led to an alliance between humans and Yautja. In tracking the evolution of the technologies in the franchise, we can see how subjection is produced visually while also getting a sense of how the production of films like those in the franchise are so intertwined with vast networks of industrial, creative, and technological agents. The merger between the *Alien* and *Predator* franchises, for example, shows that beyond the narrative alignment, the two assemblages of filmic narratives also share material relationships that reach into dozens of other film and television franchises.

However, the circulation of *Predator* technologies—cloaking and thermal vision—is not restricted to film or even the film industry. *Predator* technologies are also trafficked through military and security control mechanisms throughout the US settler citizenship control assemblage. Just as these technologies of visibility have advanced over nearly three decades to make alien affects more intense in cinema through the *Predator* franchise, they have become more widely used to produce alien affects on migrant bodies, criminal bodies, terrorist bodies, and many others coded as settler antitypes by citizenship control in the US today. The next section goes into more detail about *Predator* technologies and how they are trafficked between cinema and border security apparatuses.

PREDATOR TECHNOLOGIES AND BORDER SECURITY

According to the US Border Patrol's *Strategic Plan* for 2012–2016:

> Border Patrol agents' use of technology continues to be an important capability and force multiplier for the Border Patrol and its partners. The Border Patrol leverages various forms of technology to gain situational awareness to better detect, identify, monitor, and respond to threats to the Nation's borders.[34]

This idea that technologies of visibility are a "force multiplier" has driven the private surveillance technology sector to develop the latest surveillance technologies to meet the demands of the highly militarized national frontier. In an article instructing the surveillance technology industry on how to attract bids from US Customs and Border Protection, John Merlino repeats the need for better technologies to provide "the relevant situational awareness that the border protection staff need for actionable use and intelligence gathering."[35] In these cases, force multipliers are synonymous with the expansion of state power. "The goal now appears to focus on creating frontier force multipliers by strategically deploying infrastructure along remote borders to house technical equipment and staff and aggregate intelligence from multiple systems."[36] In other words, mobilizing "frontier force multipliers" in the citizenship control assemblage requires the trafficking of technologies to the border and throughout the nation.

Today, the US Border Patrol operates more than 115 aircraft, 9 unmanned aerial vehicles (UAVs), more than 11,000 underground seismic sensors, nearly 40 mobile surveillance systems, and more than 270 remote video surveillance systems.[37] Many of these technologies that are multiplying state power are *Predator* technologies. The focus of this section is to situate the *Predator* franchise—in particular the two primary technologies of visibility used to create alien affects in the films—within the context of settler citizenship by describing their emergence and behavior with relation to border security mechanisms. This approach offers a glimpse of how technologies are produced and distributed in the US. The *Predator* technologies discussed in the previous section, for example, emerge and evolve within the environment of the cinematic—a mode of settler narrative production. The *Predator* technologies described in this section have emerged and evolved outside of that arena, in the modes of population production now extended throughout the US settler states and in places around the globe where the US is exerting its settler colonial power.

THE ORIGINS OF THERMAL SENSING

German astronomer William Herschel is widely credited with discovering infrared energy. In an experiment with prisms and sunlight, Herschel took Isaac Newton's findings about the fragmentations of light (also using a prism) and concluded that each visible color of light had a unique wavelength, but varied in temperature. Herschel also measured the temperature of the area just beyond the visible red ray, concluding that this region just beyond the visible red—the infrared—had a higher temperature than the visible spectrum. He went on to use this scientific breakthrough to pioneer a technique for determining the elemental composition of planets and stars using their temperature signatures.[38] This science is also the basis for the thermal detection and thermal imaging technologies that emerged in the middle of the twentieth century. However, these technologies were not developed for the sake of scientific discovery. They were designed for war.[39]

A primitive version of thermal imaging technology was developed in 1929 by Hungarian inventor, Kálmán Tihanyi for use in aerial night surveillance by British airships. However, the process to render readable images from the thermal data involved many steps and was not always suitable for combat situations. It was not until nearly three decades later that the technology advanced enough to be useful for the US military.[40] In the late 1960s and early 1970s, companies competed for military contracts to develop and patent the first thermal imaging system that could be used for nighttime combat situations. Eventually, Raytheon (a subsidiary of Texas Instruments at the time), Honeywell, and FLIR Systems were all awarded contracts to develop front-facing thermal imaging cameras that would be used on military aircraft.[41] From the time Tihanyi developed the slow prototype for the thermal sensor until 1965, thermal imaging technology had had a number of shortcomings. First, most thermal imaging systems faced downward when mounted on a plane. This did not provide a very dynamic image. Second, the image generated by the thermal sensors was not available in real time, so even if the image was dynamic, it would not be seen by anybody until even days after it had been taken. Finally, thermal imaging devices were very expensive and not in great demand after the Korean War.[42]

Then, in 1956, researchers at the University of Chicago in collaboration with the US Air Force developed the first real-time, forward-looking infrared (FLIR) sensor for the purpose of night surveillance. It wasn't until about a decade later, though, that two separate projects involving a military and private industry partnership sparked an era of innovation for thermal imaging. In the first half of the 1960s, Texas Instruments (the parent company of Raytheon) and the US Air Force collaborated to develop a FLIR camera that would be widely used in the US aggression against Vietnam.[43] In 1965, the Hughes Aircraft Company (which eventually merged with Raytheon in 1997) and the US Navy joined forces to develop and test a separate FLIR camera that would serve many purposes including combat, firefighting, and electronics repair.[44] "From that point on, the FLIR business burgeoned, and between 1960 and 1974 at least sixty different FLIRs were developed and several hundred were produced.... [T]he term FLIR now properly connoted any real-time thermal imager."[45] As a result of the collaboration between the US military and numerous interconnected private industries, the capacity of the technology to see subjects in the field of battle drastically increased.

By the end of the 1970s, the FLIR industry largely relied on barium strontium titanate (BST) infrared detectors. These BST sensors, developed by Raytheon and Honeywell, were part of the first wave of thermal sensors that were compact and efficient enough to be equipped onto military aircraft, but that also could be used in civilian industries like firefighting and energy infrastructure.[46] In 1978, FLIR Systems was founded solely focused on the increasing demands of the commercial market. McTiernan and Hopkins used FLIR Systems' BTS cameras in *Predator* and *Predator 2*, respectively, to capture the thermal images of the actors that were eventually layered over the standard film images.[47] By the mid-1980s, Raytheon, Honeywell, and FLIR Systems all advanced thermal imaging capabilities, by now relying on new techniques of sensing infrared energy and rendering images that correlated. Honeywell became the first major thermal imaging company that developed military imaging technology to make the move to the private sector, and by the late 1980s it had created a sensor that relied on vanadium oxide (VOx) microbolometer technology, a more efficient sensor with a higher resolution.[48] The thermal vision scenes in the two *AVP* films were shot using microbolometer cameras, using a FLIR Systems Rainbow LUT (this refers to the color spectrum used to render heat images).[49] Incidentally, 2007, the year *Alien vs. Predator: Requiem* was released, was when FLIR Systems made the leap into the military surveillance industry; it was awarded a $250 million contract to equip US Army helicopters with VOx thermal cameras.[50]

The purpose of this brief history of FLIR technology is to demonstrate how material components of assemblages are organized and trafficked across an array of industrial, military, and scientific industries and of course in cinema. Technology of visibility is a mobile component in a multitude of arenas that constitute settler citizenship control assemblages. However, the example of FLIR technology also illustrates how the adoption and development of the infrared technology of visibility in numerous areas helped increase the capacity of those technologies to territorialize through subject making within the various arenas of the settler citizenship assemblage. FLIR technology made war more intense. It made the capacity to battle large fires greater, and of course, it made alien affects more visible in the *Predator* film franchise. It has since also become a "force multiplier" for US Customs and Border Protection.

THERMAL SENSING ON THE BORDER

FLIR technology first appeared in border security mechanisms in the United States, including US seaports, in the late 1990s. This newly added technology was part of the federal government's ongoing technological surveillance support to the Border Patrol, which by 1990 included closed-circuit television and seismic sensors.[51] In 1997, the Department of Justice and the Immigration and Naturalization Service (INS) established a program called the Integrated Surveillance Intelligence System (ISIS), which comprised three distinct technological components to create a "shield" at the border.[52] Beyond seismic sensor technology and an integrated computer-aided network, ISIS relied most on the implementation of remote video surveillance technology that could see in the dark: thermal imaging.[53] After the passage of the Homeland Security Act of 2002, which established the Department of Homeland Security, the US Border Patrol became one of twelve agencies reorganized under this newly formed, cabinet-level executive department (under President George W. Bush).[54] For FLIR and other surveillance technology companies, this meant a new stream of federal defense dollars with a new imperative to subject migrants as foreign threats.

One example of this mobilization of FLIR technology at the border during the ISIS initiative came in the form of remote vehicle surveillance (RVS) units. The RVS systems were simply eighty-foot poles with a standard color video camera and a FLIR camera mounted to the top, attached to all-terrain vehicles that could traverse the natural topography of the borderlands.[55] This technology mimics the very same techniques used by the makers of *Predator* and *Predator 2*: the standard film images are layered with infrared thermal images to produce a composite image of a body traversing a backdrop that is often the same temperature as the bodies. A thermal camera alone would not be able to achieve this effect, but paired with a standard camera, the image stands out. By 2005, there were more than 250 RVS camera systems located in the southwestern US—some as far as one hundred miles away from the US/México border.[56]

Also in 2005, ISIS became America's Shield Initiative (ASI) and was subsumed in the Secure Border Initiative (SBI), which was tasked with integrating physical, technological, and law enforcement components into a single, networked system. DHS estimated that the SBI would require $1.5 billion over five years to establish a security network on the southern border; the network would enhance border security with thermal imaging on both mobile, remotely operated surveillance towers and on unmanned aircraft.[57] For example, in 2005, DHS awarded General Atomics Aeronautical Systems (a subsidiary of General Dynamics) $14.1 million "to deliver, operate, and maintain one Predator B UAV platform and sensor package."[58] Apart from sharing a name with the Predator alien (the first *AVP* film had been released a year earlier), the MQ-9 Reaper Predator B UAV also relied on thermal sensing and camouflage to see and subject the bodies of migrants and others along US border regions. By 2009, there were six MQ-9 Reaper Predator B UAV surveillance systems in use by the Border Patrol. Today, CBP operates a fleet of nine Predator B drones that fly missions out of North Dakota, Florida, Texas, and Arizona.[59]

In 2011, FLIR Systems was given its largest contract, worth nearly $102 million, to develop mobile imaging technology specifically for the Border Patrol.[60] And in 2015, FLIR Systems was awarded a $19 million contract by DHS to continue development of long-range FLIR cameras that could be used for both aerial surveillance and mobile tower camera surveillance.[61] Along with FLIR Systems, General Dynamics has also been awarded nearly $100 million in contracts from DHS to upgrade and maintain much of the RVS surveillance infrastructure and to install thermal sensing cameras at several points along the México/US border.[62] Thus, since 2011, FLIR systems (the makers of the thermal cameras used to film *Predator* and *Predator 2*) and General Dynamics (the makers of the MQ-9 Reaper Predator B drone and the RVS dual-mounted FLIR/standard image cameras) have remained two companies who are working most closely with the Border Patrol to produce alien affects on migrant bodies (and others) using *Predator* technologies.

While thermal imaging technologies were not invented for the *Predator* franchise, there is evidence here of how this technology migrated between the cinematic and military-industrial assemblages of settler production. The material tracks that are left behind by the mobile technologies of visibility, those that perpetuate the cycles of settler subject production, can be seen moving between the filmic narrative productions of settler invasion and the population productions of settler antitypes on the México/US frontier. There is also evidence to show that as the technology migrated between these arenas, it grew in capacity. The evolution of infrared thermal imaging technology for the US military, US border security, and filmmaking mechanisms demonstrates how trafficking flows of funds and technologies subject bodies according to the desired settler citizenship production mode. Since the establishment of the Department of Homeland Security, the US has channeled billions of dollars into the citizenship control assemblage in order to deploy technologies like FLIR and others as a means to subject migrant bodies in the alien persona (a settler antitype) by casting their bodies with alien affects. These subjections are mobilized in a powerful assemblage of settler citizenship control as personae and structure the sets of power relations between settlers and their antitypes.

CLOAKING

Throughout the *Predator* franchise, the Yautja Predator aliens are all equipped with an electrical camouflage system that allows them to blend into the background of an environment, be it the jungles of fictional Central American countries, Colorado mountain towns, or the streets of Los Angeles. It wasn't until the "light-bending" device was turned off in the films that the Predator alien became "visible" to other characters, although the alien remained visible to audiences onscreen as a result of the production of the cloaking alien affect. Unlike the aliens' thermal vision, though, this *Predator* technology was not imagined by the military for use in combat. This technology seems to be a product of the science fiction imagination.

H. G. Wells's *The Invisible Man*, written in 1897 (a year before *The War of the Worlds*), may be the earliest example of science fiction cloaking technology.[63] In the novel, Wells's protagonist uses chemicals and light waves to render himself invisible to others. In 1966, the technology reappeared in the *Star Trek* television series when the Starship *Enterprise* comes under attack from a cloaked Romulan spacecraft. The show's writer, Paul Schneider, made the technology a regular part of the series, and in 1968 it was first called a "cloaking device" in the show.[64] Also in 1968, Ukrainian theorist Victor Veselago predicted "the possibility of building metamaterials that act as light accelerators," although metamaterial technology would not be realized for nearly four more decades.[65] Then, in 1987, *Predator* was released, giving audiences a first glimpse of an alien hunter cloaked in a light-bending, electric cloak killing an entire special ops unit. According to physicist David R. Smith, this rendering—accomplished through filming techniques and layering—was a "fairly realistic" depiction of the way metamaterial technology works today.[66]

By the time the first *Predator* film was released, thermal imaging technology was well in use; the FLIR camera and other military technologies aided its adaptation into the film's narrative. With respect to light-bending cloaking technology, on the other hand, its appearance in cinema to create alien affects in *Predator* preceded the emergence of the technology in use for combat or national security. In 2006, Duke University physicists became the first to design and test a workable metamaterial cloaking device that can bend microwaves around an object. However, the highly inefficient experiment was unable to bend visible light, so objects in the test were still visible.[67] Then, in 2008, Xiang Zhang at the University of California, Berkeley, developed a pair of metamaterial surfaces that were able to bend visible light and low-level infrared light in much the same ways as the experiments at Duke two years earlier.[68] Since that time, several other cloaking technologies have been developed, mostly to help military agencies camouflage their soldiers, aircraft, and land vehicles. Most recently, the US Army and Canadian military officials have collaborated with HyperStealth Biotechnology to develop and test Quantum Stealth, the latest in metamaterial technology, which can fully conceal a person by covering them in light-bending camouflage that adapts to the environment.[69] So, considering that there are currently no working cloaking technologies being implemented by the US military in combat (at least known to the public), there are also no examples of light-bending cloaking being adopted by border security officers to hide themselves.

The closest thing to the cloaking invisibility used on the border may just be a technology that has already been discussed in this section. General Atomics' MQ-9 Reaper Predator B drone system is an unmanned aircraft used by the US Border Patrol to monitor high-traffic zones along the México/US border. The Predator B, without camouflage, is invisible to the naked eye when flying at optimal heights (above fifteen thousand feet).[70] It is able to simultaneously use numerous technologies to monitor movements across the region—including FLIR technology—while remaining undetectable to those being monitored. The Predator C drone, developed by General Atomics as the next-generation UAV, was unveiled in 2009 and uses stealth technology developed at the end of the Cold War.[71] While it is not clear whether the

Border Patrol plans to upgrade to the stealthier Predator C Avenger model, the air force, who previously supplied MQ-9 Reaper Predator B drones to DHS for use by CBP, has already upgraded to the Predator C Avenger.[72]

In the case of these two *Predator* technologies—infrared thermal detection and light-bending cloaking—the previous examples demonstrate that both technologies of visibility are moving back and forth between the arena of settler narrative production in the *Predator* film franchise and the arena of settler subject production at the border. They are strategically trafficked, in both the cinematic and the national security assemblages, to make alien affects visible when cast upon the backdrop of an occupied national territory that has been recoded with settler ideological production. Again, as *Predator* technologies were trafficked in and out of various corners of the citizenship control assemblage, they evolved. Their capacities grew, and continue to grow, in the process of producing visible, feelable settler antitypes within the settler population production economy.

PREDATOR TECHNOLOGIES AND THE POLITICAL ALIEN ANTITYPE

The alien settler antitype that is produced in the US citizenship control assemblage is a political figure. Again, its purpose is to define what the settler citizen is not. Reagan invoked the term "human predator" in his 1981 speech to describe this dehumanized figure of the Black and/or brown noncitizen, and it became the new code for the rejectable exogenous settler antitype. This happened precisely at a time when the US settler state was shifting national security and military funds to securitize the border under the guise of a war on drugs. Therefore, as assemblages tend to do, the settler citizenship control assemblage produced a new coding for the subjective persona of alien—the predator—and in doing so targeted a new frontier of territoriality that would generate dozens of opportunities for land and labor exploitation. I argue that the US government's role in this process is not to express a particular national sovereignty over its border region but to support the settler colonial modes of production that mobilize localized, privatized violent extraction events. This is evidenced in the emergence of a private, for-profit detention infrastructure, the appropriation of government funds for technology companies producing alien affects, and numerous examples of violence against Native and Mestiza/o/x migrant bodies along the México/US border. This section describes the political mobilization of the alien antitype over nearly a century in US legal discourse and how recasting this antitype time and again has perpetuated and grown the capacity of the US settler citizenship assemblage. Eventually, this discursive antitype became a material, affective antitype, thanks to *Predator* technologies.

IMMIGRATION LAW AND THE ALIEN ANTITYPE

In 1924, several federal legislative actions swiftly and permanently transformed the dynamics of citizenship in the United States. Most notably, Congress passed An Act to Limit the Immigration of Aliens into the United States, and for Other Purposes (also known as the Johnson-Reed Act or the Immigration Act of 1924), which created a quota system for immigrants based on numbers of residents from any particular nation living in the US in 1890. Only 2 percent of the number of migrants from a given national population already living in the US in 1890 would be allowed in annually.[73] So, if there were ten thousand Swedish migrants living in the US in 1890, for example, the US government would allow two hundred visas for Swedish migrants wishing to enter the US annually beginning in 1924. Considering that the largest migrant populations to the US before 1890 were northwestern Europeans, this law was intended to preserve a specific cultural "heterogeneity" of the bodies within the citizenship at the time.[74] For many southern and eastern Europeans, as well as for many Asians and others who did not migrate to the US until after the turn of the twentieth century, this meant near exclusion. Still, for other migrants from Asian nations who had already been prohibited from entering the US, the Johnson-Reed Act only reinforced their outright exclusion.[75] These exogenous groups excluded from citizenship in the settler states were thus constituted as the alien personae addressed in the bill's title; this subjection preceded the attachment to the migrants' body.

Legislative acts, particularly those regarding the establishment of citizenship rights, are themselves assemblages of governmentality, organizing persons and materials like geographies, access to government institutions, and the resources that those institutions distribute.[76] The Johnson-Reed Act, for example, is one such arrangement. The discursive expression (coding) of alienhood is used to subject exogenous migrants and divide them from the settler bodies that are naturalized onto the occupied geographies of the US. Those who are subjected as alien cannot be naturalized. This subjection organized access to the benefits of US citizenship at the time, including the capacity to vote and own land. Furthermore, it took the expressions of coding and territorialization—both sayable expressions of alienhood and seeable encounters with alien affects—and redistributed them into law. Subsequent federal immigration laws followed suit.

In the 1924 Labor Appropriations Act, Congress officially established the US Border Patrol (USBP) through the Labor Department.[77] The USBP's mission initially was simply "enforcement of the laws regulating immigration of aliens into the United States."[78] Many volunteer Border Patrol officers in El Paso, for example, had been unofficially protecting the border from mostly alien Chinese migrants for almost two decades before the Labor Appropriations Act.[79] However, the formalization of the group now meant that federal funds were going to be used to protect the border from unwanted foreigners from North America. This also meant that for the first time, we see the criminalization that was written into the Johnson-Reed Act materialized onto the migrant body as the "illegal alien" subject.[80] For its first several decades, the Border Patrol was relatively low-tech, relying mostly on tracking methods and horse patrols to surveil the borderlands between ports of entry along both the northern border with Canada and the southern border with México.[81] The role of the Border Patrol, to surveil the border for unauthorized foreign entry and smuggling, stayed relatively the same until the 1950s.

During this period, The US also entered into a formal agreement with the Mexican government creating a guest worker program called the Bracero program. From 1942 until 1963, the program invited millions of braceros, or migrant laborers, to the US to meet the demand for labor in agriculture and the rail industry that was created when soldiers left to fight in Europe.[82] This had two major effects: first, it vastly increased the flow of Mexican migrants into the US and inspired the first legal attempts to limit the numbers of migrants from México. Even after the war ended, the program continued to recruit agricultural laborers while trying to control their numbers. The second effect, which likely resulted from the first, was the widespread adoption of the term "illegal alien" to describe a migrant who was recruited to the US but remained jobless, unable to contract labor due to the termination of a work agreement by the employer. The agreement between the US and México set a quota (roughly fifty thousand yearly at the start of the program and close to eight hundred thousand at its height in 1951), which was often exceeded by migrants and poorly managed by the US.[83] By the end of the program in 1963, millions of the braceros who had been brought to the US as a result of program remained, and they were quickly subjected as the (illegal) alien settler antitype. The Bracero program, which had been created by the US government to support the exploitative agricultural and industrial labor practices of settler citizens (farmers, ranchers, etc.), manufactured the "illegal alien problem," and government agencies have since been trying to fix it.[84] This attempt to solve the "problem" has become the standard framework for the US government's approach to policing migrants: the mass removal of aliens and the sealing of the border to protect from further invasion.

In 1952, Congress passed the Immigration and Nationality Act (the McCarran-Walter Act), which consolidated all the legal actions taken by the federal government regarding immigration, naturalization, passport requirements, and matters regarding migrant aliens.[85] The act also formally concluded exclusion provisions for Asian nations, ending the practices legislated in the Chinese Exclusion Act of 1882 and other legal attempts to keep specific ethnic groups out of the national citizenship flow, but upheld the quota system from the 1924 Johnson-Reed Act that overwhelmingly granted visas to migrants from northwestern European nations.[86] So, while specific racial distinctions for desirable migrants were no longer articulated in this bill, the racial composition of the settler antitype arranged by global region was still motivated by white supremacy. Beyond the racial component, though, the language of the 1952 act also targeted communists, anarchists, "alcoholics," "drug addicts," the "feeble-minded," those with any mental health issues, the "insane," those with disabilities, "beggars," "prostitutes," those entering the US to "commit immoral sexual acts," and many others whose lifestyles were not compatible with the settler lifestyle.[87] Then in 1965, the federal government passed a new Immigration and Nationality Act (Hart-Celler Act), which replaced the four-decade-long quota system with an overall cap (twenty thousand) and lottery.[88] The act ended a system that unfairly kept many Asians and Africans from migrating to the US in large numbers but also placed the first limits on migrants from the Western Hemisphere, including the millions of "illegal aliens" produced by the Bracero program.[89]

The settler antitype of the alien (and eventually the illegal alien) materialized in the enactment of the US's first antimigrant legislation and continues to organize personae within the settler citizenship control assemblage. The settler governance structures subjected each new generation of exogenous migrants arriving in the US settler nation to antitypes in order to control their capacity to contribute to the settler production modes. We also see during this time the permanent attribution of the "illegal alien" persona to the Mestiza/o/x migrant as a result of the Bracero program's inability to manage the large numbers of invited guest workers. Nearly all of the US's current migration policy, especially efforts to seal the border and deport undesirable migrants, stems from the failures of the US to control its exogenous populations after World War II. The next section describes how technologies of visibility (namely *Predator* technologies) appear in legislative efforts to implement that migration policy.

MOBILIZING PREDATOR TECHNOLOGIES

Prior to the 1950s, the funding for Border Patrol technology was largely limited to transportation costs for agents. Officers were given a modest salary and basic rations but not much else; each patrol officer was responsible for providing their own horse and saddle.[90] However, the McCarran-Walter Act and Hart-Celler Act both make appropriations for deportation transportation technologies like trains, airplanes, and boats. For the first time since the creation of a national Border Patrol, deportation technologies allowed the US to actively expel those who had entered without authorization. This meant that the deportation mechanism in the US could now remove undesirable exogenous populations, growing the capacity for the settler state to both produce and control populations and maximize the value of the labor extracted from them. Along with providing a deportation infrastructure, federal immigration legislation in the 1950s and 1960s also funded the first aircraft for the Border Patrol to surveil the coast along the Gulf of Mexico and the México/US border region. These technologies, though, only allowed Border Patrol agents to monitor and apprehend unauthorized migrants and smugglers who were also using aircraft technology to enter the US and not necessarily those who were trekking on foot or driving automobiles.[91] More advanced surveillance technologies like video cameras and thermal imaging would not be widely used to actively surveil the border until the 1990s.

So, by the 1980s, the legal mechanisms that had limited the number of authorized migrants from México and Central America led to an overwhelming number of Mexican and Central American migrants entering and living in the US without authorization. Reagan's extractive, interventionist policies in Central America only further drove migrants to seek asylum in the US, so by the time the Immigration Reform and Control Act (Simpson-Mazzoli Act) of 1986 was passed, the goal was twofold.[92] The act granted nearly three million unauthorized migrants residency with proof they had paid taxes, could speak English, and otherwise were going with the flow—an elevation into the settler class for those exogenous groups willing to live the settler lifestyle. The act also bolstered the capacity of the US Border Patrol by dramatically increasing both the number of officers and the amount of congressional funding to enhance immigration enforcement. This meant that appropriations for enforcement assets—including surveillance technology—doubled between 1982 and 1987.[93] This also meant that the state equipped its border agents with additional surveillance technology, like "22 helicopters for all nine sectors (up from a total of two helicopters in just one sector) and hundreds of night-vision scopes, night vision goggles, and surveillance systems."[94] By

1992, the Border Patrol had used the increased funds to implement advanced technologies of visibility like ground microphones, ground infrared sensors, night-vision technology, and others to surveil and control migrants.[95]

Therefore, by the time the *Predator* technologies had been developed and adopted by the border security mechanisms in the last decade of the twentieth century, the legal mechanism of citizenship had already been coding exogenous migrants as alien for nearly a century. Again, in societies of control, capture of the subject is about knowing the subject. This requires a layer of visibility that is superimposed on the discursive coding. So in order to capture migrants and subject them as alien, the settler citizenship control assemblage in the US needed an affective layer of alien visibility. Thus, since the 1990s, the citizenship control assemblage has been producing and trafficking *Predator* technologies to surveil the movements of migrants crossing the border with México. For example, since about the time *Predator 2* was released, the number of FLIR systems and UAVs used to surveil the border had grown dramatically. FLIR technology was eventually adopted for regularly patrolling the México/US border in the mid-1990s, when Border Patrol initiatives like Operation Hold the Line in El Paso and Operation Gatekeeper in San Diego were conducted with a specific objective to stop the influx of migrants at those particular points in the border before they had crossed.[96]

In 2002, the last year the US Border Patrol was under the jurisdiction of the Immigration and Naturalization Service before being moved to the newly created Department of Homeland Security, funding for border security mechanisms through the Border Patrol was $1.3 billion (up from $230 million in 1989). During President Barack Obama's administration (2009–2017), the annual budget for CBP grew close to $4 billion, nearly triple what it had been in 2003.[97] After DHS was created and the funding for the Border Patrol tripled, the capacity to traffic *Predator* technologies became nearly limitless. In 2005, a year after the release of *Alien vs. Predator*, General Atomics was contracted by the Border Patrol to create a drone surveillance program that would be used to monitor unauthorized migrant movement across the southern border. Since then, the US has spent nearly $600 million to purchase and operate up to ten predator drones along the southern border with México.[98] This does not include the $96 million contract General Dynamics was given in 2013 to fashion night vision and infrared technologies on the Border Patrol's mobile surveillance vehicles, both Predator drones and RVS mobile surveillance towers.[99]

Also, between 2005 and 2015, FLIR Systems was awarded more than $145 million in federal contracts to arm border security agents with the latest in thermal imaging technologies, including handheld thermal cameras and long-range infrared cameras for their mobile surveillance vehicles. One of these contracts, as mentioned above, was for more than $100 million to manufacture infrared and night-vision imaging technologies for the Border Patrol's mobile surveillance units.[100] Each of these contracts came out of funds appropriated by House and Senate committees with the specific intent to enhance the Border Patrol's "situational awareness" by providing them with the most advanced, force-multiplying technologies available. Force multiplying—or increasing state power through knowing the captured subject—is a practice rooted in the capacity to produce a visible alien persona to layer with a settler constitutive citizenship code. Trafficking in surveillance technologies will only continue to grow as the citizenship assemblage continues to operate uninterrupted.

More than ever, the US is channeling resources into border security mechanisms, including an astounding investment in technologies that produce alien affects on migrant bodies. The investment in these two particular *Predator* technologies of visibility—technologies that are established in other arenas like extraterrestrial cinema—are organized by legislative apparatuses in the US to have the same effect in the citizenship control assemblage: to make alien personae more visibly intense. And since the beginning of the Donald Trump administration, requests for border security and infrastructure again almost doubled. Some estimates for fiscal year 2019 requests to Congress from the executive branch approach $10 billion. While much of these funds were allocated to the "wall" and more detention facilities, nearly $600 million was for "border technologies and non-wall infrastructure," including $183 million for "aircraft and other aviation assets" and another $182 million for "surveillance technology, such as towers, radars, cameras, and sensors."[101]

Therefore, the MQ-9 Reaper Predator B drone, equipped with infrared imaging technologies and operated by CBP, is the embodiment of the *Predator* technologies of visibility that have been trafficked throughout the US settler citizenship assemblage. The drones, the RVS systems, and a number of other technologies are force-multiplying territorial assemblages that produce alien affects in order to cast exogenous migrants as alien antitypes. The fusion of technologically produced visibility with discursive alien subjectivity, which coincides with the distribution of settler narratives, gives us a glimpse of how the diffuse and complex assemblage of settler citizenship control spans time and space. It is itself composed of a multitude of industries, ideologies, and agents whose material components shape the relationships between the alien persona and the settler persona to maximize the settler's capacity to violently exploit the alien migrant.

THOUGHTS ON *PREDATOR* TECHNOLOGIES

In chapter 1, I mentioned the MQ-9 Reaper CBP-104, the Predator B drone that was called to fly over Minneapolis in 2020 to surveil the anti–police brutality protests in the wake of George Floyd's murder. This particular drone is one of nine MQ-9 Reaper Predator B drones that are currently in operation along the México/US border, but as we can see, its operational range is considerable. So, when settler production modes assemble power with a nearly limitless capacity to mobilize technologies that produce subjective antitypes, anyone can become an alien. Just like in the films in the *Predator* franchise, the deployment of settler population economies began in a faraway place, then appeared at the border, and eventually found their way into the lives of people in cities across the US. They are trafficked from the battlefield to the border and then to our backyards to first produce terrorists, then aliens, then criminals.

Settler production modes manufacture the alien antitype in legislation, in film, and eventually through technologies of visibility that evolve as they move between various arenas of the citizenship control assemblage. These relationships have increased the capacity of the state to expand its power over both US citizens and migrants by illuminating their bodies with alien affects in order to know them, capture them, and exert state power over them. Today, *Predator* technologies are still widely distributed in order to capture migrant bodies into the persona of the alien and channel them into cycles of apprehension, detention, and removal—all adding to the state's economic and political capacity to violently extract value from them. With added legislative support, the election of presidents who scapegoat migrants, advancements in technological capacity, and the increased mobilization of border security mechanisms throughout the national landscape, it is safe to say that citizenship control is only growing more efficient in its ability to capture and exploit migrants (and even some citizens) who are cast with alien affects.

Predator technologies are just one kind of technology in the settler state's citizenship machinery. They contribute to the layering of visible alien affects onto articulable expressions of belonging/nonbelonging that are formalized in the legal codes of citizenship, but are realized in the production of alien visibility. The next chapter looks more closely at different technologies of visibility, specifically those emerging in the *Men in Black* cinematic universe, which also produce alien affects that subject exogenous migrants as undesirable aliens. As with *Predator* technologies, the citizenship control assemblage organizes *Men in Black* technologies throughout the US with the goal of producing settler antitypes.

Chapter Three

MEN IN BLACK ASSEMBLAGES

After Bill Clinton was elected president in 1992, he implemented Operation Hold the Line (1993) and Operation Gatekeeper (1994), which delivered the first *Predator* technologies to the México/US border around ports of entry in El Paso and San Diego. "Agents and technology were concentrated in specific areas, providing a 'show of force' to potential illegal border crossers."[1] These efforts marked a reinvestment in technological infrastructure embedded within the anti-immigration policies enacted by the Reagan administration and carried through the George H. W. Bush administration. Hold the Line and Gatekeeper trafficked alienhood to the border, both in terms of the discursive *alien* (or *illegal* alien) settler antitype representing the undesirable exogenous migrant but also in the form of alien affects—material expressions of political subjection that are produced by technologies of visibility to cast migrants in the persona of dangerous alien. As I described in the previous chapter, these two US Border Patrol operations mobilized force-multiplying technology to surveil the border and produced a subjective alien antitype to know and control.

Then, in his 1995 State of the Union Address, Clinton described the ways he planned to refine the mechanisms for controlling the exogenous population economy:

> All Americans, not only in the states most heavily affected, but in every place in this country, are rightly disturbed by the large numbers of illegal aliens entering our country. The jobs they hold might otherwise be held by citizens or legal immigrants. The public service they use impose burdens on our taxpayers. That's why our administration has moved aggressively to secure our borders more by hiring a record number of new border guards, by deporting twice as many criminal aliens as ever before, by cracking down on illegal hiring, by barring

welfare benefits to illegal aliens.... [W]e will try to do more to speed the deportation of illegal aliens who are arrested for crimes, to better identify illegal aliens in the workplace.... It is wrong and ultimately self-defeating for a nation of immigrants to permit the kind of abuse of our immigration laws we have seen in recent years, and we must do more to stop it.[2]

So, while Reagan's strategy was to mobilize the machinery of settler production at the México/US border, Clinton's strategy was to take that extraction-driven logic of subject making and distribute it to cities and towns throughout the US. His comments point directly to what seems like an irony: that "a nation of immigrants" would seek to limit migration. However, when considering the US as a nation of settlers whose population economy produces subjects such as alien antitypes, his words point to the state's desire to maintain order over the material relations between settlers and their antitypes. These efforts led to the implementation of many of the violent and exploitative migrant control techniques the US employs to subject what it considers undesirable migrants today—those mostly those from México, Central America, the Philippines, South Asia, and East Africa. They include the creation of Immigration and Customs Enforcement (ICE), the expansion of a for-profit detention infrastructure, the development of large-scale deportation apparatuses, the wide-ranging collection of biometric data used by border agents, and other techniques and technologies to find and remove unauthorized migrants.

Then, a year after Clinton's State of the Union remarks on "illegal immigration," the US Congress passed the Illegal Immigration Reform and Immigrant Responsibility Act (IIRIRA), which materialized the Clinton administration's vision for a US secure from aliens.[3] It should be noted that the bill makes reference to "aliens" 1,795 times, relying consistently on the discursive antitype to build a justification for reassembling the machinery of the population production economy both at the border and throughout localized municipalities in the US. IIRIRA, for example, consolidated the US's immigration hearing and deportation machinery into a single "removal" apparatus. This eventually became the Office of Enforcement and Removal Operations, which was subsumed under the purview of ICE in 2003. It currently accounts for more than half of ICE's budget.[4] This is the population economy enforcement apparatus of DHS and ICE. Section 287, Amendment (g) of the bill provides the legal basis for ICE after the formation of DHS, giving the bureau overarching jurisdiction both internationally and domestically, and also provides a memorandum of understanding (MOU) between the US attorney general and local and state police that allows local police to make immigration-related arrests. Clinton's approach to citizenship control was to use the alien as a figure who was already living and working in cities across the US, not just in the border region.

Moreover, in addition to providing the legal framework for ICE and its MOUs, IIRIRA also took two other important steps. It created a twenty-five-mile border zone along all land and water boundaries of the US (which eventually became a one-hundred-mile zone in 2006), which territorializes a constitution-free region where those suspected by border agents of being in the US illegally are subject to search and seizure that would in other circumstances violate the Fourth Amendment.[5] IIRIRA also implemented the first national database for migrant workers, now called E-Verify. E-Verify, along with other databases that were used to verify asylum claims to find domestic and criminal records, was used by US government agencies to identify, track, and remove migrants deemed undesirable by the settler state. Essentially, Congress had created an office to manage a secretive group of deputized immigration agents, with no specific associations to local or federal law enforcement, to track and remove undesirable aliens. It also gave these agents broad access to biometric databases and the power to detain and deport those moving through the border zone without authorization.

Less than a year after Clinton signed IIRIRA into law, Columbia Pictures released *Men in Black*, a film in which a clandestine group of extraterrestrial enforcement agents called the Men in Black (MiB) track the movements of all alien life on and off the planet.[6] They are equipped with weapons, biometric data scanners, and a virtual wall that surrounds Earth to alert them if an alien is entering without authorization. For more than two decades, the franchise has organized a settler narrative of population production economy among humans, desirable aliens, and those aliens that pose a threat to humans. In order to organize settler colonial personae on screen, the four films in the franchise—*Men in Black*, *Men in Black II*, *Men in Black 3*, and *Men in Black: International*—utilize an array of technologies to pursue, apprehend, and even kill bad aliens while often teaming up with good aliens along the way.[7] For example, there are several high-powered weapons that the Men in Black use to stun, blast, vaporize, melt, or otherwise eliminate threatening aliens. The MiB detain and process aliens who have violated interplanetary migration laws in their secret headquarters and will often deport them back to their home planet for posing a threat to the (white) human race (in the United States). One technology that the MiB use often is a neuralyzer to erase any memory of their actions, allowing them to follow a more acceptable narrative to those watching.

This chapter describes *Men in Black* (*MiB*) technologies of visibility—biometric tracking, a virtual wall, and flashbulb narration, all technological components of the *MiB* franchise that are eventually trafficked through a number of citizenship control assemblages in the US. Again, I rely on a materialist assemblage framework to explain how the US adopts and recirculates *MiB* technologies, first through the settler narrative of alienhood in film, then in the production of alien affects in political subjections of migrants in airports, schools, and workplaces, and in nearly every interaction with the US government. So, while a number of material components in the *MiB* universe may connect to other security and military machinery (turbocharged vehicles, advanced weapons, stylish sunglasses, etc.), I study just the technologies of visibility (and invisibility) that are connected to the franchise. As in the previous chapter, here I move through the machinery of alien invasion cinema, border security, and the state's legal system to describe how *MiB* technologies move and evolve.

MEN IN BLACK

The opening scene of *Men in Black* is disturbing to watch. A white van driven by a white, US American man (Nick, played by Jon Gries) is speeding down a winding desert road. In the back of the van are a dozen or so migrants: brown-skinned and sweaty-faced folks cast as migrant laborers huddled together nervously staring out the windshield (fig. 3.1). Just then, the van pulls around a bend, and there are four sets of headlights waiting to intercept it. Border Patrol agents, with shotguns cocked, pull the van to the side of the road; Nick rolls down his window. One agent (played by Fredric Lehne) approaches:

> BORDER PATROL AGENT: Well, Nick the Dick! What a surprise. Where are you coming from Nick?
> NICK: Fishing in Cuernavaca.
> BORDER PATROL AGENT: I'm sure you were. What do you say we take a look at your catch, huh?[8]

Nick gets out of the van and walks around back to open the rear doors. Upon opening the doors, the agent then shines a light on the migrants and remarks: "O me, I would have thrown 'em back. Bájense todos, formen una línea aquí por favor [Everyone down, form a line here please]."[9]

Just then, Agent K (Tommy Lee Jones) and his partner, Agent D (Richard Hamilton), arrive on-scene to take the case. They tell the border agents they

Figure 3.1. Film still from Barry Sonnenfeld's 1997 *Men in Black*; the opening scene of the film depicting several migrants huddled in the back of a smuggler's van.

are with INS Division 6 and proceed to interrogate the migrants. The border agents just go along with it. After some banter in broken Spanish with the migrants—including Agent K welcoming the group and telling them it's a pleasure to see them there—he then zeroes in on one man.

> AGENT K: ¿Y tu? ¿Qué dices que si rompa la cara? [And you, what do you say if I break your face?] [the man laughs] ¿Eres muy feo, no? [You are very ugly, no?] [the man continues to laugh] ¿Y no hablas ni una palabra del español? [And you don't speak a word of Spanish?][10]

Agent K turns to his partner, knowing they have their alien. He detains the man and lets the other migrants go free, to the chagrin of the Border Patrol agents. After a small argument, he dismisses the agents, mockingly telling them to "keep protecting us from the dangerous aliens."[11]

The scene takes a grim turn. Agents K and D pull the man—who is an extraterrestrial in disguise whom they call Mikey—into the desert. They pull off his disguise and begin to arrest him for trying to enter the planet without authorization, even though he asks for political asylum (fig. 3.2). During his arrest, Mikey spots the original border agent who had pulled the van over; he turns and runs toward the agent. Agent K pulls out his laser gun and shoots Mikey in the back, spilling his blue blood and guts all over the desert landscape. From the outset, the film franchise aligns its narrative with the US population production economy of exogenous migrants by

Figure 3.2. Film still from Barry Sonnenfeld's 1997 *Men in Black*; Mikey, a wanted space outlaw, is caught trying to enter the US disguised as an unauthorized migrant.

dividing "good" aliens from "bad" aliens. The good aliens (and migrants, as demonstrated by Agent K's willingness to welcome and encourage the other migrants in the van to find work) are allowed to enter the US to participate in the US economy (usually as easily exploitable labor). The bad aliens are eliminated—detained, deported, and like Mikey, maybe even killed.

Throughout the franchise's four films, the Men in Black track, surveil, and control the movements of extraterrestrials who visit or seek refuge on Earth (although the films suggest that the overwhelming majority of those aliens end up in New York City). To create the alien affects in the first three films of the franchise, Rick Baker from Cinovation Studio (no longer in operation) was hired to design and create the alien puppets and models (Jeremy Woodhead was hired for *Men in Black: International*).[12] All four films have major and minor alien characters, which required filmmakers to produce a wide variety of alien affects to represent the pantheon of alien species featured in the films. Usually, extras were used as minor characters, human actors made up to look like aliens. For other, more prominent characters, CGI was used to enhance the actors' alien affects. George Lucas's Industrial Light and Magic (ILM) added computer-generated visual effects to some of the major alien characters, including the film franchise's first three antagonists.[13] Beyond imagining what aliens look like, though, filmmakers were also tasked with imagining what technologies MiB agents would need to control alien populations.

For example, the MiB track all movements of all aliens on Earth at any given time with a large, computerized mapping system. All aliens are

Figure 3.3. Film still from Barry Sonnenfeld's 1997 *Men in Black*; Agents J (Will Smith) and K (Tommy Lee Jones) at the alien tracking database interface.

registered through the MiB office and then tracked as they move about the planet. In *Men in Black* (1997), the giant map is operated by Idikiukup and Bob, twin aliens from another solar system (each with ten arms) who demonstrate that good aliens can even find a role in the alien control machinery of the US government (fig. 3.3). Using the map, agents are able to enter the name or identification number of any alien and immediately know where they are in the world (though the map shows only the US) and where they are going at any given time. Agent K and Agent J (Will Smith) use this tracker at one point to find an alien leaving the planet without authorization. They also use this technology to get a general sense of the movements of the alien groups on Earth to note any suspicious behavior. Ironically, the film suggests that many celebrities who were considered to be strange humans are in fact extraterrestrials by showing video images of them on the map. They include both Spielberg and Lucas. Therefore, the *MiB* population economy centers around the ability of some aliens to transfer into an accepted class, given their ability to blend with the dominant visual racial features and cultural performances of US Americans. Those that are nontransferable get removed. In other words, the alien biometric tracking system featured in the franchise is a technology imbued with settler colonial population production logics—it manages which aliens are admitted to visit and work on the planet and which aren't.

Again, the Men in Black are a clandestine group. They maintain their anonymity with the help of another prominent technology: the neuralyzer, a handheld device that flashes a bright light into the eyes of bystanders

Figure 3.4. Film still from Barry Sonnenfeld's 1997 *Men in Black*; Agent K (Tommy Lee Jones) with a neuralyzer.

who have observed an interaction between the MiB and extraterrestrials. The neuralyzer uses a bright flash that "isolates and measures the electronic impulses in your brain, and specifically, the ones for memory."[14] The bright flash affects anyone looking into the device; MiB agents are shielded from its effects because they are wearing customized Ray-Ban sunglasses (coincidentally, the line of sunglasses developed by Ray-Ban for the film was marketed as the Predator 2 series and the Predator J series).[15] With a flash, MiB agents erase any trace of alien affects by narrating another truth. This technology also erases from the minds of onlookers the agents' involvement in apprehending and often killing aliens. For example, after Agent K kills Mikey in the opening scenes of *Men in Black*, he uses a neuralyzer to convince Border Patrol agents that they did not witness the murder of an alien, but rather an exploding "underground gas vein" that was ignited by a bullet from one of their firearms (fig. 3.4).[16] Agent K was able to erase the memories of the half-dozen agents with a flash of light and then rewrite their experiences. Also, after recruiting Agent J to the MiB, K neuralyzes him to erase his memory as a New York police officer. When Men in Black retire, like Agent D at the beginning of *Men in Black*, they are also neuralyzed. Throughout the franchise, agents rely on this technology to instantly renarrate events in ways that obscure the alien population economy managed by the MiB. Neuralyzers, then, are technologies of instant settler consciousness production.

In *Men in Black II*, Agents J and K take up the same mission to protect the world from alien invasion, this time against the threat of destruction by a dangerous worm alien. Sarleena (Lara Flynn Boyle) is an invasive, slimy extraterrestrial who takes human form to blend in on Earth. However, in the scenes where she is killing humans, her body morphs into hundreds of worm-like tentacles. This alien affect is created using CGI produced at ILM. Just as in the first film, the agents utilize the two technologies of visibility discussed above—the tracker map and the neuralyzer—with some slight upgrades. The tracking map now includes handheld biometric scanning devices that can immediately determine an alien's status. This technology gives agents immediate mobile access to information found on the tracking map that allows them to more effectively track the movement of aliens. For example, when Agent J goes to find K (who had been previously decommissioned as an MiB agent and neuralyzed), he uses one of these handheld devices to identify aliens who are working at a post office where K is employed. Agent J uses the device to scan the face of the postal worker he suspects of being an alien. Within seconds, he receives confirmation that the person is an alien and begins talking to them in their native language (fig. 3.5). The scanning device relies on CGI graphics to replicate the facial-scanning application and portray for audiences the alien affects on the bodies of the postal workers as they are one by one outed as aliens.

The neuralyzer the MiB use in the second film to cover their tracks and erase the presence of alien affects has also evolved (for one, the light flash is blue in the second film, not red). For example, Agent J uses the device to erase the memories of many of his new potential partners whom he is dissatisfied with. The agents even have the capacity to wipe out the memory of an entire city, as demonstrated at the end of the film, when the MiB activate the Statue of Liberty as a giant neuralyzer (fig. 3.6). This scene, like the opening scene of the first film, squarely arranges the narrative of the franchise around the population production practices of the US. The Statue of Liberty, the symbol of exogenous migrant transfer into the US citizenry, is operationalized to obscure the rejection of undesirable aliens by secretive government agents.

In general, agents in the second film readopt both alien tracking technologies and neuralyzing technologies to see how aliens are moving extensively (on and off of the planet) and how they move intensively (biometric information)—all while remaining unseen to the general human public. *Men in Black II*, released a year before the creation of US Immigration and Customs Enforcement, depicts a group of clandestine government agents whose technological capacity to control populations and rewrite history is essential for the US American way of life. This narrative arc of the first two *MiB* films is in fact the same narrative arc that is completed with the creation of ICE. In the mid-1990s, there was express desire by the US settler state to

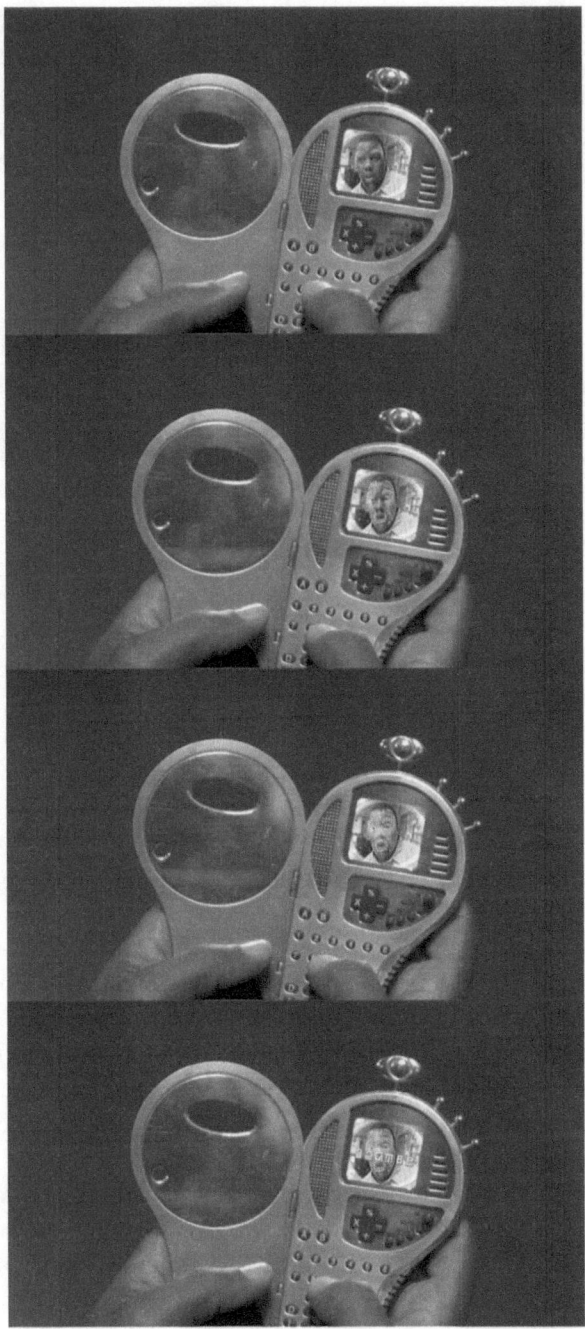

Figures 3.5a, 3.5b, 3.5c, and 3.5d. Series of film stills from Barry Sonnenfeld's 2002 *Men in Black II*; Agent J (Will Smith) with a face scanner, verifying the extraterrestrial identity of a postal worker (Biz Markie).

Figure 3.6. Film still from Barry Sonnenfeld's 2002 *Men in Black II*; Agents K (Tommy Lee Jones) and J (Will Smith) use the Statue of Liberty as a neuralyzer on all the residents of New York City.

mobilize population production technologies throughout the US, not just at the border. After 9/11, this desire was formalized into a government agency that traffics technologies, controls exogenous population economies, and covers its tracks with flashbulb narration.

In 2012, *Men in Black 3* revisited the *MiB* narrative universe and its array of technologies. Agent J goes back in time to save his partner, Agent K (this time played by both Tommy Lee Jones and Josh Brolin), from being killed in the past by a vengeful insect-alien named Boris the Animal (Jemaine Clement). The character of Boris was created using special effects makeup and was augmented with CGI technology. The tracker map is again updated, now a holographic globe that functions as before, to keep tabs on all the aliens on Earth at any given time. It is not expressly used in the film, mostly because a large part of the film takes place in 1969, but it is depicted in a scene in which Agent J decides to go back in time. In this film, though, unlike in the previous two, the tracking map is entirely CGI.[17] The neuralyzer also makes a cameo. After a small crowd witnesses a giant fish-like alien being apprehended, they are told not to flush goldfish down the toilet.

Men in Black 3 also introduces audiences to a new technology—the Arcnet, a shield that surrounds Earth to protect earthlings from dangerous invading aliens (fig. 3.7). The underlying tension in the film revolves around the fact that Agent K is killed in the past and the Arcnet that was installed in 1969 has been stolen, meaning that Earth is now vulnerable to a Boglodite invasion in the present. MiB agents must relaunch the Arcnet—Earth's virtual border technology—in 1969 to ensure the survival of the planet. The

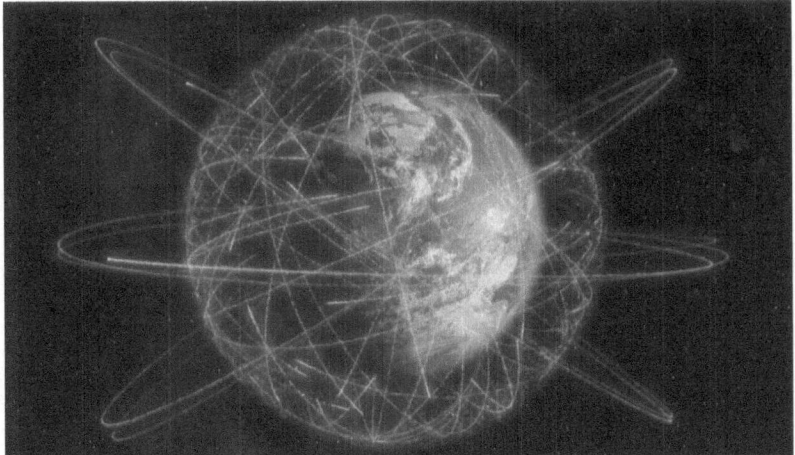

Figure 3.7. Film still from Barry Sonnenfeld's 2012 *Men in Black 3*; the ArcNet around Earth.

device is the size of a pocket watch, but outside the atmosphere, it turns into an impenetrable shield that allows MiB agents to effectively control all movement onto Earth—it's what feeds data into the biometric alien tracker featured in the first two films. It is assumed that since this technology has been in place since 1969, it has been a regular part of MiB operations. That is, MiB population economy practices depend on the subjection of aliens as they cross the virtual border and then the management of those aliens once they are on the planet. Reinstalling that technology is of upmost importance to the agency.

Finally, *Men in Black: International* recycles the MiB narrative, this time to track aliens around the world (even though the film is set only in Italy, Morocco, the United States, and the United Kingdom). The film reemploys the global migrant tracking system along with the handheld digital data tools and, of course, the neuralyzer. In this latest iteration of the franchise, Agents H (Chris Hemsworth) and M (Tessa Thompson) fill the persona of alien border agent to apprehend shapeshifting, nonwhite aliens threatening the world (but really only Europe and the US) with violence. As a film, *Men in Black: International* illustrates the ways technologies of visibility used in the service of finding and apprehending migrant alien bodies are mobilized between state assemblages, namely European nations. As these technologies evolve, they become more mobile and contribute to an array of mechanisms of control both in the US and abroad. This latest film in the franchise makes clear that the narrative production machinery of film is linked to the population production machinery of settler colonialism, especially when it comes to how populations of exogenous migrants are economized into alien subjectivities and organized by cagey government agencies with vast technological resources.

In the years since President Clinton signed IIRIRA into law, makers of the *Men in Black* franchise have narrativized the ways the US government produces alien population economies. In doing so, the films have imagined and materialized a number of technologies that have adopted the mission of population production. *MiB* technologies are ubiquitous. Because of these technologies, the MiB track aliens, capture aliens, and can obscure their actions anywhere: in the US, in other nations, at the border, in airports, at work, on the streets, and even in one's own home. Framed in the context of settler citizenship control, *MiB* technologies of visibility participate in a systematic organization of personae to enforce a set of logics rooted in a settler colonial constitutive citizenship paradigm. This logic is economic; it organizes alienhood to maximize extraction.

In general, the *Men in Black* franchise and the technologies of visibility developed in it manufacture alien affects while also masking the capacity of the state to make aliens disappear. In the film franchise, filmmakers narrate settler population economics. However, *MiB* technologies are not contained only within the filmic arena but have since been trafficked into other arenas that participate in citizenship control. After all, a global, virtual tracking system for migrants using biometric data has been a goal of the US since the early 2000s. Such technologies as developed in the *MiB* franchise and in the Department of Homeland Security parallel one another. Neuralyzing technology, or what I call flashbulb narration, has also become a common tool used by technology industries and governments to publicly code nonwhite migrants as a threat while obscuring their own violences against migrant groups.

MEN IN BLACK TECHNOLOGIES AND TRACKING ALIEN ANTITYPES

MiB technologies are force multipliers. They let the US settler state know the alien subject, and thus control the alien subject's movements. They force the alien persona into violent and extractive relationships with the settler state: as exploitable labor, bodies for private detention beds, and other relationships that perpetuate a legacy of settler racial violence. The following section describes *MiB* technologies through the citizenship assemblage by describing their emergence and behavior with relation to border security mechanisms. The technologies described here have also emerged and evolved outside of cinema and can be found in the modes of population production throughout the US settler state.

I first describe the emergence of the computerized bordering systems that began as the Integrated Surveillance Intelligence System (ISIS) and eventually became the virtual border initiative called the Secure Border Initiative Network (SBInet). These technologies, along with other biometric monitoring technologies, have been adopted by ICE to manage the exogenous population economy in the United States. They allow border agents to track the movements of migrants throughout the US by turning those movements into computable data. Aliens are coded so they can be tracked in nearly every interaction with the state—they are constantly surveilled both at the border and in communities.

The second part of this section discusses flashbulb narration, which appears as the neuralyzing technology from the *MiB* franchise. Flashbulb narration refers to a process that masks both the violences against migrant communities and the US government's operation of the citizenship control assemblage by mobilizing the bright lights and narrative machinery of a corporate media gaze. This technology is an example of instant settler narrative production that, as described before, produces settler consciousness. As a result, the citizenry of the US remains oblivious to the extent US government agencies are committing violences against migrants subjected as aliens.

TRADITIONAL SURVEILLANCE TECHNOLOGIES

Thomas Edison and William Dickson, two inventors of the late nineteenth century, are credited with developing the kinetoscope, a primitive video recording device.[18] The technology developed in 1888 was based on Edison's theory that an invention could do visually what his phonograph could do aurally: string together a series of images to achieve a movement-image. Almost immediately, the technology was adopted in the prison systems in European countries and the US to monitor the movements of incarcerated prisoners. Soon after, video surveillance technology was adopted by the militaries of those same countries to monitor one another.[19] During World War II, both handheld video recording technology and closed-circuit television (CCTV) were further developed. Both Allied and Axis forces relied on these technological advancements in surveillance for the purposes of counterintelligence, combat preparedness, and securing weapons testing sites.[20] By the 1960s, video surveillance technology had become common in public spaces throughout the United States and the United Kingdom, aiding law enforcement officials in monitoring the actions of citizens.[21] In today's society of control, video surveillance technology is found nearly everywhere from ATM machines and airports to city street corners and even the handheld electronic devices nearly everyone carries around with them.

For nearly four decades, video surveillance technology has also been widely organized by the citizenship control assemblage in the US to make alien migrants and their movements more visible to border control agents. In the early 1980s, The US Border Patrol first started using underground seismic sensors and basic closed-circuit television technology to monitor migrant movements through highly trafficked areas along the US/México border region.[22] In 1988, Intelligent Computer-Aided Detection (ICAD) was developed by the US Immigration and Naturalization Service (INS) to record the data from the early video and sonic surveillance equipment and analyze the unauthorized entry of migrants along the nearly five-thousand-mile border between the US and Canada and the nearly two-thousand-mile border with México. ICAD would also store the data in a secured, centralized location where agents could parse through the information and relay instructions back to agents in the field.[23] Since Operation Hold the Line and Operation Gatekeeper in the early 1990s, the US Border Patrol has relied on video surveillance, ground sensors, thermal imaging, and other technologies to surveil migrants even before they reach the border between México and the US.[24] Agents in El Paso and San Diego were able to see and sense the movements of migrants across the border and alert Border Patrol agents to the likely location migrants would be crossing. This allowed them to anticipate unauthorized entry before it happened, taking a proactive approach to migration enforcement. So, since CBP added technologies of visibility to their array of antimigrant machinery (vehicles, radios, firearms, checkpoints, etc.), they have multiplied the force the state has in producing the alien settler antitype and in reorganizing the material sets of relationships between the various personae (citizens, migrants, border control agents).

By the 1990s, the Border Patrol had implemented video surveillance along with thermal and seismic sensor technology all along the border with México in order to track, record, and respond to the movements of migrants. These technologies were trafficked to the border as part of Operation Gatekeeper, Operation Hold the Line, and other federal operations. To house and process the vast amounts of data collected by these technologies, the US also invested in computer-aided analysis systems that would allow the INS and eventually ICE to mobilize a response to migrants seen by these technologies in real time. In 1997, year *Men in Black* was released, the INS launched the Integrated Surveillance Intelligence System (ISIS), the first of many government initiatives funded to collect and store data from border surveillance technologies on a national level. The goal of the ISIS program was "to provide continuous monitoring of the borders in all weather conditions. When fully deployed, ISIS was to establish a fully integrated network combining sensor detections with camera video identification capability."[25] ISIS comprised surveillance aircraft, RVS vehicles mounted with cameras (both discussed in chapter 2), seismic sensors, and the ICAD system. This integrated technological approach to securing the settler borderlands would soon be adopted across the nation to monitor and subject migrants as alien antitypes and track their movements.

From 1997 to 2005, the US funded the ISIS project with more than $429 million to develop and maintain an integrated, computerized tracking system that would monitor migrant movements at the border and in the border zone.[26] Of that, more than $239 million was awarded to the Integrated Microwave Corporation (IMC) to install and maintain the RVS and ICAD systems.[27] IMC is an electronic wireless communication systems and defense electronics manufacturer whose contract came under scrutiny after it was discovered that the group failed to implement all of the surveillance technology promised to the INS. In some cases, the equipment was faulty or never arrived at all.[28] There was also speculation of impropriety with the contract given to IMC, considering they employed all three children of former Border Patrol chief and then US congressman Silvestre Reyes, although no formal charges of corruption were ever filed.[29] In 2002, IMC was purchased by L-3 Communications, another defense company, which was responsible for fulfilling the contractual obligation to install RVS and ICAD technologies (the latter operated by HAZMED, another private security firm) for the US Border Patrol on behalf of IMC.[30] This was during the same time that the Border Patrol was moving from the INS to the Department of Homeland Security. By 2004, L-3 Communications was the sole contractor operating the ISIS program.[31]

When DHS took over US Customs and Border Protection in 2003, the promise of a virtual border—the US's digital migrant tracking network—was nearly realized. This marked the moment in US history when the entire border security apparatus was integrated with the US military. Despite previous efforts by the INS and DHS to consolidate border technologies under one program, and in response to a scathing 2004 Office of Inspector General report indicating gross misuse of federal funds, inadequate implementation of surveillance technology, and a lack of oversight, DHS launched a new program called the America's Shield Initiative (ASI) to oversee the execution of the surveillance functions of the ISIS program.[32] DHS launched ASI in October 2004 and pledged to rectify the INS's shortcomings in developing

ISIS.³³ However, just like the initial ISIS program, the ASI program was short-lived; it failed to increase the "force-multiplying" effect of border enforcement for the amount of federal dollars being spent to implement it.³⁴ Failures by Integrated Microwave and L-3 Communications along with government inaction led to the eventual dismantling of the ISIS and ASI projects. Shortly thereafter, the US made one last attempt to develop a virtual border that would widely track all unauthorized entry across US land borders.

In 2005, with authorization from President George W. Bush, DHS launched the Secure Border Initiative (SBI) as a way to unify the roles of the various government agencies tasked with surveilling and controlling migrants throughout the US. This unified the functions of both the Border Patrol and ICE to "include securing and patrolling US borders, expanding programs for detention and removal of deportable aliens, updating technology, and increasing worksite enforcement to target employment of unauthorized workers."³⁵ SBI brought together all antimigration enforcement at ports of entry, between ports of entry, in airports, and in cities throughout the US under the newly formed DHS and expanded the technological capabilities of the DHS to better monitor both authorized and unauthorized migrant movements. The Secure Border Initiative Network (SBInet) was a program under SBI tasked with taking the preexisting border surveillance infrastructure (what was left over from ISIS and ASI) and rearranging the technology to consolidate the infrastructure into a single nationwide migrant-tracking network. To implement the first version of SBInet, the US awarded Boeing more than $1.2 billion between 2006 and 2009.³⁶ Boeing promised to upgrade the US's border surveillance technology (including the deployment of unmanned drones to surveil the border) and to manage the border agencies' centralized computer network (what was left of the ICAD system).

Many of the *Predator* technologies discussed in chapter 2, for example, were deployed to the border regions in the US through DHS's activation of SBInet. SBInet upgraded the RVS technology from the ISIS program to create a mobile video surveillance system (MVSS). Boeing subcontracted General Dynamics and FLIR Systems to develop the thermal imaging technology for the MVSS.³⁷ Boeing also deployed the MQ-9 Reaper Predator B surveillance drones (subcontracted through General Dynamics), which were to be integrated into the surveillance network.³⁸ The entire SBInet program, contracted through Boeing, was the third attempt by the US government to integrate a national migrant tracking network to control the entry of migrants who could be economized by the classification of some as unauthorized and others as authorized. However, like the first two programs, Boeing's SBInet lacked the proper oversight and direction to secure any part of the border, much less the entire two-thousand-mile span between the US and México.³⁹ SBInet ultimately failed and was scrapped by DHS in 2010.

Today, the US Border Patrol and ICE rely on surveillance of the US/México border region that is customized for each sector. After former DHS chief Janet Napolitano deemed Boeing's SBInet ineffective, DHS channeled funds toward situational enforcement in localized parts of the border. This meant that each sector, like the San Diego sector or the El Paso sector, would be responsible for developing its own surveillance strategy, much like they had done during Operations Hold the Line and Gatekeeper. While a considerable amount of the technological infrastructure remains in place, it is now decentralized and used by individual sectors to monitor unauthorized movements. Despite the admitted past failures of a virtual border and migrant-tracking network, DHS continues to fund the development of mobile and remote surveillance technology, unmanned drone surveillance technology, ground sensors, and other surveillance infrastructure. In 2015, DHS requested $373.5 million from the federal government to "maintain and recapitalize border infrastructure," including border technologies, and in 2019, DHS requested another $600 million for border security technologies alone.⁴⁰

Along the border and now in communities throughout the US, DHS is organizing technologies of visibility that track and monitor the movements of migrants in order to code them as alien. This allows them, through agencies like ICE, to manage the settler population production economy that arranges migrants into alien antitypes—those that are desirable and can transfer into the citizenry, those that can stay and be exploited, and those that must be removed. Again and again, the integrated tracking systems have failed, but this has not deterred the Department of Homeland Security from continuing to invest billions in the virtual border that makes aliens visible to border agents.

BIOMETRIC DATA TRACKING

Along with traditional surveillance technologies of visibility used by the US's citizenship control assemblage, biometric technologies have also been developed and trafficked to organize the exogenous population of alien antitypes. While the surveillance technologies adapted in the failed SBInet programs were largely used to monitor the movements of migrants, biometric technology is able to identify, locate, and track individual migrants based on their unique qualitative characteristics as they interact with the technology. In other words, biometrics are intensive movements that are recorded by the state, converted into storable data, coded, and used to identify personae as they continue to move about the occupied territory of the settlement. They are data that are illuminated so that the state can better know individual migrant subjects.

> Considering the complexities of a border crossing—or the similar challenges of airport screening—which often includes country clearances, checking for contraband and identifying individuals on a watch list—technology, of necessity, becomes a critical force multiplier. Technologies that can match an image with a known watch list can greatly reduce human error. Knowing that they have the support of these increasingly reliable and sophisticated systems lowers security agents' stress and enables them to function for longer periods of time with increased situational awareness.[41]

In terms of population production, biometric surveillance technologies allow both Border Patrol and ICE agents to define and identify migrants instantly, at the border and in communities throughout the US, to produce them as aliens.

For one thing, biometric collection and data management technologies can rapidly identify the people entering and leaving a country. Fingerprints, iris color and shape, facial shape, palm prints, and DNA are all micromovements of the body that generate different patterns. Even pheromones and radioactivity (discussed in chapter 2) can be considered biometric information and be detected by technologies at borders and security checkpoints.[42] Fingerprints, for example, are measured and compared to one another using software that analyzes a number of points on the print to calculate the variations in distance. This information is matched with biographical information in a database (like ICAD), identifying the person who produces that pattern. Facial features, like fingerprints, can also produce readable patterns, including elements of color and tone. By linking intensive alien affects with biographical information, border security agents can more easily track migrant movements and multiply their force over the alien antitype production economy—alienhood can be produced anywhere. Today's technologies allow border agents to scan fingerprints, facial features, and other data more quickly and efficiently than in decades before. After all, "speed is a force multiplier."[43] Speeding up the process of biometric data collection and recall allows agents to more quickly decide whether bodies moving through the mechanisms of state citizenship control can be coded as threatening aliens or not, and then be organized as such.

In 1994, the US implemented its first national biometric collection and data management program to assist federal and state law enforcement in keeping track of migrants. The Automated Biometric Identification System (IDENT) was developed for the INS with the purpose of gathering fingerprints and photographs—and eventually information like facial scans and iris scans—in order to track those who enter the US from abroad. Border agents and ICE agents rely on IDENT to verify the identities of those who are already in the database.[44] After the creation of DHS in 2002, the IDENT program (along with nearly all aspects of citizenship control) was absorbed into the department.

> Today, IDENT is the primary DHS-wide system for the biometric identification and verification of individuals encountered in DHS mission-related processes. IDENT is primarily a back-end system that conducts identification or verification services on behalf of numerous Government programs that collect biometric and associated biographic data as part of their mission.[45]

DHS agencies like CBP, ICE, the US Coast Guard, and the Transportation Security Administration (TSA), and others like the Department of Defense, input biometric data into IDENT to keep tabs on foreigners, authorized and unauthorized, at nearly every interaction with the agency or department. Biographical information is added to accompany the biometric data, including nationality, gender, citizenship status, threat level, number of interactions with DHS, and number of interactions with other law enforcement agencies.[46]

Today's biometric tracking and database technologies are shared by law enforcement agencies across the US, all under the umbrella of IDENT. This includes the national fingerprint and mug-shot databases that have been in place since the 1990s. Adding to those technologies, the FBI developed and implemented a national facial recognition database in 2012 in which facial dimensions, obtained from photographs and videos, can be used to identify an individual.[47] Then, in 2015, DHS rolled out its mobile, handheld biometrics systems in airports across the US and along the US/México border. The technology allows border agents to scan fingerprints and take photos of those entering and exiting the US to match them against any law enforcement agency database while accumulating a sizable database of biometric information from millions of foreigners.[48]

Border Patrol agents have also begun to collect scans of irises to match with photos, fingerprints, and biographical information, thus enhancing the identification and verification mechanisms within the current IDENT framework.[49] In December 2015, for example, DHS began collecting biometric facial scans and iris scans of both citizens and migrants entering the US at the Otay Mesa Port of Entry near San Diego. In February 2016, DHS implemented the second phase of the project, which scanned citizens and migrants exiting the port. Together, the two phases are an attempt to compound large amounts of detailed biometric data as a pilot for a national biometric system that is to be installed at all ports of entry, including international airports and seaports.[50] Since 2011, Accenture—a private management consulting, technology, and defense corporation—has been the primary contractor, having been awarded nearly $10 billion in DHS contracts since 2004 to implement biometric and biosurveillance technologies.[51] This in an indication of the US's continued investment not only in making migrants alien antitypes visible to agents, but also in making some citizens visible by surveilling, recording, and tracking their biometric affects.

Together, traditional camera surveillance and biometric surveillance technologies are making it possible for ICE and CBP to produce, monitor, and organize the alien antitype into a population economy, both at borders and in cities, airports, and other public spaces. Camera surveillance allows migration control agents to track the movements of migrants across the border zones. Biometric surveillance technologies allow migration control agents to observe, record, and quantify the intensive movements of migrants. These technologies are force multipliers. They enhance the capacity of migration control agents by giving them immediate access to biometric data—they can know the exogenous migrant instantly and make a judgment about that person's transferability into the settler citizenry. Camera and biometric surveillance technologies add the layer of visibility the state needs to organize its logics of settler colonial constitutive citizenship.

FLASHBULB NARRATION

Up to this point, I have focused on how developing tools to produce alien affects can help manufacture settler colonial narratives. However, technologies of visibility can also keep specific mechanisms of control from being seen. Like the neuralyzer in the *MiB* franchise, flashbulb narration on televised and computerized screens today use a combination of light technology and narrative articulation to make alien affects more intense while erasing the mechanisms organizing citizenship control in the US.[52] Flashbulb narration technologies mask the extent to which border security, local law enforcement, certain industries, and other state mechanisms exploit and expel unauthorized migrants. Instead, what is often mediated through video news reportage are sensational narratives of alien encounters and state action against the harms associated with them. The systems of lights and computer-generated images characterizing today's corporate media gaze function like neuralyzers: they use the lighting technologies of cinema and a self-defensive narrative of alien invasion to keep the average settlement citizen unaware of the extent to which the state's citizenship assemblage controls and rejects groups of migrants.

Today's news coverage of migration in the US is largely done via internet and TV technologies—which consist of lights, cameras, and other technologies of visibility described above. These technologies circulate exaggerated and untrue narrativized expressions to mask citizenship control. Moreover, the ubiquity of TV and internet technologies in homes and throughout communities makes their reach vast.[53] As camera, lighting, and broadcast technologies improve, largely aided by advancements in CGI and other computer-aided functions discussed in the previous chapter, television news is now accessible around the clock in a number of electronic media formats. This means that there is a constant stream of visual, narrativized accounts of alienhood that manufacture settler consciousness in real time, reacting to the changing dynamics of the alien antitype population economy.

The evolution of cinematic technologies, like those used in CCTV systems, has allowed for televised news reporting to cover unfolding events at the moment they occur—a voyeuristic and consumable segment of the US surveillance society. News cameras and lighting equipment have grown smaller and more mobile, giving news organizations the ability illuminate, film, and broadcast events nearly anywhere to create visible images that will be superimposed onto a layer of news narrative describing the events though scripted tropes about settlers and their antitypes. Televised and online video news formats create live movement-images on small screens through systems of lights and tell us what we are witnessing. They are deployed at precise moments in time to create a sense of urgency, but in reality, they prioritize certain events to maximize viewership. This is exemplified in the ways former president Trump used a sensationalized account of migrant "caravans" before the 2016 national election, or how he used false narratives of migrant violence against women to sensationalize a nonexistent threat for political theater.[54] Flashbulb narration holds our attention for just long enough to allow for the passage of other events not reported by the news agency. For migrants, flashbulb narration functions like other technologies of alien visibility: it makes alien affects more visibly intense while mobilizing national flows of information and resources to strengthen state power, define the narrative about the subjection of migrants, and control the ways the relationships between settler subjects and their antitypes are organized.

Corporate news mechanisms today are responsive to market forces and are no longer indicative of the relative importance of a particular issue or its worthiness of coverage. Network and local news organizations have "produced many troubling practices, from the furious pace of modern news to a tendency for journalists to scramble like politicians onto the bandwagon of the latest wave of popular sentiment."[55] Although the current debate over migration and criminality is not a new one, in much of Europe and the US, "the latest wave of popular sentiment" is increasingly antimigrant.[56] In times when the sentiment may be more pro-migrant (e.g., during World War II, when migrant labor filled in for deployed soldiers in factories and on farms as part of the Bracero program), news media tends to de-intensify alien affects on the national surface, allowing migrant laborers to more easily mobilize where demand requires them. Today's news reporting focuses on the criminality of migrant communities, the dangers they pose to citizens, and the lack of security mechanisms in place that can control their influx (like a border wall, for example). Flashbulb narration of alien affects uses digital and traditional camera technology in concert with articulations of criminality to sensationalize how menacing migrant communities threaten citizens while casting a shadow over the violent and exploitative mechanisms of state citizenship control—like child separation and detention, tent cities, sexual abuse, and even death. Flashbulb narration is a technology of visibility. It mediates flows of highly calibrated news information structured around a settler population production mode to circulate these unrealistic narratives pregnant with codes of settler ideology that reach millions of television and internet viewers every day. During election years and times of economic uncertainty especially, the mobilization of narratives of alien invasion visualized on top of images of alien affects channel bodies into voting booths and the money of millionaires into antimigrant political campaigns. These technologies are arranged at precise times to draw our collective attention away from what is happening and toward a carefully crafted narrative coded by settler citizenship modes.

Together, *MiB* technologies—flashbulb narration, migrant surveillance technology, biometric technologies, and others—are mechanisms of control that rely on a balance between producing subjective alien antitypes and obscuring the violences of state control over migrant populations. They are widely distributed throughout the citizenship control assemblage in the US, not just at the borders but also in cities and towns throughout the country. Like other alien cinematic mechanisms, *MiB* technologies are mobile, and with each iteration, become better at producing intense alien affects. They have drifted from the machinery of cinematic narrative production into the political and industrial security arenas of settler population production. In the next section, I describe how US state political and legal mechanisms deploy *MiB* technologies to organize the sets of political relationships between settlers and their alien antitypes.

MEN IN BLACK TECHNOLOGIES AND THE POLITICAL ALIEN ANTITYPE

The settler population production economy created the alien antitype, first as a border crossing figure that threatened US sovereignty. This was the "human predator" figure that Reagan invoked to justify his war on drugs and hypermilitarization of the México/US border region. The alien antitype invoked in the 1990s by the Clinton administration is an alien who is already here, living and working among the US citizenry. This framing justified the way the US mobilized *MiB* technologies to set up the settler population economy in nearly all aspects of US life. As I demonstrated above, the US government has been heavily investing in private industry to develop and implement highly advanced surveillance technology for several decades—and as these technologies evolve, so too does the capacity of border security mechanisms to capture and expel migrants. Therefore, in this section, I explore the specific state legal mechanisms that have organized financial and human resources into the development and distribution of *MiB* technologies to produce the alien political antitype. This description demonstrates how the US's desire to organize migrant population economies led to the materialization of *MiB* technologies on screen, on the border, and in the hands of migrant control agents in cities and towns throughout the country.

MIGRANT POPULATION CONTROL LEGISLATION

For more than a century, the US legal machinery has been using citizenship control laws to organize populations of migrants from Europe, Asia, and Central and South America onto the geographies of the settler-occupied US. This, of course, is in addition to the nearly five centuries of forced migration and control of enslaved peoples, mostly from Africa. As a result of legislation such as the Johnson-Reed Immigration Act (1924), the McCarran-Walter Immigration Act (1952), and the Hart-Celler Immigration Act (1965), the numbers of migrants entering the US have been tightly controlled to dramatically limit the natural flows of migrants from non-European countries. As described above, the Johnson-Reed Act set up a quota system for immigrants to the US, opening the doors for those migrants from European nations who had already moved to the US in large numbers prior to the turn of the twentieth century. By restricting the numbers of Asian, African, and eastern European migrants, US legislative mechanisms ensured that the US would remain a homogeneous, ethnically northwestern European nation. It was also at this time that the US legislature established the Border Patrol, the agency responsible for enforcing the strict limitations on migrants at the international borders. This created a demand for technological resources, which have been used for over a century to surveil and control the movements of migrants.

The McCarran-Walter Act of 1952 also significantly shaped US citizenship by further tightening regulations against migrants deemed undesirable to the US economic system and by making the federal government solely responsible for the control of migration. This legislation restricted the entry of poor migrants, the physically and mentally ill, and those whose political ideologies were not in line with the dominant western European, Christian, neoliberal values of the mid-twentieth century.[57] By the time the US legislature passed the Hart-Celler Act in 1965, the mobility of white citizens throughout the country was effortless, and the free flow of nonwhite migrants had been vastly limited. So, while many credit the Hart-Celler Act for eliminating a quota system, in reality, the US territory had already been shaped to restrict migrants. The act was unnecessary. In fact, for migrants from México, Central America, and South America, the Hart-Celler Act set a cap on the number of entrants into the US, again shaping the landscape of citizenship in the US.

Simply put, US state legal apparatuses have been limiting migrants from nonwhite cultural and ethnic areas for more than a century by carefully augmenting the flows of bodies to best suit the momentary political and economic needs of the settler nation. In doing so, the US arranges a set of economic relationships for the manufacturing and distribution of the technological machinery that provides Customs and Border Protection (and other agencies) with the capacity to control migrants as a way to maintain the desired levels of movement necessary for the settler population economy. These technologies include both the *Predator* technologies of surveillance as well as the *MiB* technologies of visibility described above.

TRAFFICKING MIB TECHNOLOGIES

With the help of state legal mechanisms in the US, *MiB* technologies—like SBInet computer networks, biometric collection systems, and cable news reporting—have been manufactured and trafficked for nearly three decades to both produce alien affects and to obscure the actions of agencies like ICE and CBP. Corporate agents like L-3 Communications, Accenture, and various news conglomerates have benefited tremendously from the multi-billion-dollar investment by the US to produce alien antitypes. As the US transitioned from ISIS, to ASI, and eventually to the failed SBInet, billions were spent to equip migration control agents with surveillance technologies, including handheld biometric scanners, used to track every migrant moving into and throughout the landscape of the nation. Yet, despite the three-time failure of the nationwide computerized alien tracking system, the US continues to invest billions to traffic alien tracking technology throughout the border regions and into local communities.

First, computerized alien tracking technologies in the US emerged late in the twentieth century. Even though federal legislation created the Border Patrol in 1924, it wasn't until the 1980s that military surveillance technologies were widely used in securing the border. After Reagan's declaration of a war on drugs and the subsequent militarization of the México/US border, the US military's role in controlling migrant populations at the border was cemented.[58] Then, in the last decade of the twentieth century, funding for surveillance technology and computer-aided tracking technologies grew to support federal efforts both to combat drug trafficking at the México/US border and also to manage migrant populations in workplaces and in interactions with local law enforcement. In 1998, the Intelligent Computer-Aided Detection (ICAD) system was funded through the Office of Border Patrol (still under the auspices of the Immigration and Naturalization Service) as part of the Integrated Surveillance Intelligence System. ICAD and ISIS cost the US more than $429 million between 1998 and 2005, before the projects were rolled into the SBInet program that was spearheaded by Boeing in 2006.[59] Specifically, the goal of ICAD was to create a centralized computerized tracking system that would allow border agents to monitor the movement of those entering the US between ports of entry at the border and eventually at international airports around the country. The technology used to implement the detection systems was borrowed from military combat technology, and despite the consistent failure of ISIS, ASI, and SBInet, they continue to cost US taxpayers hundreds of millions of dollars every year.[60]

After the Homeland Security Act of 2002 was passed, the US Border Patrol was moved into the newly created Department of Homeland Security, permanently linking the US citizenship control assemblage with the US military.[61] In doing so, the US Senate and congressional appropriations committees dramatically increased border security funding from 1980s levels. Border security funding by DHS grew by nearly $1.1 billion, from about

$230 million in 1989 to about $1.3 billion in 2003, a year after the creation of DHS. By 2009, that number had tripled to nearly $3.7 billion a year, and it has remained constant ever since.[62] In 2006 alone, DHS spent more than $1.2 billion on a failed virtual border designed and implemented by Boeing in an attempt to create a computer-aided national tracking system that would make migrants more visible to the state at any given time.[63]

Second, along with advanced surveillance technologies and computerized tracking technologies, the Border Patrol is beginning to implement biometric data collection technologies. These technologies allow border agents to add data like fingerprints, iris scans, face scans, and others to a set of biographical data used to locate and monitor noncitizens as they move through the national territory. Although fingerprint collection has been readily used by law enforcement and border agents for decades, the investment in more advanced biometric data collection has only recently entered the national legislative conversation. In the *9/11 Report*, the commission recommended that DHS develop an entry and exit biometric data collection and reference system that would allow the US to easily track those entering and exiting the country at borders and airports.[64] The system would build on the US Visitor and Immigrant Status Indicator Technology (US-VISIT) used at ports of entry (including international airports) to mandate that customs and border agents collect biometric data of those leaving the country, *citizen and noncitizen*. The cost of implementing the biometric monitoring program—which at the time consisted almost entirely of fingerprints and was proven to be faulty—was between $750 million to $1.5 billion annually, depending on the number of entries or exits.[65] The first such biometric scanners for border exits were implemented in southern Arizona and southern Texas in 2016.[66]

Since then, DHS has installed and tested biometric scanning equipment at nearly every port of entry and airport in the US with the goal of collecting all entry data, and has begun the process to collect exit data at some locations.[67] Today, there are at least two programs testing facial recognition cameras at ports of entry at the México/US border as well as in airports in seven major US cities (Atlanta, Houston, Las Vegas, Los Angeles, Miami, New York, and Washington, DC).[68] Since the *9/11 Report*, the House and Senate have passed three laws that require US Customs and Border Protection to develop and implement entry and exit mechanisms to collect biometric data from foreign travelers.[69] In S. 744, the Senate's comprehensive immigration bill passed in 2012 (but ultimately rejected by the House), the Senate encouraged provisions for a mandatory exit and entry biometric data collection system.[70] In June 2013, the House Judiciary Committee passed the SAFE Act (H.R. 2278), which was "a straightforward provision requiring implementation, as required by current law, of a biometric exit within two years at every land, air, and sea port of entry."[71] Finally, in September 2013, the House introduced H.R. 3141, the Biometric Exit Improvement Act, which would essentially make the provisions of S. 744 and H.R. 2278 federal law.[72] Thus, DHS's development and distribution of biometric tracking systems along with its surveillance technologies have given the agency the capacity to create and organize an alien antitype production economy channeling desirable migrants into pathways toward citizenship, keeping others as exploitable labor without a chance to transfer into citizenship, and marking still others as threatening and subject to the extreme violences of the settler state. These technologies produce alienhood throughout the state, meaning that the exogenous migrants (and even some citizens) are susceptible to population control at the border, at work, at the airport, and in interactions with local police.

LEGAL PROTECTION OVER FLASHBULB NARRATION

Lastly, just as federal legislation has mobilized migrant tracking and biometric *MiB* technologies, federal legislation has also mobilized flashbulb narration technologies throughout the US landscape. For one, the First Amendment to the US Constitution ratified in 1789 directly addresses such protections. The amendment states that "Congress shall make no law . . . prohibiting the free exercise thereof; or abridging the freedom of speech, or of the press."[73] This protection of the press was later extended to news media and visual media, including televised and internet news reportage, despite the varying characteristics of new media formats that emerged in the twentieth and twenty-first centuries.[74] So even if cable and internet news media, those entities practicing flashbulb narration, were not intended to be protected in 1791, federal courts in the US have upheld protection of visual news media to report on and depict anything that does not directly violate the rights of US citizens.[75] In other words, mainstream news reportage of migrants and border crossings today do not need to truthfully illuminate the circumstances of migrants to be protected under the First Amendment of the Constitution. While the state legal apparatus is not directly funding corporate television and internet media newsmakers through appropriations, they are protecting the rights of the news media to profit from the sale of exaggerated and untrue narratives of alienhood, offering little to no protection for those whose images are misused and circulated by the network media machinery. Take, for example, the precarious relationship between the Trump administration and the Fox News group. Mounting evidence shows that much of the discourse, including hateful antimigrant messaging communicated via social media and press releases by the administration, was borrowed from Fox News.[76] Media propaganda such as this is one example of flashbulb narration and is demonstrative of the ways in which assemblages of state and industrial settler narration production can become intertwined.

In general, the *MiB* technologies described here—the virtual border, biometric tracking, and flashbulb narration—are territorializing settler citizenship modes onto the bodies and geographies of a US occupied by settlers. After President Clinton signed IIRIRA in 1996, *MiB* technologies have made intense alien affects more visible, have widely distributed alien populations along stratified antitype economies throughout the US, and have masked the ways state mechanisms exert violent power over migrant groups. The organization of *MiB* technologies by the US is accelerating as the technological capacities of surveillance and the media increase. This growth in capacity, or "force multiplication," completes the citizenship control assemblage loop. As federal agencies further invest in population production technologies, they grow their capacity to manage the extractive economies of private, localized exploitation over exogenous populations in the form of labor exploitation, private detention, and others. Flashbulb narrations, like the alien invasion cinema described in this book, are rapid forms of settler narrative production that naturalize the processes of settler citizenship control. Technologies of flashbulb narration are constantly producing settler consciousness on a loop and trafficking it throughout the numerous media available to citizen consumers.

THOUGHTS ON *MEN IN BLACK* TECHNOLOGIES

Once again, I return to May 2020 when the MQ-9 Reaper Predator B drone, CBP-104, flew over Minneapolis during anti–police brutality protests. That particular MQ-9 Reaper had been requested by an ICE agent who was on the ground in Minneapolis in the days after the protests. The secretive migrant control agent, relying on the *Predator* technology of visibility, was said to be seeking "situational awareness" over the protests. In reality, the agent and their colleagues were using the technology to manufacture a visible antitype that the US could layer with the discursive subjections of "criminal" and "terrorist," subjections that can be used to deny a citizen protester their constitutional rights. Again, this is the risk when the technologies of visibility escape the confines of the cinematic and are adopted to produce alien antitypes: settler citizenship agents can easily traffic them into manufacturing other antitypes that have the potential to be transferred out.

This chapter demonstrates how today's settler citizenship control assemblage (itself comprising numerous networks and sets of relationships) is organized to subject migrants as alien antitypes by casting them with alien affects and then tracking their movements throughout the nation—channeling desirable aliens into violent exploitation and unwanted migrants into the mechanisms of expulsion. This process is aided by the distribution of *MiB* technologies of visibility, allowing for a nationwide network of population producing technologies to be mobilized in the service of the settler population economy. Just as the Clinton administration moved away from a border-centric migration policy implemented by the earlier Reagan administration, the focus of the settler narratives in the US's most popular alien invasion franchise also shifted toward a narrative arc that placed secret government agents in charge of managing the complex economies of alien antitypes that are already here, living among us. ICE, CBP, and other migrant control groups have access to wide-ranging federal, state, and local databases that allow them to easily locate, detain, and remove migrants whom they decide are undesirable.

In general, the materialist assemblage framework I have utilized thus far has provided a new way to study the growing relationship between the military, border security industries, and cinema industries in the US. It is useful for describing how technologies of visibility have evolved, moved, and even merged with other technologies in various modes of settler colonial production. The continued distribution of *Predator* and *MiB* technologies enlarges the capacity of the state to territorialize the sets of relations between noncitizen personae and the settler citizen persona, setting the conditions for an exploitative relationship rooted in histories of perpetual settler violence. The next chapter looks at the ways resistive power might be lodged against settler statecraft through a process of nomadic assemblage. Namely, I am interested in ways activists and artists in the spirit of nomadism are also trafficking technologies of visibility to illuminate the violent processes of citizenship control, intervene in the modes of settler population production, and deterritorialize the geographies of settler citizenship.

Chapter Four

SLEEP DEALER, NOMADIC ASSEMBLAGES, AND DETERRITORIALIZATIONS

For eleven nights in November 2019, the skies over Ciudad Juárez, México, and El Paso, United States, glowed. Eighteen bright, white searchlights—three sets of three lights beaming across the border from both countries—crisscrossed each other through the foggy evenings (fig. 4.1). These two cities, divided by miles of fencing marking the international boundary, share a mountainous backdrop that served to frame the dramatic scene. Although this region is accustomed to the presence of surveillance technologies, including many of those described in this book, these lights were not organized by the border security agents or military of either country. They had been installed as part of *Border Tuner*—an interactive, multimedia art installation. The project was designed by Rafael Lozano-Hemmer, a Mexican-born artist whose goal was to create communication channels between those on either side of the México/US boundary. Participants in the installation could guide a set of three lights across the border fencing; if the lights were met by those emanating from the other side, then intercom devices would activate at each site, allowing the participants controlling the lights to speak with one another.[1] The lights, in this case, served as a technology of humanization instead of a technology of capture.

The increased securitization and militarization of the México/US border over the past half century has made this once international community the scene of countless negative narratives of violence, criminality, and death.[2] However, as Lozano-Hemmer pointed out, "the absolutely most important objective of this project is that new narratives about the border emerge."[3] So, for those eleven nights, the border region between the two mountain

Figure 4.1. An image of the *Border Tuner* multimedia art installation by Rafael Lozano-Hemmer spanning the México/US border from Ciudad Juárez to El Paso in December 2019. Photo by Monica Lozano.

cities in the Chihuahuan Desert became a site where technologies of visibility connected those who are otherwise organized by the settler population production mode in the US to be permanently divided from one other. The *Border Tuner* project, even if just briefly, deterritorialized the relationship between subjectivities on colonial, nationalist borders using technologies of visibility—reterritorializing momentarily a new set of possibilities for subjectivity mediated through technology. While technologies of visibility are usually used to divide border groups into sets of settler personae, Lozano-Hemmer trafficked searchlights to the border to arrange relationships in which national subjectivities could be momentarily suspended. What lasting effects will the installation have? That might be hard to say, but what is certain is that events like this demonstrate that deterritorialization—rejecting the logical and material occupation of the sets of relationships between lands and peoples produced by colonial power—is possible.

This is an example of what Thomas Nail calls a relative positive deterritorialization, or a "process of change that does not reproduce a pre-established assemblage, but does not yet contribute to or create a new assemblage either."[4] These deterritorializations have the capacity to rearrange sets of relationships, but more likely they are perceived as anomalous phenomena that will eventually get coded out of (or into) the assemblage.[5] That is not to say that these phenomena can't organize long-term and material deterritorializations—or decolonizations for that matter. And, as small, purposeful anomalies in the flows of assemblages, or cuts as Brian Massumi suggests, these relative positive deterritorializations contain the codes for building more sustained deterritorializations/decolonizations against what has manifested as the US settler citizenship control assemblage.[6]

I begin this chapter by opening a conversation about deterritorializations of assemblages. I am particularly interested in the distinction between relative positive deterritorializations, which make individual or isolated cuts into an assemblage, and absolute positive deterritorializations, which are characterized by the complete redistribution of the sets of relations between the materials and personae of an assemblage. I then describe *nomad thought* as an expression of positive deterritorialization, both individually in its capacity to spark relative positive deterritorializations and collectively in its capacity to spark absolute positive deterritorializations. Nomad thought's positive deterritorializing potential, in turn, can organize the conditions by which the material and personae of an assemblage might be reorganized to resist arrangements into subjects and objects of territorial/state/capitalist assemblages.

Then, I look at many who are sparking relative positive deterritorializations by rearranging how technologies of visibility might be deployed against the citizenship control assemblage. I start with a description of the film *Sleep Dealer*—a cinematic assemblage that redistributes popular Hollywood narrative elements to tell a resistance story.[7] Alex Rivera—digital artist, activist, and the film's director—has spent nearly two decades using film and digital technology to challenge the exploitation of migrants in the US. *Sleep Dealer's* use of camera, lighting, and CGI technology to cut into the dominant flows of alien science fiction film sheds light on the assemblage of citizenship control. The film and its filmmakers offer audiences a glimpse of a future in which the cycles of exploitation and violence brought upon migrants might be eradicated using the very tools the state has employed to set those cycles in motion in the first place.

As I move through an analysis of *Sleep Dealer*, I also look at other expressions of art and activism that, like the film, produce relative positive deterritorializations. While the previous two chapters demonstrated how the US's territorial-state assemblages develop and organize technologies of visibility to code alien affects and produce alien antitypes, this chapter turns attention to how nomad thought might rearrange technologies of visibility to make cuts into the flows of territorial-state assemblages. These cuts deterritorialize settler citizenship coding by disrupting the production of alien affects. The cases all involve people who use technologies of visibility to expose the state's border security mechanisms—artists, activists, hackers, and even motorists. As it turns out, these people are demonstrating that the machinery of light and surveillance used to organize bodies near the México/US border into personae that suit the settler production modes can be adopted to disempower the settler state's control over migrants, even if briefly. So, this chapter considers how pro-migrant artists and activists are developing and deploying technologies of visibility that open potentials for resistance against settler colonial constitutive citizenship production modes.

NOMAD THOUGHT, NOMADIC ASSEMBLAGES, AND DETERRITORIALIZATIONS

Up to this point, I have described the US settler citizenship assemblage as a set of logics that are organized in order to maintain a distinct relationship between the settler and the state that was formed to protect the sovereignty of the settler—the United States. However, not all assemblages are motivated by the same sets of desires, and Nail's analytic framework provides a way to detail the contours of the settler citizenship assemblage that is characterized by a tension between territorial arranging and state arranging. This is not to say that describing the contours of an assemblage is quite as cut and dried; the kinds of "assemblage are never pure; all assemblages are composed of a mixture of . . . four types to different degrees. In order to understand how an assemblage works . . . we need to be able to map out its different tendencies and political types."[8] These four types of assemblage are territorial, state, capitalist, and nomadic.

Thus far in *Visions of Invasion*, I have focused on the territorial-state assemblage of citizenship control assemblage and how it organizes settler antitypes using technologies of visibility that have been trafficked from Hollywood's extraterrestrial invasion narratives into US antimigration security policy. Nomad thought, though, is an ontology that can resist the coding of alien affects produced by the machinery of the settler state; it rejects the power driving the dominant population production processes of citizenship in today's control society. In today's citizenship assemblages, nomad thought can be a strategy that cuts into the flows trafficking materials (like discourses and technologies) and personae between the assemblages that often channel alien antitypes into violence, exploitation, and expulsion. Nomad thought, I argue, is the organizing logic of nomadic assemblages. This section also explains the types of deterritorializations and what they mean in the context of the US's citizenship control assemblage. This leads into an explanation of how nomadic assemblages have the capacity to spur both relative and absolute deterritorializations.

NOMAD THOUGHT

Instead of thinking about migrants and citizens from a paradigm of constitutive citizenship subjectivity—settler populations imagined through national citizenship codes—I understand alien affects as products that emerge from within a citizenship control assemblage that cast bodies into various personae. Some are cast as citizens, some noncitizen antitypes. As I described in the previous chapters, being cast as an antitype has degrees: from pressure for assimilation to economic and sexual exploitation, incarceration, and in some cases death. I have also described how the process of casting antitypes along a settler population economy concurrently produces the settler citizen type, which is everything the antitypes are not. Doing so actualizes settler sovereignty—or what I described previously as the settler citizens' capacity to move through the settler state with little resistance (like having access to passports and driver's licenses, and having freedom from law enforcement stop and seizure), enact extractive economic mechanisms (like fracking and urban gentrification) almost anywhere in the settler state, and maintain social and political structures that center the "rights" of the settler citizens over the lives of antitypes (like stand-your-ground gun laws, antifacemask activism during the COVID-19 pandemic, and qualified immunity for police officers who commit on-duty violence). Thus, one's movement depends on the ways this citizenship control assemblage codes one's body.

Nomad thought, though, has the potential to rearrange the ways technologies of visibility cast bodies as aliens to make this intervention.[9] Nomad thought draws from the margins to challenge the codes centralized by dominant systems of power. In the case of Lozano-Hemmer's *Border Tuner*, the artist's activism was not trying to openly reject or defy the desires of the citizenship assemblage, but rather he rearranged the technological and human mechanisms of the territorial assemblage, for just a few days, to imagine what an uncoded set of relationships between groups of people might feel like in that place. Inevitably, though, the imperial/colonial despot recodes the territories captured in violence to a system of imperial/colonial thought.[10] This oscillation between what is territorialized and deterritorialized is in many cases spurred by the actions of those like Lozano-Hemmer. "[O]n the periphery, the communities embark on another kind of adventure, display another kind of unity, a nomadic unity, and engage in a nomadic war-machine, and they tend to come uncoded rather than being coded over."[11]

Deleuze positions nomad thought as an ontological and methodological way of knowing the world that meets colonial empire with a sustained, mobile, and uncodable resistance. It is not as much a logic of a particular political identity per se (e.g., of migrants or Indigenous peoples), but more of a logic of resistance to state coding (like settler colonial subjectivities). "[N]omads are unhappy in our regimes: we use any means necessary to pin them down, so they lead a troubled life. . . . [However,] the nomad is not necessarily someone who moves around: some journeys take place in the same place, they're journeys of intensity."[12] That is to say, nomad thought is a process of mapping intensities as they subject us. It vaguely formalizes a logic of elusiveness theorized from bodies who move outside of the prescribed arrangements ascribed to personae in societies of control.

Thus, in the current US settler situation, a multitude of apparatuses of US citizenship perpetually subject migrant communities as aliens and force them into intense and violent conditions. But nomad thought reminds us that just as personae are produced, they might be unproduced, or reproduced, to readjust pressures applied by the assemblage, especially on the margins of imperial territory, like borderlands:

> "Nomad thought" does not immure itself in the edifice of an ordered interiority, it moves freely in an element of exteriority. It does not repose on identity; it rides difference. . . . The concepts it creates do not merely reflect the eternal form of the legislating subject, but are defined by a communicable force in relation to which their subject, to the extent that they can be said to have one, is only secondary. They do not reflect upon the world but are immersed in a changing state of things.[13]

Nomad thought resists the dominant ways of knowing implicit to the state: segregation, state subjectivities, international borders, and so on. It operates outside of the logic from which settler colonialism, citizenship legislation, immigration enforcement, and antitype subjection are conceived, and in doing so realizes possibilities outside of their constraints. Nomad thought is creative; it opens spaces "to reconcile partiality and discontinuity with the construction of new forms of interconnectedness and collective political projects."[14] It resists the subjectivities states apply to bodies; it is a logic of elusion.

Nomads, though, are not necessarily migrants, and migrants don't necessarily express nomad thought. Rosi Braidotti differentiates the experiences of nomadic subjects from those of migrants (though I look to the nomadic expressions that occur within migrant groups in the US specifically because of the ways citizenship control assemblages organize their bodies in relation to state power).[15] She contends that nomad thought (or "nomadic consciousness") is a "way to explore and legitimate political agency while taking as historical evidence the decline of metaphysically fixed, steady identities."[16] It decenters assumptions about subjectivities and resists "more localized but . . . exploitative power formations" that emerge as the US's territorial assemblages further subjugate bodies.[17] Nomad thought, therefore, can reject coding that happens through the settler population production economy and might open spaces for nomadic assemblages to emerge that can lead to positive deterritorializations.

NOMADIC ASSEMBLAGES

Nomad thought can be considered an organizing logic of a nomadic assemblage. It reorganizes the personae of an assemblage, even if just briefly, to make cuts into the flows of population production inherent in the assemblage. Nomad thought also rearranges the materials of an assemblage into different sets of relationships. Deleuze and Guattari, in describing nomadology, discuss the ways in which nomads adopt the tools (technologies) of the "empire they communicate with, conquer, or integrate with."[18] The tools of the state that the nomad adopts are separated from the desires of the assemblages they employ, meaning that tools used for state control don't have to only be used for state control. They can be refashioned to carve a place for nomads and exert power back onto the state. Or, as Deleuze and Guattari might remark: "There is a schizophrenic taste for the tool that moves it away from work toward free action, a schizophrenic taste for the weapon that turns it into a means for peace. A counterattack and a resistance simultaneously."[19]

The process of a nomadic assemblage

> is revolutionary in the sense that instead of applying solutions to pre-given problems, such as how to make sure everyone is represented fairly in a presupposed state, or simply affirming that "other problems are possible," particular problems are themselves transformed directly by those who effectuate them and who are affected by them.[20]

These types of assemblages are unlike territorial and state assemblages in that they are not bound to a set of relationships (territorialities) that operate in the service of an ideology (like settler colonialism). They are free-form arrangements. "Nomadic assemblages are arranged in such a way that the conditions (abstract machine), elements (concrete assemblage), and agencies (personae) of the assemblage are able to change and enter into new combinations without arbitrary limit or so-called 'natural' or 'hierarchical' uses and meanings."[21] Nomadic assemblages are change assemblages; they rearrange logics, materials, and bodies to deterritorialize sets of relations in order to "offer a political alternative absolutely incompatible with the territorial hierarchies based on essentialist meanings."[22]

For instance, surveillance and light technologies used in citizenship control are not themselves imbued with the logic of state power but rather are trafficked by the state to satisfy the desire of the assemblage—the capture of migrants and the ultimate territorialization of settler-state power. For activists challenging citizenship control, adopting the same surveillance and lighting technologies in order to change the organization of state personae demonstrates how one might reapply the empire's tools to deterritorialize statehood to be inclusive of those who are cast with alien affects, or to not even traffic the technologies that produce alien affects in the first place. Despite their limited access to advanced technologies in comparison to the state, these activists are making cuts into the flows of the US citizenship control assemblages by using technologies of visibility to recode the ways the assemblage makes alienhood visible on the surface of US statehood. It may not be an equal force, but resistive cuts have the capacity to alter the emergent properties of the citizenship assemblage. Activists are demonstrating just how exploitative the territorial-state assemblage of citizenship control can be for migrants once they have been divided from the citizenry. Those resisting the state's control of alienhood are opening new possibilities for those once cast with alien affects to move more freely within the state. These new possibilities are positive deterritorializations.

FOUR DETERRITORIALIZATIONS

For nomads—especially those who resist coding under US settler statehood—navigating the uneven sets of relationships implied in the settler citizenship production economy can be difficult and dangerous. Since assemblages are not static, they tend to autoproduce the sets of relations between personae and materials to keep the assemblage inclining toward its abstract desires, even when cuts are made. More precisely, assemblages of state power carve striated landscapes of imperial territoriality that act upon bodies to control their movements, but they have to keep readjusting those territories to account for changing materials and bodies. "It is a vital concern of every State not only to vanquish nomad thought but to control migrations and, more generally, to establish a zone of rights over the entire 'exterior,' over all of the flows traversing the ecumenon."[23] In the case of the territorial-state citizenship control assemblages described in this book, the control of exogenous migrants is deeply rooted in maintaining the flows of settler citizens and limiting the flows of their antitypes toward sets of relationships that are localized, extractive, exploitative, and violent.

This capacity to adjust to the changing elements of the assemblage's material and personae is the first kind of deterritorialization Nail describes: it is a process called "relative negative deterritorialization... by which pre-established assemblages adapt and respond to changes in their relations by incorporating those changes."[24] This is the way power is able to adapt, over time, to maintain territorializations over changing subjects and objects. By contrast, "absolute negative deterritorializations" are characterized by the complete destabilization of all political assemblages. They are negative because they are characterized by the complete subordination of personae under the power of those who have acquired resources specifically to undermine all types of organizations that distribute power. After all, "staying stratified—organized, signified, subjected—is not the worst that can happen; the worst that can happen is if you throw the strata into demented or suicidal collapse, which brings them back down on us heavier than ever."[25] An absolute negative deterritorialization totally unearths the foundations of possibility for political organization and keeps the parts from reorganizing in any manner (total destruction).

Nomad thought, though, is a logic of deterritorialization that evades the state's attempt to control the flows of bodies while also resisting absolute collapse. "If the nomad can be called the Deterritorialized par excellence, it is precisely because there is no reterritorialization *afterward* as with the migrant, or upon *something else* as with the sedentary."[26] Nomadism does not desire transfer into personae; nomads are always in transitory spaces, meaning that they wage a constant challenge to the state by resisting subjection, which interrupts coding, which in turn unorganizes striated spaces of territoriality. Nomads are always moving against the tendencies of territorial and state assemblages, with no real interest in creating new ones.

So, just like there are two kinds of negative deterritorializations, there are also two kinds of positive deterritorializations, which I argue are motivated by nomadic organizing logics to make cuts into territorial and state assemblages. The first type are relative positive deterritorializations, described as a process of "ambiguous change" that can open spaces for reorganizing materials and personae within an assemblage.[27] Relative positive deterritorializations are momentary and take considerable effort to sustain. "Everyone recognizes that a new element or agency has escaped the established assemblage, but it is not yet clear whether it will cause a radical transformation of the whole assemblage or whether it will be incorporated into an already established assemblage through a relative negative deterritorialization."[28] However, even if they don't always result in radical transformation, they still provide a glimpse of the strategies one might use to scramble the organizing logics of a territorial-state assemblage. These strategies, which include decoding personae and rearranging technologies of visibility, are nomadic. Like the *Border Tuner* installation described above, Rivera's film *Sleep Dealer*, and the other examples from this chapter, all exemplify relative positive deterritorializations.

Finally, there are absolute positive deterritorializations. These deterritorializations mobilize the radical and often "revolutionary" nomadic assemblages—formations that are entirely new sets of relationships between personae and materials. They are "creative process[es] that [produce] something new from the subjects and objects that are continually escaping from all assemblages. Absolute positive deterritorialization is therefore the kind of change that is capable of creating and sustaining a revolutionary movement."[29] Relative positive deterritorializations can become absolute positive deterritorializations with a sustained effort to resist the recoding of subjection (reterritorialization). Absolute positive deterritorializations are world builders. They are not destructive in the sense that they deconstruct any assemblage, but rather they engage in a permanent, metamorphic deterritorialization to reorganize elements of past assemblages into new potential relationships.

I will speak more about absolute relative deterritorialization in the concluding chapter. Here, though, I describe how activists are deterritorializing the US state's citizenship control assemblage by utilizing technologies often associated with capture that result in momentary, relative positive deterritorializations. The cases here offer a glimpse of strategies rooted in nomadic thought that produce small cuts into the territorial-state assemblages of citizenship control in the US. More specifically, I once again use a materialist method to show how artists and activists employ technologies nomadically against today's migrant control assemblages to deterritorialize the settler citizenship population production mode in the US. These groups are trafficking technologies of visibility, too. However, technologies like those described in this chapter can cut into the flows of assemblages if they are programmed to; they already have the capacity to be tools of deterritorialization even after being used as tools for state territorialization.

THE *SLEEP DEALER* ASSEMBLAGE

Why Cybraceros? is a short film directed and produced by Alex Rivera in 1997 that depicts a future in which robots operated via remote control by laborers in México can pick oranges and fill baskets on farms in the US (the word *cybracero* is a play on the words cyber-bracero, a reference to the federal labor agreement between México and the United States I discussed in chapter 2).[30] The five-minute short uses a combination of film images taken of farmworkers harvesting food and basic CGI images of robots to express what Rivera satirically believes will be the next phase in migrant labor (fig. 4.2). The film insinuates that as a result of the heightened political and economic tensions brought on by large numbers of immigrant populations living and working in the US—along with advancing computer and networking technologies—it is possible to import migrant labor without having to import the migrant. Rivera's vision of a world where migrant laborers, gig workers, media makers, and security forces are all linked together via body implants imagines a (not-so-distant) future in which bodies separated by austere geographical bordering apparatuses are still brought together in a biopolitical economy of exploitation via the internet.[31] It's a vison of a sort of extractive techno-neoliberalism. In other words, "[u]nder the Cybracero Program, American

Figure 4.2. Film still from Alex Rivera's 1997 *Why Cybraceros?*; an image of an early CGI representation of a robot picking oranges.

farm labor will be accomplished on American soil, but no Mexican workers will need to leave Mexico. Only the labor of Mexicans will cross the border ... and that means quality products at low financial and social cost."[32]

For Rivera, *Why Cybraceros?* was the beginning of a more than decade-long project that culminated in the release of *Sleep Dealer* in 2008. At the heart of both *Why Cybraceros?* and *Sleep Dealer* is the narrative that migrant labor could be imported into the US via digital networks, allowing Mexican workers to send their labor across the México/US border in the form of robots operated remotely from outside the US. However, over the eleven years Rivera spent making the film, the technologies of visibility he used to make *Sleep Dealer* evolved tremendously, resulting in an imaginative and visually stunning filmic expression of resistance to settler-state power. The filmmaker arranges articulable and visible expressions that adopt nomad thought to shed light on the assemblage of citizenship control, cutting into the US's territorial-state power and deterritorializing the cinematic production of alien affects. Specifically, *Sleep Dealer* relies on many of the same technologies of visibility used by the creators of the *Predator*, *Men in Black*, and other alien invasion franchises to make his film. *Sleep Dealer*, however, rearranges the sets of relations between technologies and personae in visual relative positive deterritorialization to change how film produces personae at borders.

SLEEP DEALER

The film opens with a rapid sequence of shots featuring Memo Cruz (Luis Fernando Peña), the protagonist of the film, connected to several wires attached to his arms and legs and wearing a mask covering his mouth and ears. He and dozens of other workers are lined up in a row in a factory, all plugged into the blue wires and masks of the "sleep dealer"—the technologically advanced maquiladoras where they work. He is narrating his experience working in the sleep dealers, describing the ways he and others will hallucinate and often collapse from exhaustion. Memo, a migrant from Santa Ana del Río, Oaxaca, México, must travel north to the border near the United States to work in the sleep dealers. The film builds on Rivera's conceptualization of robotic migrant labor from *Why Cybraceros?* and adds narrative components that challenge the economic and political forces in the US that exploit migrants and commit violence along the border (fig. 4.3). *Sleep Dealer* carefully reorganizes personae and visibilities to recast the viewer's orientation toward the México/US border.

The film then takes the viewer to Oaxaca. Memo is helping his father retrieve water from the corporate water suppliers, Del Rio Water, to keep

Figure 4.3. Film still from Alex Rivera's 2008 *Sleep Dealer*; a shot of Cybracero, the maquiladora where Memo works.

the family's very small farm from going bankrupt. Del Rio has dammed the natural water flow of the river to maintain control of the supply. In his spare time, Memo uses recycled radio and computer equipment to hack into cell phone calls and other radio signals from his bedroom. "Memo dreams of the enchantments percolating in the connected world and tries to cope with his mounting feelings of disconnection and entrapment by obsessively tapping into it through his homemade computer console."[33] Paula Straile-Costa writes that "Memo's obsession with hacking demonstrates the powerful influence of North American media around the world. He intercepts conversations of node workers gainfully employed remotely in locations through the U.S., fueling his curiosity and alienation from his home."[34] Often, he would hear the phone calls of the many rural Mexicans who are talking to relatives working in sleep dealers. This is when he first learns about nodes and the interconnected networks of transnational labor. One night, he stumbles upon a signal of a remote aerial drone operator from the US who is conducting patrols at Del Rio Water, and he gets caught. As a result, Memo and his family are targeted as "aqua-terrorists," a subjection immediately assigned by the techno-settler state that justifies the deployment of Del Rio Water's fleet of aerial drones to destroy the family's home, killing Memo's father. Memo, who is attending a birthday party at a friend's house at the time, watches the entire drone attack on television; the show *Drones* (with crosshairs replacing the *o* in the word) is broadcasting a live feed of the attack (in English) celebrating the drone pilots and deriding the aqua-terrorists for bringing this harm upon themselves (an example of flashbulb narration). Even though Del Rio

Figure 4.4. Film still from Alex Rivera's 2008 *Sleep Dealer*; Memo and his father are interrogated by a remote-controlled guard at Del Rio Water.

has occupied Oaxaca and extracted its water, they take a self-defensive position against Memo and his family. After his father's funeral, Memo makes the tough decision to migrate north to find work in sleep dealer factories to support his widowed mother and brother.

These scenes from Oaxaca are certainly significant to the narrative of the film, but they are also where Rivera first visualizes a sci-fi landscape of Oaxaca to reveal a possible technological future in which the US extends "tendrils of technology [until they] have infiltrated the environment."[35] For example, when Memo and his father retrieve water from a Del Rio reservoir, they interact with an assault rifle attached to a camera and intercom system that connects the two men to a customer service agent (likely in the US) (fig. 4.4). This image—a border agent persona embodied in the assembled machinery of a camera-gun-microphone-speaker—appears several times in the film and demonstrates how Rivera arranges certain cinematic elements in his nomadic assemblage. Thus, *Sleep Dealer* offers a stinging a critique of drone technology and the role it plays in carving political, economic, and geographic landscapes on both sides of the US/México border. The scenes shot in Oaxaca provide audiences with their first encounter with drones. These images portray the deadly, violent expressions of territorial-state power using technologies of visibility that expand the power of corporate colonial empire. Rivera's drones (rendered using CGI technology) track and kill the "aqua-terrorists," resulting in the death of Memo's father.[36] With his own cinematic technologies, Rivera is able to amplify the intensity of those violent drone strikes much like the technologies of visibility in the *Predator* and *Men in Black* franchises amplify alien affects. The production of CGI drones in the first twenty minutes of the film creates highly intensive images of violent state control.

In general, *Sleep Dealer* is about the current state of transnational political and economic technologies and how they impact both the US and México.[37] The Oaxaca scenes demonstrate Rivera's understanding of both the emancipating and subjugating potentials of technological innovation. Commenting on this tension, Rivera states: "We live in a moment when the military is using technology to wage remote war. Corporations are using technology to move extraordinarily quickly around the globe to take advantage of weak environmental standards and weak labor standards."[38] He also suggests, though, that social movements can be activated using the same global networks, "in this moment when we don't know who will be more empowered by the connectivity and by new technology."[39] Network technologies depicted in the film used to strengthen corporate enclosure over material and digital landscapes might simultaneously be adopted to emancipate network users from the constraints of neoliberal state power.

> [T]he film poses an alternative interpretation of connectivity whereby the limits of capital are exposed through various forms of resistance, which in turn lay bare unexpected weaknesses in the infrastructure of global corporate power. As the film proceeds, these exposed faults are increasingly brought into contact with each other and help to spread into other parts of the system.[40]

Sleep Dealer, thus, narrates a series of relative positive deterritorializations that eventually spawn an absolute positive deterritorialization. Throughout, Rivera portrays the relationship between emancipating and capturing technologies to show how the US controls economic, political, and social flows at the border and in communities in both the US and México, but also how some who are subjugated by this machinery resist by recoding the same machinery with nomad thought.

After Memo journeys to the México/US border, for example, he searches for a job at a sleep dealer. On his journey north to Tijuana via bus, he meets Luz Martínez (Leonor Varela), a journalist and blogger who eventually helps him get his nodes. Nodes are implants placed on the legs, arms, neck, and back of the body that connect people to virtual reality interfaces. Among other things, nodes allow users to connect to the sleep dealers, where they can operate labor drones that complete a number of tasks like construction, farmwork, and housekeeping. Luz, who also has nodes, uses hers to plug into

Figure 4.5. Film still from Alex Rivera's 2008 *Sleep Dealer*; Luz uploads Memo's memory to TruNode.

TruNode, a marketplace for memories that are sold and traded by its members. After she tells him how to get nodes, Memo tells Luz the story about his family and his village in Oaxaca (fig. 4.5). Later, she sells that same memory on TruNode to Rudy Ramirez, the drone pilot who lives in the US who was responsible for killing Memo's father. This transaction starts a chain of events that culminates in a friendship between the three and the beginnings of a nomadic assemblage in the film. Thus, the nodes act as the conduit into the flows of dominant exploitation and violence, like Rudy's drone or Memo's job at the sleep dealers. However, nodes also become a technology that makes the film's ultimate deterritorialization possible.

Another prominent example of how technologies can be both capturing and emancipatory are the sleep dealers themselves. When Memo gets his nodes installed, he quickly finds a job in a sleep dealer factory, where he is able to remotely control a construction robot in San Diego. In an homage to Rivera's short film, the name of the company where Memo finds a job is called Cybracero. Memo plugs the blue wires of the migrant labor machinery into his nodes, puts on his mask, and inserts two blue contact lenses into his eyes that allow him to see from the perspective of the labor drone that is constructing high-rises across the border in San Diego (fig. 4.6). This technology inserts Memo into the transnational economy via the settler colonial production process of gentrification in the US while his body remains in México, bound by national borders. The sleep dealer technology gives Cybracero the capacity to extract labor from Memo and thousands of others while keeping their bodies physically removed from the spaces of citizenship in the US.

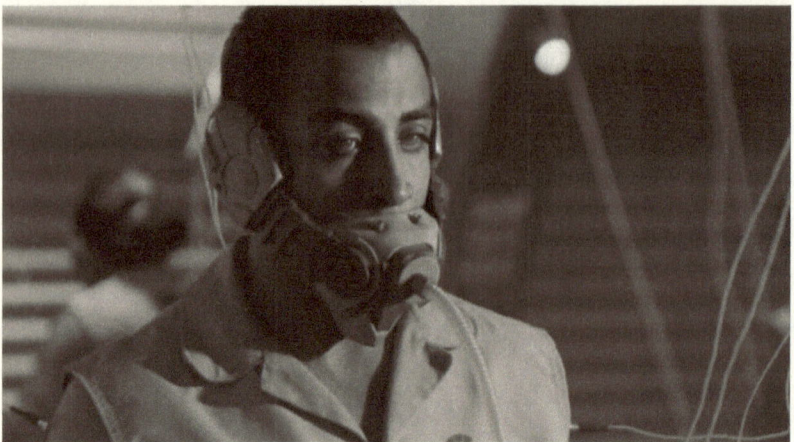

Figure 4.6. Film still from Alex Rivera's 2008 *Sleep Dealer*; Memo plugged into Cybracero via nodes implanted in his body.

The commodification of memories through the TruNode platform also creates an economy around the buying and selling of visual memories, a third technology Rivera features. This technology of visibility appears as an interface on Luz's desktop computer that she uses to manage her account after she uploads her memories via her nodes. She, too, is plugged into the transnational economy, but her labor is done by collecting narratives layered on top of memory images and selling them to others—converting technology captures into economic flows. This technology of visibility, unlike flashbulb mediation, allows the multitudes with internet access a chance to see an unmediated narrative of migration from a first-person vantage point—adding emancipatory qualities to the technology as well. TruNode is also what eventually brings together the group of protagonists from stratified personae to reject their political types and enact a nomadic assemblage. Luz sells Memo's memory to Rudy, who had killed Memo's father. Seemingly out of guilt from having just watched the memory, Rudy tries to connect with Memo to reconcile his actions. It is in this moment of nomadic reorganization that the seeds of resistance are planted. Rudy purchases a memory in the US through Luz's website (which she operates from a border town) that depicts something that happened to Memo in Oaxaca. Their new relationship transcends rigid national and economic subjections and opens an opportunity to enact positive deterritorializations against the territorial-state assemblage depicted in the film.

Sleep Dealer concludes when Rudy crosses the heavily fortified border into Tijuana and attempts to meet up with Luz and Memo. At the border

Figure 4.7. Film still from Alex Rivera's 2008 *Sleep Dealer*; Rudy encounters a remote-controlled guard as he tries to cross into México from the United States.

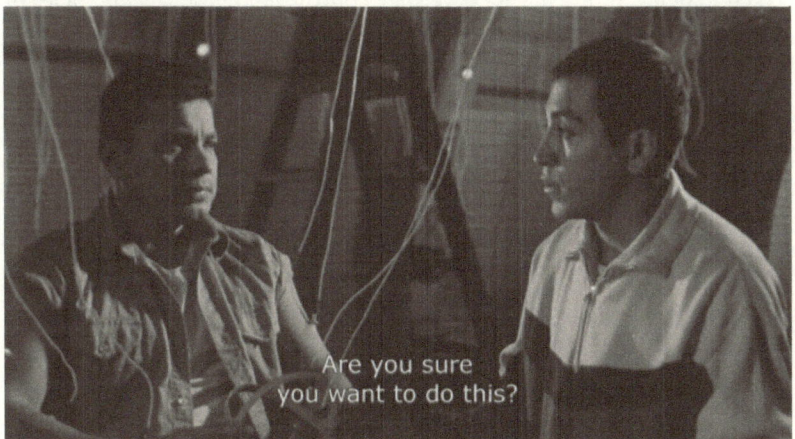

Figure 4.8. Film still from Alex Rivera's 2008 *Sleep Dealer*; Rudy and Memo use links at Cybracero to hack into a Del Rio Water drone.

checkpoint, Rudy encounters the same camera-gun-microphone-speaker apparatus featured earlier in the film, which initially prevents him from leaving the US, indicating that the bordering project is just as much about keeping citizen-types in as it is about keeping citizen antitypes out (fig. 4.7). The voice behind the device even informs Rudy of the grave danger he faces in traveling to México but fails to dissuade him from crossing. Once Rudy makes contact with Memo and Luz, the three break into the Cybracero factory and plug Rudy into the sleep dealer network via his nodes (fig. 4.8). Memo once again hacks into Del Rio Water's security drone system, allowing

Rudy to remotely control the drone, fly it to Santa Ana del Río, and shoot a hole in the river dam. This act, conducted over the network, floods the valley with water and ultimately revives the small town's local economy.

In general, Rivera's film narrates a series of relative positive deterritorializations that eventually culminate in an absolute positive deterritorialization, which resets the relations between Memo's family and the land in Oaxaca that was being exploited at the film's start. Like other films discussed in this book, *Sleep Dealer* arranges a number of political conditions, material elements, and personae into a cinematic expression. However, unlike other mainstream Hollywood expressions of alienhood, Rivera's film imagines a way to turn the technologies of subjugation into technologies of emancipation by reorganizing the cinematic tools available to the director. The film itself acts a relative positive deterritorialization that narrates for audiences what a nomadic assemblage might look like, while also shedding light on a technological future of excessive state control, ubiquitous technologies of visibility in border spaces, and the continued disembodiment of migrants from their labor. This demonstrates how Rivera's art and activism challenge the settler colonial constitutive citizenship paradigm in the US today by arranging technologies of visibility to make a cut into the dominant production flows of the territorial-state assemblage.

A NOTE ON DRONE HACKING

In *Sleep Dealer*, activists adopt nomad thought to cut into the citizenship control assemblage by hacking drones. More than a decade after *Sleep Dealer* and Rivera's prediction that drone technology would become more readily available to the consumer public, the technology has indeed become ubiquitous. Federal, state, and local law enforcement agencies throughout the US, in particular, have invested billions of dollars in unmanned aerial drones to maximize their securitization force.[41] However, drones used by the US government in citizenship control on the México/US border are now being hacked in order to disrupt the daily business of US border agents.[42]

Timothy Bennett, a program manager with DHS, suggested in 2016 that "[t]he bad guys on the borders have lots of money, and what they're putting money into is in spoofing and jamming of GPS," which was allowing hackers to hijack or destroy DHS drones.[43] Not all drones are as susceptible to hacking as others, though. The DHS uses large, encrypted drones in many high-traffic border areas (like the MQ-9 Reaper Predator B described in previous chapters), which are much less likely to be targeted by hackers given their advanced security features. The majority of the drones being hacked on the border are smaller surveillance drones that are typically operated remotely and often used by border agents to monitor the movements of migrants and drug traffickers across the México/US border.[44] Several local and state law enforcement agencies along the border also utilize small-scale drone technologies in support of the efforts of DHS and the Border Patrol. With seemingly limitless funding appropriation and networks of corporate agents, the US citizenship control assemblage will likely continue to have broad access to these "force-multiplying" technologies.

That said, there are a number of ways that hackers can interrupt the operations of a surveillance drone. The first is called spoofing, "a technique where a signal sent by hackers impersonates the signal a drone had been receiving, effectively relinquishing control of the drone."[45] Spoofing allows a hacker to redirect the drone, potentially taking ownership of it, giving the hacker access to the data stored on board as well as to the drone's design specifications. This is what Memo, Luz, and Rudy did to the Del Rio Water drone in *Sleep Dealer*. For many, this is the greatest risk that drone hacking poses—a spoofed drone has the potential to be weaponized against the US military or other security interests in the US.[46] Despite the fact that border drones (both large and small) are not equipped with firearms or explosives (yet), many observers suggest that a spoofed drone would pose a public safety hazard, and some have even called for legislative action to prevent this scenario.[47]

Other methods for hacking drones include jamming and skyjacking. "Jamming is when someone uses a device to jam the GPS signal so that the drone loses its ability to determine its location or altitude."[48] Jamming often uses radio signals or other frequency waves to block the signals transmitted from the operator to the drone. Typically, this results in a crash or a loss of the drone. However, unlike spoofing, the hacker cannot take over operations and control the drone, only disrupt it. Currently, the practice of jamming is illegal in the US and is enforced by the Federal Communications Commission and the Federal Aviation Administration.[49] Finally, skyjacking a drone is when a hacker uses one drone to attach to another, midflight. Locating and docking with another drone requires quite a bit of flight skill and radar technology. This capacity, though, allows hackers to access the data stored on the hijacked drone and potentially take ownership of it, but it does not allow for the control access like spoofing might.[50]

In any case, the widespread practice of hacking drones has made it harder for the Border Patrol and DHS to surveil the heavily trafficked routes along the México/US border. The nomadic practice of repurposing drones allows those crossing through the border region to circumvent the technologies of visibility organized by the US's territorial assemblage of citizenship control. Those engaged in hacking border drones can locate and track the very machinery that is designed to surveil those settler antitypes on the fringes of the US settler state. By reorganizing the relationships between antitype subjectivities and drone technologies, hackers have the potential to deny the US the ability to subject them as antitypes. It allows the antitype to know the territorial-state assemblage, a direct expression of force that challenges settler colonial power. Like in Rivera's *Sleep Dealer*, the deployment of drone technology within citizenship control assemblages allows the US to multiply its military, industrial, and ideological power over Mestiza/o/x migrant communities. In the case of antimigrant control activists and others who are trying to make nomadic cuts into the US settler empire, hacking has been and likely will continue to be a practice that mobilizes relative positive deterritorializations.

ALEX RIVERA'S NOMADIC MIGRANT ACTIVISM

Rivera's efforts in producing *Sleep Dealer* are twofold: he narrates a deterritorialization against a territorial-state-capitalist assemblage while also trafficking nomad thought to audiences watching the film. *Sleep Dealer* might be a relative positive deterritorialization, but it provides a glimpse of how others might be able to decode settler citizenship personae to mobilize nomadic assemblages beyond cinema. Early in the process of making *Sleep Dealer*, Rivera was challenged with the task of visualizing his science fiction robots building skyscrapers and doing farmwork, his weaponized drones, and other visual effects, on a small budget.[51] The film relies on special effects and CGI technologies to make the citizenship control assemblages visible, just like the makers of the *Predator* and *Men in Black* films used them to make alien affects.

However, unlike the producers of the Hollywood blockbusters, Rivera did not have the financial resources that filmmakers typically do when embarking on a science fiction project requiring so many special and visual effects. He only had a budget of about $2 million, most of which was in the form of a grant to finalize the film.[52] To animate both the labor drones and the security drones, Rivera first sketched out drawings on paper and used consumer-level animation software called Poser to create the movement-images of mechanical robots, which are set upon the backdrop of rural México and the México/US border region. Once filming had wrapped and the computer-generated images were rendered, Rivera edited and finished the film using Final Cut Pro, another consumer-level software package.[53] Like the characters in his film, Rivera tapped into the consumer flow of goods and labor to make a small cut in the larger assemblage with technologies that are reasonably accessible to independent filmmakers. Yet, despite the limited resources available to the makers of this film and despite competition from mainstream Hollywood sci-fi blockbusters, *Sleep Dealer* manages to make a cut into cinematic flows. It was made by an activist who broke from the dominant cinematic organizations of personae and technologies to render a successful and transgressive science fiction film.[54]

In fact, after the release of *Sleep Dealer*, the Pentagon reached out to Rivera to better understand the nature of nonstate actors and others who may either develop drone technology or hack into the existing technologies created by the US military.[55] Almost immediately, the US government wanted to organize Rivera's technologies into their own territorial assemblage (an example of relative negative deterritorialization described above). Rivera himself mentions that it is not strange to see the Pentagon fund Hollywood's science fiction films in order to forge a bond between security machinery and cinematic machinery. He describes the extraordinary presence of the US military in Hollywood with this example:

> *Transformers: Revenge of the Fallen* was the first Hollywood production with all four branches of the military: Army, Air Force, Navy, and Marines all working on it. . . . There's this extraordinarily complex exchange between the fantasies of war, the process of recruiting, the technologies of war that appear in the films, and the technologies of visualization that get invented by the military and passed down to the entertainment sphere. 3-D graphics get developed in the military, then get used to project films, but these are often action films focused on still other military fantasies, all of it, on screen and off-screen, in many ways written by the Pentagon.[56]

Despite this tendency of the film industry, Rivera uses his films and art to draw attention to the settler colonial forces that invite migrant labor into the flows of national commerce while simultaneously erecting bigger and more technologically advanced barriers for migrants. For Rivera, *Sleep Dealer* "is a myth of sorts, simplifying and visualizing these oddly symmetrical global flows. . . . [T]elepresent/transnational exchanges, including the military drone, accelerate and exaggerate already existing neocolonial exchanges."[57]

From this statement, Rivera seems well aware of the ways the bonds between state military mechanisms and corporate entertainment mechanisms are supporting one another to multiply settler state power. His film is an expression of that awareness. But it's also an expression of nomad thought that has found a way to reappropriate the tools of the state to recode migrants away from the alien persona and to deterritorialize settler colonial citizenship relationships. Rivera's characters accomplish this on the screen, and he accomplishes this as an activist filmmaker.

Sleep Dealer speaks directly to how technologies impact people's movements in societies of control and how transnational politics alienates bodies from their own value. Rivera's film foretells a technocolonial future that was set in motion nearly five centuries ago. The film also expresses a unique paradox in which technologies that subjugate bodies to the dominant national flows of labor and citizenship contain in themselves the potential to make deep cuts into those dominant flows. These technologies are trafficked by activists both to illuminate the assemblages of control that capture them and to organize new ways for bodies to interact with the material components of the state outside of the subjugation of territorial, state, and corporate power. Again, Rivera himself keenly comments on how some are able to make cuts into the forces of state power by rearranging the technologies of visibility. The nomadic adoption of technologies, even drone technologies, "all seem like organic and predictable developments. Once [people] get a hold of technology like drones, artists and activists will redefine and redeploy it."[58] These cuts have the capacity to develop inventive and imaginative nomadic assemblages that take technologies organized for other purposes elsewhere and employ them as a mode of resisting settler colonial modes of population production.

THOUGHTS ON MAKING CUTS

In the fall of 2019, folks at the University of California, Berkeley, started noticing small, black robots with four rugged tires scooting around campus. These robots were tasked with delivering fast food and coffee to people around campus, who would pay a small surcharge or maintain a monthly subscription to the service.[59] There are now more than six hundred thousand Kiwibots, mostly in the San Francisco Bay Area, which deliver food and drinks to folks at schools, airports, and other places.[60] But soon after the robots grew in popularity, reports surfaced that the operators of the bots were "drivers" in Medellín, Colombia, who were being paid about two dollars an hour to manage the fleet of bots that were in the US.[61] That is to say, Kiwi Campus, the company that set up the robot delivery service, materialized precisely the kinds of relationships between alien antitypes, robotic technologies, and information technologies that Rivera imagined both in *Why Cybraceros?* and then in *Sleep Dealer*. What was once a narrative situated in the realm of the cinematic was trafficked into the settler population production economy. This is another demonstration of the capacity of the territorial-state assemblage of citizenship to adapt to challenges to its power. While relative positive deterritorializations (like those described above) make cuts, in the absence of a sustained nomadic deterritorialization, those cuts mend. So, it is one thing to know how to use nomad thought to make cuts, but moving toward nomadic assemblages that produce absolute positive deterritorializations requires organization on another scale.

Today, hackers are disrupting border surveillance technologies—on the border and in film. The characters in Rivera's film use technologies of visibility to launch a nomadic attack on the dam in Oaxaca, deterritorializing the striations of US power over Indigenous lands and cultivating practices. Rivera's film relies on technologies of cinematic visibility to circulate his filmic activism, which illuminates the contradictions between the free flow of transnational labor and colonial citizens of those nations on one hand, and the entrapment of migrants into control apparatuses on the other. Sure, small hacks and low-budget films are only isolated deterritorializations, but taken together, we may encounter them as sparks of something bigger on the horizon. Certainly, one film will not stop the churning of citizenship control in the US. However, infrared technology alone does not keep migrants from México and Central America trapped in antitypes that lead to cycles of violence. It is through the assemblage of security apparatuses that technologies like infrared have a force-multiplying effect. It is when infrared technology is adopted in multiple arenas and in relationship to other technologies and personae that the technology of visibility has the capacity to impose political power. Thus, individual technologies mobilized in relative positive deterritorialization are also parts of potentially larger nomadic movements. When nomadic assemblages emerge, they, too, might multiply political force, a force with the capacity to deterritorialize absolutely toward a more emancipatory set of relationships between materials, lands, peoples, and desires for an anticolonial sovereignty.

This chapter has shown that a materialist assemblage approach can yield both a critical framework for the study of colonial power as well as an affirmative framework for studying how activists and artists are resisting colonial power. We must accept that technologies have the potential to capture bodies in cycles of control, but they also have the potential to untangle those same bodies from the processes of population production that have locked them into settler colonial antitypes. Technologies of visibility are not inherently tools of subjugation, nor are they tools of emancipation, but rather, technologies of visibility are ways to project an affective register onto articulable expressions of subjection to organize power—territorial or nomadic.

CONCLUSION

In the 1996 film *Mars Attacks!*, a group of Martian invaders infiltrates the US Capitol Building and shoots members of Congress with heat ray guns on live TV (fig. 5.1).[1] Most members are either killed or captured by the Martians, while Americans at home reel from the shock of the violence. In the aftermath of the attack, President James Dale (played by Jack Nicholson) makes a bold speech to his military leaders (fig. 5.2):

> Now, I want the people to know that they still have two out of three branches of the government working for them, and that ain't bad. I want the people to know that the schools will still be open, ok? And I want the people to know that the garbage will still be carried out. And I want a cop on every corner, which incidentally, we would already have if they listened to *me* last election.[2]

Dale then turns to his press secretary and asks to get on the air. In the next scene, from the Oval Office, he addresses the television camera with an insincere tone and nervous smirk:

> My fellow Americans, it is with a heavy heart that I am coming to you this afternoon. As you know, earlier today, the Martian ambassador and his confederates attacked and killed many of your representatives on Capitol Hill. I will be conferring with other world leaders as time goes on, and rest assured, that working together, we will soon come out at a very real outcome. Thank you.[3]

The inept and arrogant leader shrugs off the destruction of Congress at the hands of Martian invaders, insisting on a return to normal. He even takes the opportunity to gripe about a grudge from a previous election, all while Martians mount their next move.

Figure 5.1. Film still from Tim Burton's 1996 *Mars Attacks!*; the alien delegation opens fire on Congress.

Figure 5.2. Film still from Tim Burton's 1996 *Mars Attacks!*; President Dale (Jack Nicholson) speaks to his advisers after the attack on Congress.

What ensues is an all-out invasion. Dozens of Martian flying saucers descend on Washington, killing scores of people and toppling national monuments.⁴ Nearly everyone, including President Dale, is killed. At the heart of *Mars Attacks!* is a critique of the metropolitans and the central US government, which both eventually fall victim to the alien race.⁵ In the end, the film's hero, Richie (Lukas Haas)—a middle-America donut shop employee—saves what's left of the planet and inherits a nation that is in need of a new political order.⁶ This sequence, as I described in chapter 1, is a narrative loop that materially fulfills the imaginary of the settler consciousness. The settlers end up on empty land, nativize themselves to it, and begin to create new political orders. In fact, in one of the film's last scenes, set upon the crumbled ruins of the US Capitol Building, Richie accepts a medal of honor from Taffy Dale (Natalie Portman), the president's daughter (fig. 5.3). He then delivers a prepared address. In a move to disavow the past and nativize the rugged,

Figure 5.3. Film still from Tim Burton's 1996 *Mars Attacks!* closing scene of the film in which Richie (Lukas Haas) delivers an acceptance speech from the steps of the destroyed US Capitol Building after being awarded a medal.

rural American man, he tells the audience: "[S]o, I guess, like, now we just have to start over and start rebuilding everything. But I was thinking maybe instead of houses, we could live in teepees, cuz, it's better in a lot of ways."[7]

For cinema scholar Paul Cantor, the film's depiction of struggle and survival for its average Joe hero "ultimately goes back to Tocqueville, the original spirit of American federalism, and a serious vision of the self-organizing power of the American people."[8] Cantor celebrates the capacity of the victims of alien invasion to go it alone, arguing that the framing of the film "insists that America is much more than its governing elites, that the human resources of the country are spread widely—and unpredictably—throughout its population and territory.... [The film] expresses a democratic faith in the basic decency and capability of the American people."[9] However, what Cantor calls the "self-organizing power" of the US citizen depicted in *Mars Attacks!* and other alien invasion films is precisely the logic of settler colonial nationalism I have described throughout *Visions of Invasion*.[10]

In fact, the trope of destroying the US capital city appears time and again in the US alien invasion genre. From the first images of Washington's destruction we see in *Earth vs. the Flying Saucers* (1956), cinematic aliens have destroyed the city to symbolize the end of US democracy in *Superman II* (1980), *Independence Day* (1996), *Transformers: Dark of the Moon* (2011), and even Steven Spielberg's 2005 version of *War of the Worlds*.[11] The narrative theme fits right in line with the anti-imperial settler consciousness I described above. This consciousness has been pervasive in conservative US politics since Reagan's speech for Goldwater in 1964, relying on the anti-Washington narrative just as much as the alien invasion genre to produce a sovereign citizen-type, usually from out "West," who is able to overcome the alien invasion when the federal government cannot. Therefore, this figure—the settler—is built in contrast to the alien antitype in recurring settler narratives and emerges, time and again, in terra nullius to build a white settler future.[12]

This, I suggest, is *Visions of Invasion*'s first and most urgent contribution to readers: that understanding the production of alien antitypes can shed light on how settler colonial nationalism in the US today is built on managing an economy of political subjectivities—settlers and antitypes; insiders and outsiders; cowboys and aliens. Settlers do not see themselves as extenders of a particular (European or US) state sovereignty; they "see themselves as founders of political orders, [and] they also interpret their collective efforts in terms of an inherent sovereign claim that travels with them and is ultimately, if not immediately, autonomous from the colonising metropole."[13] It provides endless mobility with the right to carry the tools of political violence with them wherever they go. Settlers reject an imperial colonial persona for a uniquely ambulatory, individualized, and exploitative sovereignty that is produced in that denunciation of the colonial order. In rejecting the colonial metropole, thus, the settler seeks to acquire yet "unsettled lands" (terra nullius) on which to create a new political and economic formation. But even terra nullius must be produced: settler sovereignty "attack[s] the land (the nonhuman) to eliminate Indigenous presence and make the land alienable. Making death lands is an operation of making terra nullius. Death and extraction and fungibility ride together."[14] So, even in alien cinema narratives, making "death lands" out of the US and destroying its democracy have become settler colonial tropes that lead to the establishment of another political order that centers the figural settler and their desire for unquestioned individual sovereignty.

In thinking about the US as a settler state, then, we must conceive of a government that is organized around settler sovereignty claims in which the individual rights of the settler are protected by the mechanisms of the nation-state, not the other way around. I refer to this as the *settler contract*. In a settler situation, the state and the military are present to protect these individualized/localized sovereignty claims for the settler class while intervening swiftly and immediately when noncitizen antitypes try to make similar claims to sovereignty. Settler sovereignty is not compatible with state sovereign logic precisely because it would require the settler to submit to the collective, making them vulnerable to subjection, unable to control the population economy. The settler state, and the settler state military, have become technologies mobilized in defense of individual settler sovereignty mythologized as a set of constitutional rights.[15] If settler subjectivity is characterized by a constant potential for transfer (as described in the introduction), then settler sovereignty is characterized by a constant potential for uprooting—both in the settlers' decision to move from one locality of extraction to another and in the violent dispossession of Native, Black, and Mestiza/o/x peoples at each new mobilization. This usually happens in angry and destructive fits.

Which brings me to the events of January 6, 2021, in Washington, DC. Thousands of insurrectionists attacked the US Capitol Building, looking to kill and kidnap members of the US Congress.[16] However, these murderous insurrectionists were not Martians, they were not foreigners, and they were not Black, or Indigenous, or Mestiza/o/x protesters. They were mobs of almost entirely white settler nationalists who were displeased with the election of President Joseph R. Biden. The US is at a moment of political upheaval, when the settler class—led by a network of billionaire media moguls, conspiracy theorists, and white settler nationalist militias (like the Oath Keepers and Proud Boys)—has begun to transform the US American territory into death lands. The settler citizens now want to tear down the political order and start again. Perhaps scholars across the humanities must take today's version of white settler nationalism even more seriously.

For years, groups like these have perpetuated settler narratives in the US, relying on the "invasion" of migrants, cast as aliens, to constantly question the authority of the federal government.[17] Now, these groups have taken their efforts to the nation's capital and towns across the country in an attempt to lay waste to the federal government, which they feel has broken the settler contract. For me, the rise of today's hypernationalism from vigilante groups who were once exclusively dedicated to patrolling the border is an indication that alien making isn't just a facet of settler nationalism in the US; it's central to it. Settler nationalism depends on the constant production, circulation, and reproduction of alien subjectivity in order to re-create the conditions for a renewed settler contract.

Visions of Invasion describes how the US federal government traffics technologies to produce and police the alien antitype. This, in part, is how the federal government keeps its end of the settler contract. However, one aspect that I don't detail in this book is the role the settler plays in keeping their end of the deal. The settler citizen, often without direct request, will volunteer to commit vigilante violence against antitypes. Ersula Ore, for example, describes lynching as a performative rhetoric of white nationalism, in which for generations scores of white men have committed vigilante violence to (re)enact an American (settler) identity.[18] Vigilante violence also takes the form of dozens of border militias who patrol the México/US border, apprehending migrants at gunpoint.[19] Vigilante violence manifests itself in thousands of hate crimes against Asian and Pacific Islander communities in the midst of the COVID-19 pandemic in the US.[20] And, of course, vigilante violence boiled over as a group of white settler nationalists stormed the US Capitol Building on January 6, 2021, wanting to destroy US democracy in order to create a new political order built around their perceived victimization.

Beyond this immediate call to attend to the violences manifesting in today's US settler colonial situation, a study of alien making can inform new directions for scholars in the fields of rhetoric studies, communication studies, and media studies. This takes me to this project's second major contribution. *Visions of Invasion* describes a process of rhetorical subjection that produces political personae. One's persona is organized by their relationship with the colonial political order. This book, though, offers a vision of political subjectivity that is both discursive and affective, meaning that it takes into account the ways technologies of light, surveillance, and computer-generated imaging create an affective layer of subjectivity to pair with discursive articulations of constitutive citizenship. It demonstrates that a study of the discursive is modulated by the affective and, perhaps more controversially, that at least in terms of political affects, they are inseparable from the forces of discursivity. Mostly, this direction in studying rhetorical affects—especially in manufacturing nonnormative subjectivities—would invite a critical inquiry into the theoretical turn to affect and its possibilities for rhetoric.

I also ask readers to consider moving toward incorporating a critical study of settler colonial theory into studies on migration and bordering. An approach to settler colonialism like the one in *Visions of Invasion* not only speaks to the inequities experienced by members of minoritized groups in the US, but it can also frame how many of the subjections that lead to violence and exploitation manifest in the first place. For one, the subjection of Mestiza/o/x folks as Latinx can flatten and even erase the vast linguistic, cultural, and material connections to Indigenous heritages colonized people have in what is now North and South America.[21] Rather, shifting our scholarly attention away from the representations of colonial subjectivities and toward a mutual rejection of colonial identities might allow us to reimagine the sets of relationships possible in a world built outside of settler consciousness. This would unnormalize the colonial logics of organizing peoples into ethnic phenotypes. I urge researchers throughout the humanities and social sciences to consider what it would mean to resist studying ethnic groups as variables and to instead reexamine the colonial logics that undergird the scientific method. This approach might allow more scholars to not only report on the effects of colonial violences on nonwhite communities but also unearth how the modes of population productions that sustain the sets of political and economic relationships are even pervasive in places like institutions of higher education.

Finally, *Visions of Invasion* demonstrates the value of a materialist approach to rhetoric. Specifically, my materialist method defined by assemblage theory offers readers a way to study how the production of political subjectivities generates material outcomes in a settler colonial situation. The case studies in this book unveil the intricacies of the rapidly strengthening assemblage of citizenship control in the US, which includes a cinematic narrative apparatus at its core. These findings support the fact that political assemblages have a tremendous capacity to enact a steady relative negative deterritorialization that can account for the numerous anomalies and cuts that are made to it over time. Alien making always adapts to the settler state's latest population needs and thus is able to produce alien affects that code and recode subjects using narrative tropes embedded in the invasion genre. In other words, a materialist assemblage method can account for how, over time, bodies are subjected and resubjected in political orders to produce state power.

On the other hand, the materialist rhetorical method in this book also reveals why we must begin to network deterritorializations to organize an assemblage that brings an end to settler colonial situations on this continent. To start, we might begin as Lorenzo Veracini suggests: organizing the narrative production modes of settler colonialism to imagine and materialize the end of settler colonialism.[22] This is an anti-antitype technology, which has the capacity not only to make small cuts but also to reterritorialize around new sets of relationships that restore the value of lands and labor back to the peoples from whom they have been traditionally extracted.

So, I echo Veracini: "Detecting settler colonialism and its operation, of course, is not enough, and the decolonisation of settler colonial forms needs to be imagined before it is practiced."[23] *Visions of Invasion* has demonstrated how, under citizenship control in the US, numerous and various material elements are arranged in relation to the settler citizen population economy, meaning that those cast as antitypes are organized into sets of relationships that are exploitative, extractive, and violent. The material components I have described are mostly technologies of visibility imagined and developed by the Hollywood film industry, which eventually get trafficked into the citizenship control assemblage. By tracking the movements of these technologies—from film to citizenship control assemblage—these case studies have shown that producing antitypes in a settler colonial population production economy builds the settler's capacity to produce localized, extractive violences (settler sovereignty) while simultaneously being protected by the state assemblage that was built to sustain their sovereignty. My efforts to draw attention to this political dynamic, though, are only a small step in "[d]etecting settler colonialism and its operation"; there is so much of the settler situation in the US that has yet to be unmasked.[24]

There are of course other violences that are implicit in settler population production that I did not discuss, but that are nonetheless rooted in the same organizing logic of the settler state. The US's population production economy manufactures cisgender-heterosexual-reproducing settler subjects in order to maintain a particular racial heterogeneity, which includes the subjection of LGBTQ2 groups and reproductive justice supporters as antitypes. The US's population production economy manufactures political antitypes such as socialists, communists, and antifascists as way to preserve the settler sovereignty coded into the personae of the country's two major political parties. Republicans and Democrats uphold settler sovereignty by legislating the ability of localized, extractive violences to be enacted—in the form of market deregulation, in the form of environmental deregulation for fossil fuel profits, in the form of private prisons for Black and migrant criminal antitypes, and in the form of military and financial support for international settler colonial projects, like current encroachments against Palestinian sovereignty. To say the least, detecting and describing the intricacies of this settler situation—a settler territorial-state assemblage that has grafted itself onto what is now the United States—takes a momentous effort.

However, this book also demonstrates that technologies of visibility can be organized into deterritorializations that make cuts of possibility into regimes of control. These cuts offer glimpses, even if just briefly, of how imagination can ultimately manifest in revolutionary change. Like Alex Rivera's *Sleep Dealer*, these cuts have the capacity to rearrange the elements of techno-statecraft in order to interrupt the territorial assemblages of state power. They can decode alienhood from migrant bodies that enter the US. Rivera imagines characters who break free from their personae to enact material change in a territorial-state assemblage. Again, before we can practice this deterritorialization, someone has to imagine it. Now, from cell phone cameras and personal drones to large-scale hacking and frequency jamming, nomadic assemblages mobilize techno-resistance (albeit in a small way) against the US's population production economy. While these individual moments of resistance may seem modest in relation to the magnitude of the state's citizenship control assemblages, numerous relative positive deterritorializations networked over time and space have the capacity to shape nomadic assemblages, rearranging the sets of relations dictated by white settler colonial logics.

For me, imagining different sets of relations between bodies, lands, and resources can initiate a critical and creative reorientation, one that decentralizes the settler citizen type and rejects the impulse to organize people into sets of economic relationships. I call these desubjective imaginings *antisettler personae*, and I encourage others to start to imagine what their antisettler personae can be.

NOTES

INTRODUCTION

1. National Commission on Terrorist Attacks upon the United States, *The 9/11 Commission Report: Final Report of the National Commission on Terrorist Attacks upon the United States* (New York: W. W. Norton, 2004); and Steven Spielberg, dir., *War of the Worlds* (Paramount Pictures, 2005).

2. Steven Spielberg, quoted in Travis Johnson, "'James Cameron's Story of Science Fiction' Names 'The War of the Worlds' the Greatest of All Time," Special Broadcasting Service (Sydney), September 9, 2020, https://www.sbs.com.au/guide/article/2020/09/07/james-camerons-story-science-fiction-names-war-worlds-greatest-all-time. Other critics have described the 9/11 imagery as a way for Spielberg to make a film that allows the US to grapple with the national trauma of 9/11 without directly invoking imagery of the events. See Lindsay Ellis, "Movies, Patriotism, and Cultural Amnesia: Tracing Pop Culture's Relationship to 9/11," *Vox*, September 11, 2017, https://www.vox.com/2016/9/9/12814898/pop-culture-response-to-9-11; and Paul Klein, "*War of the Worlds*: Spielberg's Film Is Actually a Meditation on 9/11," No Majesty, April 23, 2020, https://nomajesty.com/war-of-the-worlds-spielbergs-film-meditation-on-9-11/.

3. Spielberg, *War of the Worlds*.

4. National Commission on Terrorist Attacks, *The 9/11 Commission Report*. The commission recommended that in order to curb terrorism, the US would need to undertake a dramatic securitization of the US/México border, suggesting that "[e]very stage of our border and immigration system should have as a part of its operations the detection of terrorist indicators" with regard to screening procedures (385). The commission then calls for increased biometric technology to be implemented at US/México border ports of entry and for border agents to be trained in antiterrorism measures.

5. Terri Diane Halperin, *The Alien and Sedition Acts of 1798: Testing the Constitution* (Baltimore: Johns Hopkins University Press, 2016), 43.

6. Zygmunt Bauman, *Globalization: The Human Consequences* (New York: Columbia University Press, 1998); and Massimo Livi-Bacci, *A Short History of Migration* (Cambridge: Polity Press, 2012).

7. For a discussion about the ecological impacts the border wall is having on the US/México borderland, see Lindsay Eriksson and Melinda Taylor, "The Environmental Impacts of the Border Wall between Texas and Mexico," University of Texas School of Law, UT Working Group Human Rights Analysis, 2008, http://www.utexas.edu/law/centers/humanrights/borderwall/analysis/briefing-The-Environmental-Impacts-of-the-Border-Wall.pdf.

8. Bauman, *Globalization*; Livi-Bacci, *A Short History of Migration*.

9. John Urry, *Mobilities* (Cambridge: Polity Press, 2007), 36.

10. Urry, *Mobilities*, 36.

11. Urry, *Mobilities*, 188.

12. David Agren, "Remain in Mexico: Asylum Seekers at Border See Hopes Raised Then Dashed," *The Guardian* (San Francisco), March 2, 2020.

13. Bauman, *Globalization*, 86. For more on societies of control, see also Gilles Deleuze, "Postscript on the Societies of Control," *October* 59 (Winter 1992): 3–7.

14. Bauman, *Globalization*, 89.

15. For more on imagining constitutive citizenship as a political organization of only certain members of society, signaling the exclusion of others, see Richard Bellamy, "Constitutive Citizenship versus Constitutional Rights: Republican Reflections on the EU Charter and the Human Rights Act," in *Sceptical Essays on Human Rights*, ed. Tom Campbell, Keith D. Ewing, and Adam Tomkins (Oxford: Oxford University Press, 2015), 15–41. I agree with Bellamy's framing of constitutive citizenship in that its use in the US (and other settler states) as a political tool for organizing racial groups has manifested in the distribution of control mechanisms over those deemed noncitizens. So, while the US advertises itself as a nation whose citizens are granted rights through a human rights framework, citizens of the US settler state are constituted in their capacity to reproduce the political logics of white nationalism, a violently political mode for managing populations. Thus, I rely on the term "constitutive citizenship" throughout *Visions of Invasion* to refer to its overtly political dynamic of settler citizenship control.

16. Tara Tidwell Cullen, "ICE Released Its Most Comprehensive Immigration Data Yet. It's Alarming," National Immigrant Justice Center, March 13, 2018, https://immigrantjustice.org/staff/blog/ice-released-its-most-comprehensive-immigration-detention-data-yet.

17. Jason De León's study sheds light on the extreme conditions facing transnational migrants and the ways the US is complicit in the deaths of thousands. See Jason De León, *The Land of Open Graves: Living and Dying on the Migrant Trail* (Berkeley: University of California Press, 2015).

18. On April 19, 2021, US president Joe Biden signed an executive order officially changing the language that all immigration enforcement agencies in the US government use to describe unauthorized migrants. No longer will agencies refer to migrants as "illegal aliens," but rather they will refer to them as "undocumented noncitizens." Although the change is celebrated by left-leaning politicians, the order does not change any procedures for apprehending, detaining, or deporting migrants. In fact, I argue throughout this book that the political term "alien" has always been synonymous with "noncitizen," and the genre of alien invasion centers around apprehensions of maintaining a white settler citizenship in the US today. For more on the name change, see Joel Rose, "Immigration Agencies Ordered Not to Use Term 'Illegal Alien' under New Biden Policy," National

Public Radio, April 19, 2021, https://www.npr.org/2021/04/19/988789487/immigration-agencies-ordered-not-to-use-term-illegal-alien-under-new-biden-polic.

19. Sarah Ahmed, *The Promise of Happiness* (Durham, NC: Duke University Press, 2010), 49.

20. Ahmed, *The Promise of Happiness*, 157.

21. For a discussion of extensive and intensive movements, see Gilles Deleuze and Félix Guattari, *A Thousand Plateaus: Capitalism and Schizophrenia* (Minneapolis: University of Minnesota Press, 1987). Intensive movement, or what Deleuze and Guattari refer to as speed (velocity), is that qualitative difference that "*constitutes the absolute character of a body*" (381; emphasis in original). Speed is intensive; it is a qualitative movement. It is vibrational, affective, and always in-becoming. Intensities populate our environments. Each force and microforce coming into contact with our bodies registers sensation—a perception or a feeling of intensity, conscious or subconscious. Thus, subjectivity is intensive. The extended and extensive parts are the modes by which bodies move and communicate in material landscapes. The felt changes in the intensities of our environments modulate the movements of those extended parts and the bodies moving through those environments.

22. Katarzyna Marciniak, *Alienhood: Citizenship, Exile, and the Logic of Difference* (Minneapolis: University of Minnesota Press, 2006); and Charles Ramírez Berg, *Latino Images in Film: Stereotypes, Subversion, and Resistance* (Austin: University of Texas Press, 2002). In chapter 7 of *Latino Images in Film*, Berg links the Hollywood alien film industry with images of Latina/o/x migrants in the US, suggesting that "comparing the traditional Hispanic stereotype—which has a long history in American cinema—with the new Alien provides . . . a powerful critical dialectic that allows [one] to chart an interesting pattern of displacement and distortion, and gives [one] a way to resolve a troubling problem posed by the arrival of the renaissance [science fiction] Alien: Why have stereotyped cinematic representations of the Hispanic recently become so grossly debased?" (158). Marciniak's link between filmic expressions of extraterrestrials and migrants draws specific attention to visualizations of alien bodies. In other words, expressions of alienhood are not just discourses about border crossing and nonbelonging, but also expressions about what aliens look and feel like.

23. Andrew Culp, *Dark Deleuze* (Minneapolis: University of Minnesota Press, 2016). I borrow the term "autoproduce" to inform the ways settler logics are mobilized in production models to territorialize and code political conditions for noncitizens. Culp uses the term to describe the production of the "real" under capitalism.

24. See Lisa A. Flores, "Constructing Rhetorical Borders: Peons, Illegal Aliens, and Competing Narratives of Immigration," *Critical Studies in Media Communication* 20, no. 4 (2003): 362–87; and Lisa A. Flores, *Deportable and Disposable: Public Rhetoric and the Making of the "Illegal" Immigrant* (University Park: Pennsylvania State University Press, 2020). In "Constructing Rhetorical Borders," Flores describes the ways dominant narratives of migrants in popular media construct the subjective migrant as criminal, impoverished, and abject. In her book *Deportable and Disposable*, she continues describing the ways encounters with migrants produce a subjective, criminal body—this time, though, through an engagement with rhetorical subjection and performativity. Flores introduces the field to a notion of subjection that I build on in this book. See also Josue David Cisneros, "(Re)Bordering the Civic Imaginary: Rhetoric, Hybridity, and Citizenship in *La Gran Marcha*," *Quarterly Journal of Speech* 97, no. 1 (February 2011): 26–49; Josue David Cisneros, *The Border Crossed Us: Rhetorics*

of Borders, Citizenship, and Latina/o Identity (Tuscaloosa: University of Alabama Press, 2014); Karma R. Chávez, "Embodied Translation: Dominant Discourse and Communication with Migrant Bodies-as-Text," *Howard Journal of Communications* 20, no. 1 (2009): 18–36; and D. Robert DeChaine, "Bordering the Civic Imaginary: Alienization, Fence Logic, and the Minuteman Civil Defense Corps," *Quarterly Journal of Speech* 95, no. 1 (2009): 43–65.

25. Michel Foucault, *Discipline and Punish: The Birth of the Prison*, trans. Alan Sheridan (New York: Vintage Books, 1977), 194.

26. T. Carlos Jacques, "Whence Does the Critic Speak? A Study of Foucault's Genealogy," in *Michel Foucault: Critical Assessments*, vol. 3, ed. Barry Smart (London: Routledge, 1994), 97–112.

27. Jacques, "Whence Does the Critic Speak?," 102.

28. Gilles Deleuze, *Foucault* (Minneapolis: University of Minnesota Press, 1988), 47.

29. Deleuze, *Foucault*, 51.

30. Gilbert Caluya, "The Post-Panoptic Society? Reassessing Foucault in Surveillance Studies," *Social Identities* 16, no. 5 (2010): 621–33; and Deleuze, *Foucault*.

31. Caluya, "The Post-Panoptic Society?," 628.

32. Foucault, *Discipline and Punish*, 200.

33. For Foucault, "The panoptic mechanism arranges spatial unities that make it possible to see constantly and to recognize immediately.... Hence the major effect of the Panopticon: to induce in the inmate a state of conscious and permanent visibility that assures that automatic functioning of power." Foucault, *Discipline and Punish*, 200–201.

34. Rey Chow, "Postcolonial Visibilities: Questions Inspired by Deleuze's Method," in *Deleuze and the Postcolonial*, ed. Simone Bignall and Paul Patton (Edinburgh: Edinburgh University Press, 2010), 62–77; and Deleuze, *Foucault*, 67.

35. Deleuze, *Foucault*. In Deleuze's theorization of assemblages of power in contemporary control societies, assemblages replace institutions as organizers of nonlocalized manifestations of power. See also Deleuze, "Postscript on the Societies of Control"; and Brian Massumi, "The Autonomy of Affect," *Cultural Critique*, no. 31 (Autumn 1995): 83–109. Today's visible and articulable aspects of life in a control society are structured around a sort of mobile diagram evolving out of Foucault's panoptic discipline. Given that control societies are no longer composed of systems of enclosures but of open spaces of flow, power is exercised throughout the exteriority of society. It is dispersed by systems of governing assemblages, which are "the presentation of the relations between forces (visible and articulable) unique to a particular formation, [they are] the distribution of the power to affect and the power to be affected" (Deleuze, *Foucault*, 72–73).

36. Deleuze, *Foucault*, 52.

37. For Gregory J. Seigworth and Melissa Gregg, "The political dimensions of affect generally proceed through or persist immediately alongside its aesthetics, an ethico-aesthetics of a body's capacity for becoming sensitive to the 'manner' of a world . . . while also holding close to the often shimmering (twinkling/fading, vibrant/dull) continuities that pass in the slim interval between 'how to affect' and 'how to be affected.'" I read this as an important relationship between political potential—especially when talking about subjection—and how affect produced to shimmer on bodies determines the degree to which one can affect and be affected. Thus, here and for the remainder of the book, I refer to the moments of affection in which alien affects are sensible as shimmers. See Gregory J. Seigworth and Melissa Gregg,

"An Inventory of Shimmers," in *The Affect Theory Reader*, ed. Melissa Gregg and Gregory J. Seigworth (Durham, NC: Duke University Press, 2010), 14–15.

38. Patrick Wolfe, "Settler Colonialism and the Elimination of the Native," *Journal of Genocide Research* 8, no. 4 (2006): 387; and Lorenzo Veracini, *Settler Colonialism: A Theoretical Overview* (Basingstoke, Hants., England: Palgrave Macmillan, 2010).

39. Patrick Wolfe, *Settler Colonialism and the Transformation of Anthropology: The Politics and Poetics of an Ethnographic Event* (London: Continuum, 1998), 209. See also Lorenzo Veracini, *The Settler Colonial Present* (Basingstoke, Hants., England: Palgrave Macmillan, 2015).

40. La paperson, *A Third University Is Possible* (Minneapolis: University of Minnesota Press, 2017), 1–2.

41. La paperson, *A Third University Is Possible*, 12 (emphasis added).

42. Veracini, *Settler Colonialism*, 16 (emphasis in original).

43. Veracini, *Settler Colonialism*; and Veracini, *The Settler Colonial Present*.

44. For context on the colonizer/colonized binary, see Albert Memmi, *The Colonizer and the Colonized* (Boston: Beacon Press, 1991). Veracini replaces the colonizer/colonized binary with the triadic population economy model, suggesting: "Indeed, colonialism and settler colonialism should be seen as distinct especially because two is not three." Veracini, *Settler Colonialism*, 17.

45. Veracini, *The Settler Colonial Present*, 5. Veracini describes four antitypes: the "desirable co-ethnics," the "undesirable exogenous 'others,'" "assimilable indigenes," and "unassimilable Indigenous 'others.'" These types are characterized by their nativity to the settled territory as well as the possibility of their being transferred into the citizenry.

46. Veracini, *The Settler Colonial Present*, 5.

47. Veracini, *Settler Colonialism*, 20.

48. Veracini, *Settler Colonialism*, 20.

49. This conception of settler subject production differs slightly from Mark Rifkin's notion of "settler time" in which he describes the production of the figure of the Native as either an image of the past or a contemporary image defined in non-Native terms. I agree with Rifkin's critique that too often settler and Indigenous groups are seen as existing on the same timeline—a single trajectory toward a single present. This, as Rifkin points out, is a narrative that lends itself to the erasure of alternative, Native, and queer temporalities. I also agree that the Native-in-the-present-as-they-were-in-the-past visualization is a product of the settler gaze, but I contend that this is a common subjective production mode that keeps settler time in a looping arc toward the past. So, while Rifkin sees settler time as linear, I would contend that settler time loops back to a point when the settler's capacity to violently extract land and labor is at its peak. See Mark Rifkin, *Beyond Settler Time: Temporal Sovereignty and Indigenous Self-Determination* (Durham, NC: Duke University Press, 2017).

50. Veracini, *Settler Colonialism*, 22.

51. Veracini, *Settler Colonialism*, 14.

52. Veracini, *The Settler Colonial Present*.

53. Veracini, *Settler Colonialism*; and Veracini, *The Settler Colonial Present*.

54. Veracini, *Settler Colonialism*; and Veracini, *The Settler Colonial Present*.

55. Chris Dixon, "The Opposite of Truth Is Forgetting: An Interview with Roxanne Dunbar-Ortiz," *Upping the Anti*, no. 6 (2008): 57, https://uppingtheanti.org/journal/article/06-the-opposite-of-truth-is-forgetting.

56. Eddie S. Glaude Jr. uses the term "disremembering" when referring to colonial legacies of anti-Blackness. With regard to narratives, "[d]isremembering blots out horrible loss, but it also distorts who the characters take themselves to be. Something is lost.... Disremembering is active forgetting." Eddie S. Glaude Jr., *Democracy in Black: How Race Still Enslaves the American Soul* (New York: Broadway Books, 2016), 47.

57. Veracini, *Settler Colonialism*, 32.

58. Ronald W. Greene, "Another Materialist Rhetoric," *Critical Studies in Mass Communication* 15, no. 1 (1998): 21–41.

59. Greene, "Another Materialist Rhetoric," 38.

60. Greene, "Another Materialist Rhetoric," 39.

61. Ronald W. Greene, "Rhetorical Materialism: The Rhetorical Subject and the General Intellect," in *Rhetoric, Materiality, and Politics*, ed. Barbara A. Biesecker and John Louis Lucaites (New York: Peter Lang, 2009), 43–65.

62. Greene, "Another Materialist Rhetoric," 39.

63. See Richard Marback, "Detroit and the Closed Fist: Toward a Theory of Material Rhetoric," *Rhetoric Review* 17, no. 1 (Autumn 1998): 74–92; Jack Selzer and Sharon Crowley, eds., *Rhetorical Bodies* (Madison: University of Wisconsin Press, 1999); and Cheryl Forbes, "Writing the Body: An Experiment in Material Rhetoric," *Rhetoric Review* 19, nos. 1–2 (Autumn 2000): 60–72.

64. Barbara A. Biesecker and John Louis Lucaites, eds., *Rhetoric, Materiality, and Politics* (New York: Peter Lang, 2009), 1–17.

65. See Alessandro De Giorgi, "Immigration Control, Post-Fordism, and Less Eligibility: A Materialist Critique of the Criminalization of Immigration across Europe," *Punishment and Society* 12, no. 2 (April 2010): 147–67; Zornitsa Keremidchieva, "The Congressional Debates on the 19th Amendment: Jurisdictional Rhetoric and the Assemblage of the US Body Politic," *Quarterly Journal of Speech* 99, no. 1 (2013): 51–73; Victor Konrad and Heather N. Nicol, *Beyond Walls: Re-Inventing the Canada–United States Borderlands* (Abingdon, Oxon., England: Routledge, 2008); and Michael Lechuga and Sergio Fernando Juárez, "El Chamizal: Cementing National Identity with a Concrete Canal on the México/U.S. Border," in *Latina/o/x Communication Studies: Theories, Methods, and Practice*, ed. Leandra Hinojosa Hernández, Diana I. Bowen, Sarah De Los Santos Upton, and Amanda R. Martinez (Lanham, MD: Lexington Books, 2019), 163–84.

66. Deleuze and Guattari, *A Thousand Plateaus*; Manuel DeLanda, *Assemblage Theory* (Edinburgh: Edinburgh University Press, 2016); and Thomas Nail, "What Is an Assemblage?" *SubStance* 46, no. 1 (2017): 21–37. I borrow from each of these to craft an analytical framework for studying the multiple layers of an assemblage and the emergent properties of assemblages as they pertain to citizenship control.

67. Walter D. Mignolo, "Delinking: The Rhetoric of Modernity, the Logic of Coloniality and the Grammar of De-Coloniality," *Cultural Studies* 21, nos. 2–3 (March–May 2007): 449–514.

68. In the spirit of Andrew Culp's *Dark Deleuze*, then, we might think of a dark materialist rhetoric that is behind the organizing logics of settler colonialism on the North American continent. Culp questions the motives of those who take up Deleuze as a joyous philosopher, instead insisting that those invested in a Deleuzian ontology ought to rely on the darker side of Deleuze's terminology. "[I]nstead of simply appreciating the forces that produce the

World, *Dark Deleuze* intervenes in them to destroy it ... and to do so requires cultivating a hatred for it." Culp, *Dark Deleuze*, 8.

69. Culp, *Dark Deleuze*, 30.

70. For Nail, the personae of an assemblage are the "mobile operators that connect the concrete elements together according to their abstract relations" ("What Is an Assemblage?," 27). The personae, while considered "agents" by Deleuze and Guattari, "are not the origin of the assemblage and do not control or program the assemblage in advance. Rather, personae are the immanent agents or mobile positions, roles, or figures of the assemblage" (30). Personae are not individual subjects that decide how to move through an assemblage, but rather are a multitude of bodies, stripped of individual identity and reassembled collectively as a role (i.e., the [collective] voter, the abject immigrant, the law enforcement officer, etc.).

71. Carl Freedman, *Critical Theory and Science Fiction* (Middletown, CT: Wesleyan University Press, 2000).

72. See, for example, Kevin D. Haggerty and Richard V. Ericson, "The Surveillant Assemblage," *British Journal of Sociology* 51, no. 4 (December 2000): 605–22; Bart Simon, "The Return of Panopticism: Supervision, Subjection and the New Surveillance," *Surveillance and Society* 3, no. 1 (January 2005): 1–20; and Majid Yar, "Panoptic Power and the Pathologisation of Vision: Critical Reflections on the Foucauldian Thesis," *Surveillance and Society* 1, no. 3 (January 2003): 254–71.

73. Deleuze, *Foucault*; and Véronique Voruz, "The Status of the Gaze in Surveillance Societies," in *Re-Reading Foucault: On Law, Power and Rights*, ed. Ben Golder (Abingdon, Oxon., England: Routledge, 2013), 127–50.

74. Daniel O'Connor, "Lines of (F)light: The Visual Apparatus in Foucault and Deleuze," *Space and Culture* 1, no. 1 (1997): 49–66.

75. O'Connor, "Lines of (F)light," 49.

76. Mike Crang, "Rethinking the Observer: Film, Mobility, and the Construction of the Subject," in *Engaging Film: Geographies of Mobility and Identity*, ed. Tim Cresswell and Deborah Dixon (Lanham, MD: Rowman and Littlefield, 2002), 13–31.

77. Veracini, *Settler Colonialism*; Veracini, *The Settler Colonial Present*; and Anna Johnston and Alan Lawson, "Settler Colonies," in *A Companion to Postcolonial Studies*, ed. Henry Schwarz and Sangeeta Ray (Malden, MA: Blackwell, 2000), 360–76.

78. Veracini, *Settler Colonialism*, 101.

79. For more on backmasking, or the process of playing a record backward to find a hidden meaning, see Peter Blecha, *Taboo Tunes: A History of Banned Bands and Censored Songs* (San Francisco: Backbeat Books, 2004). Blecha describes how many fundamentalist Christian groups (some of whom have legacies closely tied with settler violences) decried popular rock bands of the 1970s and 1980s like Led Zeppelin for having satanic lyrics backmasked.

80. Johnston and Lawson, "Settler Colonies," 369.

81. Alex Rivera, dir., *Sleep Dealer* (Maya Entertainment, 2008).

82. Veracini, *Settler Colonialism*, 104.

CHAPTER ONE: *THE WAR OF THE WORLDS* AND ALIEN MAKING

1. For Denise Ferreira da Silva, "if one forgoes the desire for a Real that holds a historic (cultural subaltern) I and engages the Symbolic as the moment of production of the transparent I and its other, the scientific mill will have to be taken seriously as the very locus of production of the 'name of Man' and of the 'others' who fail to signify it and ask how scientific strategies, the alibis that sustain racial and colonial juridical domination and economic exploitation, populate the global space with a variety of modern subjects, who neither preceded nor are coetaneous with man, but have been produced using the same raw material assembled during the long period of his gestation." Her description of the simultaneous production of a colonial subject-type (symbolized as "man") in unison with the production of the colonial antitype under the scientific gaze frames the ways subjects are produced in this book under the technological gaze. Denise Ferreira da Silva, *Toward a Global Idea of Race* (Minneapolis: University of Minnesota Press, 2007), 12.

2. John Rieder, *Colonialism and the Emergence of Science Fiction* (Middletown, CT: Wesleyan University Press, 2008); Jessica Langer, *Postcolonialism and Science Fiction* (Basingstoke, Hants., England: Palgrave Macmillan, 2011); Lorenzo Veracini, "*District 9* and *Avatar*: Science Fiction and Settler Colonialism," *Journal of Intercultural Studies* 32, no. 4 (August 2011): 355–67; and Lorenzo Veracini, "Review: On Settler Colonialism and Science Fiction (Again)," *Settler Colonial Studies* 2, no. 1 (2012): 268–72.

3. H. G. Wells, *The War of the Worlds* (1898; Vancouver: AD Classics, 2008).

4. Craig Viveiros, dir., *The War of the Worlds*, season 1, written by Peter Harness (BBC, 2019; aired November 17, 2019, AMC).

5. Gilles Coulier and Richard Clark, dirs., *War of the Worlds*, season 1, written by Howard Overman (Fox/Canal, 2019; aired October 29, 2019).

6. Theresa Machemer, "Businesses Can Now Buy Spot, Boston Dynamics' Robotic 'Dog,'" *Smithsonian Magazine*, June 18, 2020.

7. Matt O'Brien, "Inside Boston Dynamics, the Secretive Lab Where Unnerving, High-Tech Robots Come to Life," *Spokesman-Review* (Spokane, WA), June 5, 2018.

8. Rieder, *Colonialism and the Emergence of Science Fiction*; and David Seed, "The Course of Empire: A Survey of the Imperial Theme in Early Anglophone Science Fiction," *Science Fiction Studies* 37, no. 2 (July 2010): 230–52.

9. Noah Berlatsky, "Why Sci-Fi Keeps Imagining the Subjugation of White People," *Atlantic*, April 25, 2014.

10. Stephen Hawking, in an interview with the Discovery Channel in 2010, quoted in Paul Rincon, "Stephen Hawking's Warnings: What He Predicted for the Future," BBC News, March 15, 2018.

11. Wells, *The War of the Worlds*, 14.

12. H. G. Wells, *Anticipations of the Reaction of Mechanical and Scientific Progress upon Human Life and Thought* (London: Chapman and Hall, 1902).

13. Seed, "The Course of Empire," 233–34.

14. For more on this trajectory from benevolence to monstrousness, see Michael Lechuga, "Battling Identity Warfare on the Imagined US/México Border: Performing Migrant Alien in *Independence Day* and *Battle: Los Angeles*," in *The Rhetorics of US Immigration: Identity,*

Community, Otherness, ed. E. Johanna Hartelius (University Park: Pennsylvania State University Press, 2015), 240–66.

15. Lincoln Geraghty, *American Science Fiction Film and Television* (Oxford: Berg, 2009).

16. Robert Wise, dir., *The Day the Earth Stood Still* (Twentieth Century Fox, 1951); and Christian Nyby, dir., *The Thing from Another World* (RKO Pictures, 1951).

17. Tim Dirks, "Greatest Visual and Special Effects (F/X): Milestones in Film," AMC Filmsite, www.filmsite.org/visualeffects.html.

18. Consistent with the argument that settler narratives reproduce themselves in the US, it is important to note that *The Day the Earth Stood Still* was remade in 2008 (Scott Derrickson, dir., *The Day the Earth Stood Still* [Twentieth Century Fox, 2008]); while *The Thing from Another Planet* was remade twice under the title *The Thing* (John Carpenter, dir., *The Thing* [Universal Pictures, 1982]; and Matthijs van Heijningen Jr., dir., *The Thing* [Universal Pictures, 2011]).

19. Dirks, "Greatest Visual and Special Effects."

20. George Lucas, dir., *Star Wars* (Twentieth Century Fox, 1977); and Ridley Scott, dir., *Alien* (Twentieth Century Fox, 1979).

21. While Ian Buchanan dismisses the direct comparison with "absurdist" machines like Goldberg machines, this comparison has proven to be useful to many who apply assemblage theory to realist (in Manuel DeLanda's sense) applications of the theory. Ian Buchanan, "Assemblage Theory and Its Discontents," *Deleuze Studies* 9, no. 3 (August 2015): 384. Also, see Eileen Honan, "Unplugging from the Goldberg Machine," in *Writing with Deleuze in the Academy: Creating Monsters*, ed. Stewart Riddle, David Bright, and Eileen Honan (Singapore: Springer, 2018), 31–44.

22. Roger Ebert, review of *Alien*, RogerEbert.com, October 26, 2003, https://www.rogerebert.com/reviews/great-movie-alien-1979.

23. Scott collaborated with Filmfex Animation Services to bring his aliens to life. Although Filmfex was a short-lived company, its other notable film collaboration was on Scott's *Blade Runner* (Warner Bros., 1982).

24. *Alien* Wiki, "*Alien*," https://alienfilmspedia.fandom.com/wiki/Alien#:~:text=Light%20effects%20in%20the%20egg,escapes%20in%20the%20shuttle%20Narcissus.

25. *Alien* Wiki, "*Alien*."

26. Dirks, "Greatest Visual and Special Effects."

27. Jean-Pierre Jeunet, dir., *Alien: Resurrection* (Twentieth Century Fox, 1997). For more on Blue Sky Studios, see Jake S. Friedman, *The Art of Blue Sky Studios* (San Rafael, CA: Insight Editions, 2014).

28. DeLanda, *Assemblage Theory*, 14.

29. Dirks, "Greatest Visual and Special Effects."

30. Steven Spielberg, dir., *E.T. the Extraterrestrial* (Universal Pictures, 1982).

31. Beyond the production of settler antitypes, the *Alien* franchise also imagines the Weyland Corporation (later called the Weyland-Yutani Corporation) as a colonizing conglomerate and the reason why humans first encounter the Xenomorph alien.

32. Dirks, "Greatest Visual and Special Effects"; and Paul Verhoeven, dir., *Starship Troopers* (TriStar Pictures, 1997).

33. Dirks, "Greatest Visual and Special Effects"; and Tim Burton, dir., *Mars Attacks!* (Warner Bros., 1996).

34. James Cameron, dir., *Avatar* (Twentieth Century Fox, 2009).

35. Dirks, "Film Milestones."

36. While many of the franchises that outdate CGI (like the *Alien* franchise, the *Star Wars* franchise, the *Predator* franchise, and even the *Men in Black* franchise) still feature choreographed lighting and shimmering alien figures played by actors, they often incorporate CGI to supplement the visual effects in each film. Filmmakers working on these projects seem to have found a balance between utilizing more traditional visual effects techniques and incorporating CGI, which has become a mainstay in the expression of alienhood in today's extraterrestrial invasion genre. Films that once utilized only the traditional lighting and special effects techniques of a generation ago now incorporate computer-generated glimpses of alienhood seamlessly.

37. Zolan Kanno-Youngs, "U.S. Watched George Floyd Protests in 15 Cities Using Aerial Surveillance," *New York Times*, June 19, 2020.

38. Kanno-Youngs, "U.S. Watched George Floyd Protests"; and Jason Koebler, Joseph Cox, and Jordan Pearson, "Customs and Border Protection Is Flying a Predator Drone over Minneapolis," *Vice*, May 29, 2020, https://www.vice.com/en/article/5dzbe3/customs-and-border-protection-predator-drone-minneapolis-george-floyd.

39. Kanno-Youngs, "U.S. Watched George Floyd Protests."

40. US Department of Homeland Security, "The Life Saving Missions of ICE," August 20, 2018, https://www.dhs.gov/news/2018/08/20/life-saving-missions-ice#:~:text=Bottom%20Line%3A%20U.S.%20Immigration%20and,national%20security%20and%20public%20safety.

41. K. Campbell, cited in Sasha Ingber and Riin Aljas, "Former Air Force Officer Fears Intelligence Collected on Protesters," *Newsy*, June 11, 2020, https://www.newsy.com/stories/surveillance-planes-above-floyd-protests/.

42. US Attorney General William P. Barr issued a statement on May 31, 2020, asserting that "[f]ederal law enforcement actions will be directed at apprehending and charging the violent radical agitators who have hijacked peaceful protest and are engaged in violations of federal law. To identify criminal organizers and instigators, and to coordinate federal resources with our state and local partners, federal law enforcement is using our existing network of 56 regional FBI Joint Terrorism Task Forces (JTTF). The violence instigated and carried out by Antifa and other similar groups in connection with the rioting is domestic terrorism and will be treated accordingly." US Department of Justice, "Attorney General William P. Barr's Statement on Riots and Domestic Terrorism," Press Release no. 20-500, May 31, 2020, https://www.justice.gov/opa/pr/attorney-general-william-p-barrs-statement-riots-and-domestic-terrorism; see also Susie Cagle, "'Protesters as Terrorists': Growing Number of States Turn Anti-Pipeline Activism into a Crime," *The Guardian*, July 8, 2019.

43. Koebler, Cox, and Pearson, "Customs and Border Protection Is Flying a Predator Drone."

44. Kanno-Youngs, "U.S. Watched George Floyd Protests."

45. US Department of Homeland Security, *FY 2019 Budget in Brief* (Washington, DC: US Government Publishing Office, 2019), https://www.dhs.gov/sites/default/files/publications/DHS%20BIB%202019.pdf.

46. Marciniak, *Alienhood*, 16.

47. Derrick Bryson Taylor, "George Floyd Protests: A Timeline," *New York Times*, November 5, 2021.

48. Kanno-Youngs, "U.S. Watched George Floyd Protests."

49. Michael D. Shear, "Border Officials Weighed Deploying Migrant 'Heat Ray' ahead of Midterms," *New York Times*, August 26, 2020.

50. Shear, "Border Officials Weighed Deploying Migrant 'Heat Ray.'"

51. Maggie Haberman and Charlie Savage, "Trump, Lacking Clear Authority, Says U.S. Will Declare Antifa a Terrorist Group," *New York Times*, May 31, 2020.

52. Charlie Savage, "What Could a Domestic Terrorism Law Do?," *New York Times*, August 7, 2019.

53. Savage, "What Could a Domestic Terrorism Law Do?"

54. Haberman and Savage, "Trump, Lacking Clear Authority."

55. Jonathan Levinson and Conrad Wilson, "Federal Law Enforcement Use Unmarked Vehicles to Grab Protesters off Portland Streets," Oregon Public Broadcasting, July 17, 2020, https://www.opb.org/news/article/federal-law-enforcement-unmarked-vehicles-portland-protesters/.

56. In addition to mandating that individual states issue federally approved ID cards that require proof of US citizenship (including driver's licenses), the law also has one distinct clause that eventually provided the legal framework for what the Trump administration was trying to do. The Real ID Act updated the definition of a terrorist organization in the US and gave the DHS the authority to deny entry to those suspected of engaging in terrorist-related activities with such organizations. National Commission on Terrorist Attacks, *The 9/11 Commission Report*; and Real ID Act of 2005, Public Law 109-13, Statutes at Large 119 (2005), 302–23.

57. Real ID Act of 2005, 308.

58. Real ID Act of 2005, 306–7. Along with defining a removable terrorist alien, the act also gives the DHS access to the state ID databases that contain the facial data of all those who register for state IDs. Additionally, the act gives the DHS the authority to "to waive all legal requirements . . . necessary to ensure expeditious construction of the barriers" along the México/US border. A central precedence for the Trump administration was to build the border wall he promised in his campaign. Real ID Act of 2005, 306.

CHAPTER TWO: *PREDATOR* ASSEMBLAGES

1. Ronald Reagan Presidential Foundation and Institute, "Life and Times," https://www.reaganfoundation.org/ronald-reagan/reagans-life-times/.

2. Nathan Juran, dir., *Law and Order* (Universal Pictures, 1953); Allan Dwan, dir., *Cattle Queen of Montana* (RKO Pictures, 1954); Allan Dwan, dir., *Tennessee's Partner* (RKO Pictures, 1955); William Witney, dir., *Wagon Train*, season 7, episode 2, "The Fort Pierce Story," written by John McGreevey (Universal Television, 1963; aired September 23, 1963); and Gene Autry, prod., *Death Valley Days*, seasons 13–15 (Flying A Productions; aired 1963–1965).

3. Ronald Reagan, "A Time for Choosing" (speech, Los Angeles, October 27, 1964).

4. Reagan, "A Time for Choosing."

5. Reagan, "A Time for Choosing"; see also Veracini, *Settler Colonialism*.

6. Brady Hummel, "The Return of Law and Order in America: The Ghost of Conservatism Past Is Still Alive and with Us Today," *The Policy*, July 18, 2016, https://thepolicy.us/the-return-of-law-and-order-in-america-ac7c2b6ae7e6.

7. Ronald Reagan, "Remarks at the Annual Meeting of the International Association of Chiefs of Police in New Orleans, Louisiana" (speech, New Orleans, September 28, 1981) (emphasis added).

8. Michelle Alexander explains that Reagan's push for a "war on drugs" was a political strategy to draw attention away from the privatization of prisons and the demands they created, and to win an election. See Michelle Alexander, *The New Jim Crow: Mass Incarceration in the Age of Colorblindness* (New York: New Press, 2012). In privatizing prisons, I contend, the Reagan administration increased the capacity for value extraction at localized, private organizations while also leveraging US state power to support those violent extractive projects that target Black and Latinx communities disproportionately. Also see Kristina K. Shull, "'Nobody Wants These People': Reagan's Immigration Crisis and America's First Private Prisons" (PhD diss., University of California Irvine, 2014); and Douglas S. Massey and Karen A. Pren, "Unintended Consequences of US Immigration Policy: Explaining the Post-1965 Surge from Latin America," *Population and Development Review* 38, no. 1 (March 2012): 1–29.

9. Ronald Reagan, "National Security Decision Directive no. 221: Narcotics and National Security," April 8, 1986, http://fas.org/irp/offdocs/nsdd/nsdd-221.pdf; and Bert Tussing, "New Requirements for a New Challenge: The Military's Role in Border Security," *Homeland Security Affairs* 4, no. 4 (October 2008): 1–22.

10. Tussing, "New Requirements for a New Challenge."

11. Tussing, "New Requirements for a New Challenge."

12. John McTiernan, dir., *Predator* (Twentieth Century Fox, 1987); Stephen Hopkins, dir., *Predator 2* (Twentieth Century Fox, 1990); Paul W. S. Anderson, dir., *Alien vs. Predator* (Twentieth Century Fox, 2004); Greg I. Strause and Colin Strause, dirs., *Alien vs. Predator: Requiem* (Twentieth Century Fox, 2007); Nimród Antal, dir., *Predators* (Twentieth Century Fox, 2010); Shane Black, dir., *The Predator* (Twentieth Century Fox, 2018); and Dan Trachtenberg, dir., *Prey* (Twentieth Century Fox, 2022).

13. Les Paul Robley, "Visible Invisibility for *Predator*," *American Cinematographer* 68, no. 12 (December 1987): 101–7.

14. The film costars Jesse Ventura, a former US Navy SEAL who later became the governor of Minnesota. In 2010, Ventura also wrote *American Conspiracies: Lies, Lies, and More Dirty Lies That the Government Tells Us*, which documents the ways the US government has kept secrets from its citizens to retain political and financial control. This investment in conspiracy theory, I contend, is explained by the settler consciousness, or an attempt to sow distrust in the centralized, imperial metropole to argue for the sovereign rights and knowledge production practices of the settler. See Jesse Ventura, *American Conspiracies: Lies, Lies, and More Dirty Lies That the Government Tells Us* (New York: Skyhorse Publishing, 2010).

15. Robley, "Visible Invisibility for *Predator*"; Les Paul Robley, "*Predator*: Special Visual Effects," *Cinefantastique* 18, no. 1 (December 1987): 34–42; and Ian T. Haufrect, prod., *If It Bleeds We Can Kill It: The Making of "Predator"* (Twentieth Century Fox, 2004).

16. Haufrect, *If It Bleeds We Can Kill It*.

17. Haufrect, *If It Bleeds We Can Kill It*.
18. Robley, "Visible Invisibility for *Predator*."
19. Robley, "Visible Invisibility for *Predator*," 102. A Fresnel lens is a round lens with concentric grooves, sort of like tight water ripples. Initially used for lighthouses, Fresnel lenses are used to amplify the intensity of a light.
20. Haufrect, *If It Bleeds We Can Kill It*.
21. Robley, "*Predator*: Special Visual Effects."
22. Haufrect, *If It Bleeds We Can Kill It*.
23. The second film, like the first, was written by Jim and John Thomas.
24. The techniques used to create the light-bending technologies remained consistent with those of the first film. Bryan Johnson, prod., *The Hunters and the Hunted: The Making of "Predator 2"* (Twentieth Century Fox, 2004).
25. Johnson, *The Hunters and the Hunted*.
26. Johnson, *The Hunters and the Hunted*.
27. John Davis, prod., *The Making of Alien vs. Predator* (Twentieth Century Fox, 2004).
28. Davis, *The Making of Alien vs. Predator*.
29. Mary Ann Skweres, "'Alien vs. Predator': The Battle to Merge Practical Effects and CGI," Animation World Network, August 13, 2004, http://www.awn.com/vfxworld/alien-vs-predator-battle-merge-practical-effects-and-cgi.
30. John Davis, prod., *AVP-R: The Nightmare Returns; Creating the Aliens* (Twentieth Century Fox, 2008).
31. Sam Hurwitz, dir., *Making a Scene*, season 4, episode 11, "*Predators*" (Sam Hurwitz Productions; aired September 1, 2010). Troublemaker Studios was responsible for producing the creature CGI in *Predators*.
32. The film was directed by Shane Black, who costarred in the original *Predator* film as Rick Hawkins, one of Dutch's commandos who was killed by the first Yautja Predator.
33. The film, in fact, was shot in Vancouver, Canada. *Predator, The*, Wiki, https://avp.fandom.com/wiki/The_Predator_(film)#cite_ref-Twitator_24-0.
34. US Customs and Border Protection, *2012–2016 Border Patrol Strategic Plan* (Washington, DC: US Government Publishing Office, 2012), http://www.cbp.gov/sites/default/files/documents/bp_strategic_plan.pdf. It should be noted that the *2020 U.S. Border Patrol Strategy* report cited the 2012–2016 *Strategic Plan* for its "risk-based approach . . . [n]ow, at the core of the 2020 U.S. Border Patrol Strategy [which] is a holistic, innovative approach to achieving Operational Control (OPCON) of the border." See US Customs and Border Protection, *2020 Border Patrol Strategy*, September 23, 2019, https://www.cbp.gov/sites/default/files/assets/documents/2019-Sep/2020-USBP-Strategy.pdf.
35. John Merlino, "Beefing Up Border Security: Tips on Selling Advanced Surveillance Solutions to Protect U.S. Frontiers," *Security Today*, September 1, 2013, https://securitytoday.com/Articles/2013/09/01/Beefing-Up-Border-Security.aspx?Page=1.
36. Merlino, "Beefing Up Border Security."
37. Center for Migration Studies of New York, "FY 2019 Budget Request: U.S. Customs and Border Protection," 2008, http://cmsny.org/wp-content/uploads/2018/04/FY2019-POTUS-Budget-Request-CBPupdated.pdf.

38. Jack R. White, "Herschel and the Puzzle of Infrared," *American Scientist* 100, no. 3 (May–June 2012): 218–25.

39. Bob Wimmer, "Warming Up to Thermal Imaging: History of Thermal Imaging," Security Sales and Integration, July 1, 2011, 1–7.

40. Wimmer, "Warming Up to Thermal Imaging."

41. Wimmer, "Warming Up to Thermal Imaging"; and J. M. Lloyd, *Thermal Imaging Systems* (New York: Springer Science, 1975).

42. Wimmer, "Warming Up to Thermal Imaging"; and Lloyd, *Thermal Imaging Systems*.

43. Lloyd, *Thermal Imaging Systems*.

44. Wimmer, "Warming Up to Thermal Imaging"; and Lloyd, *Thermal Imaging Systems*.

45. Lloyd, *Thermal Imaging Systems*, 5.

46. Wimmer, "Warming Up to Thermal Imaging."

47. Geiger Bot, "Thermal Cameras," https://sites.google.com/site/geigerbot/tech-info/thermal-cameras.

48. Wimmer, "Warming Up to Thermal Imaging."

49. Likely, a FLIR Rainbow LUT camera was used to film the *AVP* series in order to render alien affects onscreen. See Geiger Bot, "Thermal Cameras."

50. Alex Pulaski, "$250 Million Deal Lights Up FLIR's Future," *The Oregonian* (Portland), July 12, 2006.

51. US Customs and Border Protection, "Border Patrol History," July 1, 2020, https://www.cbp.gov/border-security/along-us-borders/history.

52. US Department of Homeland Security, Office of Inspector General, *A Review of Remote Surveillance Technology along U.S. Land Borders* (Washington, DC: US Government Publishing Office, 2005), https://www.oig.dhs.gov/sites/default/files/assets/Mgmt/OIG_06-15_Dec05.pdf.

53. US Department of Homeland Security, Office of Inspector General, *A Review of Remote Surveillance Technology*.

54. US Department of Homeland Security, "Creation of the Department of Homeland Security," September 15, 2015, http://www.dhs.gov/creation-department-homeland-security.

55. US Department of Homeland Security, Office of Inspector General, *A Review of Remote Surveillance Technology*.

56. US Department of Homeland Security, Office of Inspector General, *A Review of Remote Surveillance Technology*.

57. US Government Accountability Office, *Secure Border Initiative: SBInet Expenditure Plan Needs to Better Support Oversight and Accountability* (Washington, DC: US Government Publishing Office, February 15, 2007), https://www.gao.gov/products/gao-07-309.

58. US Department of Homeland Security, Office of Inspector General, *A Review of Remote Surveillance Technology*, 14.

59. US Government Accountability Office, *Border Security: Additional Actions Needed to Strengthen Collection of Unmanned Aerial Systems and Aerostats Data* (Washington, DC: US Government Publishing Office, February 16, 2017), https://www.gao.gov/assets/690/682842.pdf.

60. FLIR Systems, "FLIR Systems Awarded U.S. Customs and Border Protection Contract Valued at up to $101.9 Million to Support Mobile Surveillance Capabilities," GlobeNewswire,

January 5, 2011, https://www.globenewswire.com/news-release/2011/01/06/1050101/0/en/FLIR-Systems-Awarded-U-S-Customs-and-Border-Protection-Contract-Valued-at-up-to-101-9-Million-to-Support-Mobile-Surveillance-Capabilities.html.

61. FLIR Systems, "FLIR Systems Receives Production Order Totaling $19.5 Million from U.S. Customs and Border Protection to Support Mobile Surveillance Capabilities," GlobeNewswire, July 7, 2015, https://www.globenewswire.com/news-release/2015/07/07/1049722/0/en/FLIR-Systems-Receives-Production-Order-Totaling-19-5-Million-From-U-S-Customs-and-Border-Protection-to-Support-Mobile-Surveillance-Capabilities.html.

62. Calvin Biesecker, "CBP Awards Mistral $50 Million Contract for Mobile Border Surveillance Systems," *Defense Daily*, August 1, 2014, https://www.defensedaily.com/cbp-awards-mistral-50-million-contract-for-mobile-border-surveillance-systems/homeland-security/.

63. Wells, *The War of the Worlds*; H. G. Wells, *The Invisible Man: A Grotesque Romance* (1897; New York: Random House, 1996); and J. R. Minkel, "The First Invisibility Shield," *Popular Science*, September 27, 2006, https://www.popsci.com/scitech/article/2006-09/first-invisibility-shield/.

64. Chris Gayomali, "A Brief History of the Real-Life Invisibility Cloak," *The Week*, January 9, 2015, http://theweek.com/articles/466216/brief-history-reallife-invisibility-cloak.

65. Metamaterials, for example, are now at the forefront of making true invisibility cloaking a reality for soldiers in the US, the United Kingdom, and Canada. J. R. Minkel, "Unveiling the First Invisibility Shield," *Popular Science*, November 5, 2008, https://issuu.com/yufei.chang/docs/popular_science_october2006/82.

66. Minkel, "Unveiling the First Invisibility Shield," 80.

67. Gayomali, "A Brief History of the Real-Life Invisibility Cloak."

68. Sarah Yang, "Invisibility Shields One Step Closer with New Metamaterials that Bend Light Backwards," *UC Berkeley News*, August 11, 2008, https://www.berkeley.edu/news/media/releases/2008/08/11_light.shtml.

69. David Hambling, "Invisibility Cloaks Are Almost a Reality with Fractal-Camouflage Clothing," *Wired*, May 8, 2012, http://www.wired.co.uk/magazine/archive/2012/06/start/hiding-in-plain-sight.

70. Roger Connor, "The Predator, a Drone That Transformed Military Combat," Smithsonian National Air and Space Museum, March 9, 2018, https://airandspace.si.edu/stories/editorial/predator-drone-transformed-military-combat.

71. Joseph Trevithick and Tyler Rogoway, "Pocket Force of Stealthy Drones May Have Made Returning F-117s to Service Unnecessary," *The Drive*, December 1, 2019, https://www.thedrive.com/the-war-zone/26791/pocket-force-of-stealthy-avenger-drones-may-have-made-returning-f-117s-to-service-unnecessary.

72. Trevithick and Rogoway, "Pocket Force of Stealthy Drones."

73. An Act to Limit the Immigration of Aliens into the United States, and for Other Purposes, Public Law no. 68-139, Statutes at Large 43 (1924), 153–70; and US Department of State, Office of the Historian, "The Immigration Act of 1924 (The Johnson-Reed Act)," April 8, 2018, https://history.state.gov/milestones/1921-1936/immigration-act.

74. US Department of State, Office of the Historian, "The Immigration Act of 1924."

75. US Department of State, Office of the Historian, "The Immigration Act of 1924"; and Shiho Imai, "Immigration Act of 1924," *Densho Encyclopedia*, http://encyclopedia.densho.org/Immigration%20Act%20of%201924/.

76. Keremidchieva, "The Congressional Debates on the 19th Amendment."

77. Labor Appropriations Act of 1924, Public Law no. 68-153, Statutes at Large 43 (1924), 1110–30; and US Customs and Border Protection, "Border Patrol History."

78. Labor Appropriations Act of 1924, 1127. For some, the emergence of a formalized Border Patrol was a response to the need to enforce both the immigrant exclusion laws and also the Eighteenth Amendment of the Constitution, which prohibited the use and distribution of alcohol; see US Customs and Border Protection, "Border Patrol History."

79. US Customs and Border Protection, "Border Patrol History." These early unauthorized mounted patrols are a similar persona to that of contemporary minutemen patrolling the México/US border. For more on these groups of vigilante border agents, see DeChaine, "Bordering the Civic Imaginary"; and Michael Lechuga, "A Minuteman in the White House: Performing Spectacle, Mobilizing Political Affect, and Gendering Vulnerability in the United States," *Women's Studies in Communication* 40, no. 4 (2017): 324–29.

80. Mae M. Ngai, *Impossible Subjects: Illegal Aliens and the Making of Modern America* (Princeton, NJ: Princeton University Press, 2014), 64–69.

81. US Customs and Border Protection, "Border Patrol History."

82. David G. Gutiérrez, ed., *Between Two Worlds: Mexican Immigrants in the United States* (Lanham, MD: Rowman and Littlefield, 1996).

83. Gutiérrez, *Between Two Worlds*.

84. Manuel García y Griego, "The Importation of Mexican Contract Laborers to the United States, 1942–1964," in *Between Two Worlds: Mexican Immigrants in the United States*, ed. David G. Gutiérrez (Lanham, MD: Rowman and Littlefield, 1996), 72.

85. Immigration and Nationality Act of 1952, Public Law no. 82-414, Statutes at Large 66 (1952), 163–282.

86. Ngai, *Impossible Subjects*.

87. Immigration and Nationality Act of 1952, 182–83.

88. Immigration and Nationality Act of 1965, Public Law no. 89-236, Statutes at Large 79 (1965), 911–22.

89. Ngai, *Impossible Subjects*.

90. US Customs and Border Protection, "Border Patrol History."

91. US Customs and Border Protection, "Border Patrol History."

92. Joseph Nevins, "How US Policy in Honduras Set the Stage for Today's Migration," *The Conversation*, updated October 25, 2018, https://theconversation.com/how-us-policy-in-honduras-set-the-stage-for-todays-migration-65935; and Immigration Reform and Control Act, Public Law no. 99-603, Statutes at Large 100 (1986), 3359–444.

93. Deborah W. Meyers, "U.S. Border Enforcement: From Horseback to High-Tech," Migration Policy Institute, November 2005, http://www.migrationpolicy.org/research/us-border-enforcement-horseback-high-tech.

94. Meyers, "U.S. Border Enforcement," 3.

95. Meyers, "U.S. Border Enforcement."

96. US Customs and Border Protection, "Border Patrol History."

97. Carla N. Argueta, "Border Security: Immigration Enforcement between Ports of Entry," Congressional Research Service, April 19, 2016, https://fas.org/sgp/crs/homesec/R42138.pdf.

98. Bob Ortega, "Is Pricey Border Patrol Drone Program Worth the Cost?," *Arizona Republic*, updated June 21, 2015, http://www.azcentral.com/story/news/arizona/investigations/2015/06/21/border-patrol-drone-program/28999735/.

99. Biesecker, "CBP Awards Mistral $50 Million Contract."

100. FLIR Systems, "FLIR Systems Awarded U.S. Customs and Border Protection Contract."

101. Center for Migration Studies of New York, "FY 2019 Budget Request."

CHAPTER THREE: *MEN IN BLACK* ASSEMBLAGES

1. US Customs and Border Protection, "Border Patrol History."

2. William J. Clinton, "State of the Union 1995" (speech, Washington, DC, January 24, 1995).

3. Illegal Immigration Reform and Immigrant Responsibility Act, Public Law no. 104-208, Statutes at Large 110 (1996), 3009–546.

4. Heather Timmons, "No One Really Knows What ICE Is Supposed to Be. Politicians Love That," *Quartz*, July 7, 2018, https://qz.com/1316098/what-is-ice-supposed-to-do-the-strange-history-of-us-immigration-and-customs-enforcement/.

5. American Civil Liberties Union, "The Constitution in the 100-Mile Border Zone," June 21, 2018, https://www.aclu.org/other/constitution-100-mile-border-zone.

6. Barry Sonnenfeld, dir., *Men in Black* (Columbia Pictures, 1997).

7. Sonnenfeld, *Men in Black*; Barry Sonnenfeld, dir., *Men in Black II* (Columbia Pictures, 2002); Barry Sonnenfeld, dir., *Men in Black 3* (Columbia Pictures, 2012); and F. Gary Gray, dir., *Men in Black: International* (Columbia Pictures, 2019).

8. Sonnenfeld, *Men in Black*.

9. Sonnenfeld, *Men in Black*.

10. Sonnenfeld, *Men in Black*.

11. Sonnenfeld, *Men in Black*.

12. Ethan Anderton, "New 'Men in Black International' Details Promise New Aliens and Locales, Big Action and Laughs," Film: Blogging the Reel World, January 10, 2019, https://www.slashfilm.com/men-in-black-international-details/.

13. StarsInTheCity1, "'Men in Black' Making Of (in Spanish)," YouTube, September 15, 2011, https://www.youtube.com/watch?v=Jh_KA8Xaf6o; and Walter F. Parkes, prod., *The Making of "Men in Black 3"* (Sony Pictures Studios, 2012).

14. Agent K, in Sonnenfeld, *Men in Black*.

15. *Men in Black* Wiki, "List of Men in Black Equipment," https://meninblack.fandom.com/wiki/List_of_Men_in_Black_equipment.

16. Sonnenfeld, *Men in Black*.

17. Parkes, *The Making of "Men in Black 3."*

18. Rick Delgado, "From Edison to Internet: A History of Video Surveillance," Business 2 Community, August 14, 2013, http://www.business2community.com/tech-gadgets/from-edison-to-internet-a-history-of-video-surveillance-0578308#sDTpoCX8gK587DTK.99.

19. Anthony C. Caputo, *Digital Video Surveillance and Security*, 2nd ed. (Amsterdam: Elsevier, 2014).

20. Caputo, *Digital Video Surveillance and Security*.

21. Delgado, "From Edison to Internet."

22. US Customs and Border Protection, "Border Patrol History."

23. US Government Accountability Office, *Border Security: Key Unresolved Issues Justify Reevaluation of Border Surveillance Technology Program* (Washington, DC: US Government Publishing Office, February 22, 2006), https://www.gao.gov/products/gao-06-295; and US Department of Homeland Security, Office of Inspector General, *A Review of Remote Surveillance Technology*.

24. US Customs and Border Protection, "Border Patrol History."

25. US Department of Homeland Security, Office of Inspector General, *A Review of Remote Surveillance Technology*, 8.

26. US Department of Homeland Security, Office of Inspector General, *A Review of Remote Surveillance Technology*.

27. John Mintz, "Probe Faults System for Monitoring U.S. Borders," *Washington Post*, April 11, 2005, https://www.washingtonpost.com/archive/politics/2005/04/11/probe-faults-system-for-monitoring-us-borders/495248eb-2481-4938-abd8-7388842c4b3f/.

28. Mintz, "Probe Faults System for Monitoring U.S. Borders"; and US Department of Homeland Security, Office of Inspector General, *A Review of Remote Surveillance Technology*.

29. Mintz, "Probe Faults System for Monitoring U.S. Borders"; and Tom Barry, "El Paso: Where Homeland Security Meets National Security," Border Lines, TransBorder Project, Center for International Policy, September 10, 2009, http://borderlinesblog.blogspot.com/2009/09/el-paso-where-homeland-security-meets.html.

30. US Department of Homeland Security, Office of Inspector General, *A Review of Remote Surveillance Technology*.

31. US Department of Homeland Security, Office of Inspector General, *A Review of Remote Surveillance Technology*.

32. US Department of Homeland Security, Office of Inspector General, *A Review of Remote Surveillance Technology*.

33. US Government Accountability Office, *Border Security: Key Unresolved Issues*.

34. In congressional hearings, time and again, the criteria used to judge the effectiveness of a technology was whether it met the subcommittee's definition of a "force multiplier." See US Congress, House of Representatives, Subcommittee of Management, Integration, and Oversight of the Committee on Homeland Security, "Mismanagement of the Border Surveillance System and Lessons for the New America's Shield Initiative, Part I, II, and III," 109th Cong., 1st sess., 2006, 16–19.

35. Doris Meissner and Donald M. Kerwin, "DHS and Immigration: Taking Stock and Correcting Course," Migration Policy Institute, February 2009, 8, http://www.migrationpolicy.org/research/dhs-and-immigration-taking-stock-and-correcting-course.

36. US Government Accountability Office, *Secure Border Initiative: DHS Needs to Strengthen Management and Oversight of Its Prime Contractor* (Washington, DC: US Government Publishing Office, 2010), http://www.gao.gov/new.items/d116.pdf.

37. US Department of Homeland Security, *Report on the Assessment of the Secure Border Initiative-Network (SBInet) Program* (Washington, DC: US Government Publishing Office, 2010), https://www.globalsecurity.org/security/library/report/2011/sbi-net-assessment.pdf.

38. US Department of Homeland Security, *Report on the Assessment of the Secure Border Initiative-Network (SBInet) Program.*

39. US Government Accountability Office, *Secure Border Initiative: DHS Needs to Strengthen Management.*

40. US Department of Homeland Security, Press Office, "Fiscal Year 2015 Six Month Border Security Update Statement by Secretary Johnson," April 24, 2015, http://www.dhs.gov/news/2015/04/24/fiscal-year-2015-six-month-border-security-update; and Center for Migration Studies of New York, "FY 2019 Budget Request."

41. John Merlino, "Border Checkpoints Go High Tech: Science Fiction Is Quickly Becoming Science Fact," *Security Today*, March 1, 2015, https://securitytoday.com/Articles/2015/03/01/Border-Checkpoints-Go-High-Tech.aspx?Page=1.

42. US Department of Homeland Security, "Privacy Impact Assessment for the Automated Biometric Identification System (IDENT)," July 31, 2006, http://www.dhs.gov/xlibrary/assets/privacy/privacy_pia_usvisit_ident_final.pdf.

43. David Silverberg, "Identity Verification on the Border: How Fast Can It Get?" *Federal News Network*, February 5, 2016, http://federalnewsradio.com/govtechworks-articles/2016/02/identity-verification-on-the-border-how-fast-can-it-get/.

44. US Department of Homeland Security, "Privacy Impact Assessment for the Automated Biometric Identification System."

45. US Department of Homeland Security, "Privacy Impact Assessment for the Automated Biometric Identification System," 2.

46. US Department of Homeland Security, "Privacy Impact Assessment for the Automated Biometric Identification System," 2.

47. Aliya Sternstein, "Homeland Security to Roll Out Biometrics along the Border This Summer," Defense One, January 28, 2015, http://www.defenseone.com/technology/2015/01/homeland-security-roll-out-biometrics-along-border-summer/103968/.

48. US Department of Homeland Security, "Privacy Impact Assessment for the Automated Biometric Identification System"; and Sternstein, "Homeland Security to Roll Out Biometrics."

49. Sternstein, "Homeland Security to Roll Out Biometrics."

50. US Customs and Border Protection, "CBP to Begin Biometric Entry/Exit Testing at Otay Mesa Port of Entry," December 10, 2015, https://www.cbp.gov/newsroom/local-media-release/cbp-begin-biometric-entryexit-testing-otay-mesa-port-entry.

51. Eric Lichtblau and John Markoff, "Accenture Is Awarded U.S. Contract for Borders," *New York Times*, June 2, 2004, https://www.nytimes.com/2004/06/02/business/accenture-is-awarded-us-contract-for-borders.html; and Zachary R. Mider, "Tax Runaways Win Billions in U.S. Contracts Despite Bans," Bloomberg, July 8, 2014, http://www.bloomberg.com/news/articles/2014-07-08/tax-runaways-win-billions-in-u-s-contracts-despite-bans.

52. In thinking about the role of flashes in producing consumable cultural and political narratives, Krista Thompson writes that "a visual economy of light is in part a product of everyday aspirational practices of black urban communities, who make do and more with what they have, creating prestige through the resources at hand. But these very processes can have

a critical valence because they have the potential to disrupt notions of value by privileging not things but their visual effects.... Through a range of different types of photographic and videographic images, objects, spectacles, and the verbal re-creation of the moment of the picture's taking a new, ever-changing, and unpredictable community of viewers is created who reconstitute and reenvision value." Thus, for Thompson, flashes, along with verbal re-creation of an image, create reconstitutive possibilities. For flashbulb mediation, though, these possibilities are typically limited to the maintenance of citizenship control assemblages. Krista Thompson, *Shine: The Visual Economy of Light in African Diasporic Aesthetic Practice* (Durham, NC: Duke University Press, 2015), 25.

53. About 88 percent of US Americans get their news from local and national television news sources, and more than half of all Americans (51 percent) get their news from online search engines and news aggregating websites; see Media Insight Project, "The Personal News Cycle: How Americans Choose to Get Their News," American Press Institute, March 17, 2014, http://www.americanpressinstitute.org/publications/reports/survey-research/personal-news-cycle/.

54. See Lechuga, "A Minuteman in the White House."

55. Daniel Hallin, "Whatever Happened to the News?," *Media and Values*, no. 50 (1990), http://www.medialit.org/reading-room/whatever-happened-news#bio.

56. Hallin, "Whatever Happened to the News?"

57. Immigration and Nationality Act of 1952.

58. Reagan's National Security Decision Directive no. 221 and the subsequent war on drugs set the stage for the eventual incorporation of both ICE and CBP into the Department of Homeland Security, thus channeling military funds toward migrant control apparatuses.

59. John Pike, "Integrated Surveillance Intelligence System (ISIS)," Global Security, July 13, 2011, http://www.globalsecurity.org/security/systems/isis.htm.

60. Pike, "Integrated Surveillance Intelligence System."

61. Homeland Security Act, Public Law no. 107-296, Statutes at Large 116 (2002), 2135–321.

62. Argueta, "Border Security."

63. Meissner and Kerwin, "DHS and Immigration."

64. National Commission on Terrorist Attacks, *The 9/11 Commission Report*; and Daniel Morgan and William Krouse, "Biometric Identifiers and Border Security: 9/11 Commission Recommendations and Related Issues," Congressional Research Service, February 7, 2005, https://fas.org/sgp/crs/homesec/RS21916.pdf.

65. Morgan and Krouse, "Biometric Identifiers and Border Security."

66. Russell Brandom, "New Homeland Security System Will Bring Facial Recognition to Land Borders This Summer," *The Verge*, June 5, 2018, https://www.theverge.com/2018/6/5/17427150/facial-recognition-vehicle-face-system-homeland-security-immigration-customs; and Victor Tangermann, "New Facial Recognition Tech at U.S. Borders Will Scan Your Face, Whether You Like It or Not: Making Every Border Crossing Experience Just a Little Bit More Dystopian," *Futurism*, June 6, 2018, https://futurism.com/facial-recognition-us-borders.

67. Morgan and Krouse, "Biometric Identifiers and Border Security."

68. Brandom, "New Homeland Security System Will Bring Facial Recognition."

69. Janice Kephart, "10 Reasons Why Biometric Exit May Advance in 2014," Center for Immigration Studies, January 2014, http://cis.org/sites/cis.org/files/kephart-biometric.pdf.

70. Kephart, "10 Reasons Why Biometric Exit May Advance."
71. Kephart, "10 Reasons Why Biometric Exit May Advance," 5.
72. Kephart, "10 Reasons Why Biometric Exit May Advance."
73. US Constitution, amend. 1, 25.
74. Robert Corn-Revere, "Internet and First Amendment Overview," Freedom Forum Institute, First Amendment Center, November 20, 2002, https://www.freedomforuminstitute.org/first-amendment-center/topics/freedom-of-speech-2/internet-first-amendment/.
75. Corn-Revere, "Internet and First Amendment Overview."
76. Jane Mayer, "The Making of the Fox News White House," *New Yorker*, March 4, 2019.

CHAPTER FOUR: *SLEEP DEALER*, NOMADIC ASSEMBLAGES, AND DETERRITORIALIZATIONS

1. Vik Kolenc, "Border Tuner Will Open Communication between El Paso, Juarez Residents via Beams of Light," *El Paso Times*, October 18, 2019.
2. Kolenc, "Border Tuner Will Open Communication."
3. Kolenc, "Border Tuner Will Open Communication."
4. Nail, "What Is an Assemblage?"
5. Nail, "What Is an Assemblage?"
6. For Massumi, "[i]n every shift of attention, there is an interruption, a momentary cut in the mode of onward deployment of life. The cut can pass unnoticed, striking imperceptibly, with only its effects entering conscious awareness as they unroll. This is the onset of the activation." Cuts are made at the level of the microperceptual—at the level of the affective—and thus entail embodied movement. "The body figures here as a cut in the continuity of relation, filled with potential for re-relating, with a difference." Thus, I adopt the notion of *cuts* as they relate to the nomadic movements of nomad thinkers within the assemblage, who re-relate to the modes of political subjection in their art/activism. Brian Massumi, *Politics of Affect* (Cambridge: Polity Press, 2015), 53–54.
7. Rivera, *Sleep Dealer*.
8. Nail, "What Is an Assemblage?," 33.
9. Gilles Deleuze, "Nomadic Thought," in *Desert Islands and Other Texts (1953–1974)*, ed. David Lapoujade, trans. Michael Taormina (Los Angeles: Semiotext(e), 2004), 252–61.
10. Deleuze, "Nomadic Thought."
11. Deleuze, "Nomadic Thought," 258.
12. Deleuze, "Nomadic Thought," 259.
13. Brian Massumi, foreword to *A Thousand Plateaus: Capitalism and Schizophrenia*, by Gilles Deleuze and Félix Guattari (Minneapolis: University of Minnesota Press, 1987), xii.
14. Rosi Braidotti, *Nomadic Subjects: Embodiment and Sexual Difference in Contemporary Feminist Theory* (New York: Columbia University Press, 1994), 5.
15. Braidotti, *Nomadic Subjects*.
16. Braidotti, *Nomadic Subjects*, 5.
17. Braidotti, *Nomadic Subjects*, 5.
18. Deleuze and Guattari, *A Thousand Plateaus*, 404.
19. Deleuze and Guattari, *A Thousand Plateaus*, 403.

20. Nail, "What Is an Assemblage?," 33.
21. Nail, "What Is an Assemblage?," 32.
22. Nail, "What Is an Assemblage?," 33.
23. Deleuze and Guattari, *A Thousand Plateaus*, 385.
24. Deleuze and Guattari, *A Thousand Plateaus*, 34.
25. Deleuze and Guattari, *A Thousand Plateaus*, 161.
26. Deleuze and Guattari, *A Thousand Plateaus*, 381.
27. Nail, "What Is an Assemblage?," 35.
28. Nail, "What Is an Assemblage?," 35.
29. Nail, "What Is an Assemblage?," 36.
30. Alex Rivera, dir., *Why Cybraceros?* (Freewaves, 1997), http://archive.freewaves.org/video/why-cybraceros.
31. For more on the neoliberal biopolitics of *Sleep Dealer*, see China Medel, "The Ghost in the Machine: The Biopolitics of Memory in Alex Rivera's *Sleep Dealer*," *Camera Obscura* 33, no. 1 (2018): 113–37; and Ande Davis, "Consumed by El Otro Lado: Alterations of the Neoliberal Self in *Sleep Dealer*," *Chiricú Journal* 4, no. 1 (Fall 2019): 38–55.
32. Rivera, *Why Cybraceros?*
33. Fiona Jeffries, "Cyborg Resistance on the Digital Assembly Line: Global Connectivity as a Terrain of Struggle for the Commons in Alex Rivera's *Sleep Dealer*," *Journal of Communication Inquiry* 39, no. 1 (January 2015): 23.
34. Paula Straile-Costa, "Hacking the Border: Undocumented Migration and Technologies of Resistance in Alex Rivera's *Sleep Dealer* and Digital Media," *Theory in Action* 13, no. 2 (April 2020): 63.
35. Mark Engler and John Feffer, "Science Fiction from Below: Alex Rivera, Director of the New Film *Sleep Dealer*, Imagines the Future of the Global South," *Foreign Policy in Focus*, May 13, 2009, https://fpif.org/science_fiction_from_below/.
36. Alex Rivera, dir., *Before the Making of Sleep Dealer* (Maya Entertainment, 2009), http://alexrivera.com/films/.
37. Engler and Feffer, "Science Fiction from Below."
38. Alex Rivera, quoted in Engler and Feffer, "Science Fiction from Below."
39. Alex Rivera, quoted in Engler and Feffer, "Science Fiction from Below."
40. Jeffries, "Cyborg Resistance on the Digital Assembly Line," 30.
41. Patrick Tucker, "DHS: Drug Traffickers Are Spoofing Border Drones," Defense One, December 17, 2015, https://www.defenseone.com/technology/2015/12/DHS-Drug-Traffickers-Spoofing-Border-Drones/124613/; and Andrew Zaleski, "The Biggest Hijacking Threat Americans Face Today," CNBC, The Hacking Economy, February 2, 2016, https://www.cnbc.com/2016/02/01/the-biggest-hijacking-threat-americans-face-today.html.
42. Cadie Thompson, "Drug Traffickers Are Hacking US Surveillance Drones to Get Past Border Patrol," *Business Insider*, December 30, 2015, https://www.businessinsider.com/drug-traffickers-are-hacking-us-border-drones-2015-12; Robert Brzenchek, "How Gangs Are Using Drones to Disrupt Law Enforcement," American Military University Edge, May 21, 2018, https://inpublicsafety.com/2018/05/how-gangs-are-using-drones-to-disrupt-law-enforcement/; Tucker, "DHS: Drug Traffickers Are Spoofing Border Drones"; and Zaleski, "The Biggest Hijacking Threat."

43. Timothy Bennett, quoted in Zaleski, "The Biggest Hijacking Threat."

44. Tucker, "DHS: Drug Traffickers Are Spoofing Border Drones"; and Zaleski, "The Biggest Hijacking Threat."

45. Zaleski, "The Biggest Hijacking Threat."

46. Tucker, "DHS: Drug Traffickers Are Spoofing Border Drones"; Thompson, "Drug Traffickers Are Hacking US Surveillance Drones"; and Zaleski, "The Biggest Hijacking Threat."

47. Brzenchek, "How Gangs Are Using Drones."

48. Thompson, "Drug Traffickers are Hacking US Surveillance Drones."

49. Thompson, "Drug Traffickers are Hacking US Surveillance Drones."

50. Brzenchek, "How Gangs Are Using Drones."

51. Rivera, *Before the Making of Sleep Dealer*.

52. Rivera, *Before the Making of Sleep Dealer*.

53. Rivera, *Before the Making of Sleep Dealer*.

54. Despite the film's modest box office earnings (a little more than $100,000), it won several awards, including two awards at the Sundance Film Festival in 2008 (the Waldo Salt Screenwriting Award and the Alfred P. Sloan Foundation Feature Film Prize) as well as the 2008 Amnesty International Film Prize at the Berlin International Film Festival. See Internet Movie Database, "*Sleep Dealer* (2008)," https://www.imdb.com/title/tt0804529/.

55. Malcolm Harris, "Border Control," *New Inquiry*, no. 6, July 2, 2012, https://thenewinquiry.com/border-control/.

56. Alex Rivera, quoted in Harris, "Border Control."

57. Alex Rivera, quoted in Harris, "Border Control."

58. Alex Rivera, quoted in Harris, "Border Control."

59. Bradley Berman, "On Berkeley's Sidewalks, Bots with Burritos," *New York Times*, November 8, 2018.

60. Berman, "On Berkeley's Sidewalks, Bots with Burritos."

61. Carolyn Said, "Kiwibots Win Fans at UC Berkeley as They Deliver Fast Food at Slow Speeds," *San Francisco Chronicle*, May 26, 2019; and Berman, "On Berkeley's Sidewalks, Bots with Burritos."

CONCLUSION

1. Burton, *Mars Attacks!*

2. Burton, *Mars Attacks!*

3. Burton, *Mars Attacks!*

4. Paul A. Cantor, *The Invisible Hand in Popular Culture: Liberty vs. Authority in American Film and TV* (Lexington: University Press of Kentucky, 2012), 145. The scene is an homage to the 1956 film *Earth vs. the Flying Saucers* (directed by Fred F. Sears), which depicts flying saucers using laser guns to destroy Washington, DC, at the height of the Cold War. Burton's flying saucers, even though they were made with ILM's CGI technologies, are nearly identical to those seen in the invasion from Sears's black-and-white, stop-animation film. According to critics, Burton adapted his film to mimic early Hollywood alien invasion as a way to depict the hypernationalism he saw in the 1990s' US occupation of Kuwait and Iraq and the subsequent media coverage. See Fred F. Sears, dir., *Earth vs. the Flying Saucers* (Columbia Pictures, 1956).

5. Cantor, *The Invisible Hand in Popular Culture*.

6. For more on *Mars Attacks!*, see Kate Donaldson and Aaron Donaldson, hosts, "*Mars Attacks!*," Alien Movie Project, episode 17 (podcast), July 17, 2018, https://www.alienmovieproject.com/blog/amp-episode-17-mars-attacks.

7. Burton, *Mars Attacks!*

8. Cantor, *The Invisible Hand in Popular Culture*, 160.

9. Cantor, *The Invisible Hand in Popular Culture*, 158.

10. Cantor, *The Invisible Hand in Popular Culture*. Cantor's analysis also describes the film *Independence Day*, also released in 1996. Cantor suggests that *Independence Day* also puts the average US American at the center of a survival narrative in a rejection of the "elite" central government. And like in *Mars Attacks!*, a key scene in the film depicts the utter annihilation of Washington, DC, along with other major US cities like New York and Los Angeles.

11. Richard Lester, dir., *Superman II* (Columbia Pictures, 1980); Roland Emmerich, dir., *Independence Day* (Twentieth Century Fox, 1996); and Michael Bay, dir., *Transformers: Dark of the Moon* (Paramount Pictures, 2011).

12. For a description of terra nullius, see Johnston and Lawson, "Settler Colonies."

13. Veracini, *Settler Colonialism*, 53.

14. La paperson, *A Third University Is Possible*, 17–18.

15. Veracini, *Settler Colonialism*, 142.

16. Hailey Fuchs, Simon Romero, and Adam Goldman, "Prosecutors Unseal Chilling Accounts of Violence at the Capitol," *New York Times*, January 15, 2021.

17. Journalist Chase Lawrence has written about the links between the Oath Keepers and border militias like the United Constitutional Patriots, who patrol the México/US border to report undocumented migrants to border authorities. See Chase Lawrence, "Questions Remain as to Ties between Police, Border Militias and Trump Campaign in Southwest US," World Socialist Web Site, October 27, 2020, https://www.wsws.org/en/articles/2020/10/28/sout-o28.html. Several members of the Oath Keepers, at the writing of this book, are under federal investigation for conspiracy to plan the insurrection on the US Capitol on January 6, 2021. See Alan Feuer, "Oath Keeper Pleads Guilty and Will Cooperate in Jan. 6 Riot Inquiry," *New York Times*, April 16, 2021.

18. Ersula J. Ore, *Lynching: Violence, Rhetoric, and American Identity* (Jackson: University Press of Mississippi, 2019).

19. For decades, white nationalist vigilante groups have been honing their violent tactics by organizing at the México/US border. Many of these groups were also active in the 2020 presidential election campaign to misinform and intimidate voters and communities of color. See Vanda Felbab-Brown and Elisa Norio, "What Border Vigilantes Taught US Right-Wing Armed Groups," Brookings Institution, March 12, 2021, https://www.brookings.edu/articles/what-border-vigilantes-taught-us-right-wing-armed-groups/.

20. Sam Cabral, "Covid 'Hate Crimes' against Asian Americans on Rise," BBC News, May 5, 2021.

21. Kurly Tlapoyawa, "What 'Latinx' Doesn't Include," *Yes! Magazine*, November 22, 2019, https://www.yesmagazine.org/opinion/2019/11/22/latinx-indigenous-history-heritage.

22. Veracini, *Settler Colonialism*, 104.

23. Veracini, *Settler Colonialism*, 108.

24. Veracini, *Settler Colonialism*, 108.

BIBLIOGRAPHY

An Act to Limit the Immigration of Aliens into the United States, and for Other Purposes. Public Law no. 68-139, Statutes at Large 43 (1924), 153–70.

Agren, David. "Remain in Mexico: Asylum Seekers at Border See Hopes Raised Then Dashed." *The Guardian* (San Francisco), March 2, 2020.

Ahmed, Sarah. *The Promise of Happiness*. Durham, NC: Duke University Press, 2010.

Alexander, Michelle. *The New Jim Crow: Mass Incarceration in the Age of Colorblindness*. New York: New Press, 2012.

Alien Wiki. "Alien." https://alienfilmspedia.fandom.com/wiki/Alien#:~:text=Light%20effects%20in%20the%20egg,escapes%20in%20the%20shuttle%20Narcissus.

American Civil Liberties Union. "The Constitution in the 100-Mile Border Zone." June 21, 2018. https://www.aclu.org/other/constitution-100-mile-border-zone.

Anderson, Paul W. S., dir. *Alien vs. Predator*. Twentieth Century Fox, 2004. Motion picture.

Anderton, Ethan. "New 'Men in Black International' Details Promise New Aliens and Locales, Big Action and Laughs." Film: Blogging the Reel World, January 10, 2019. https://www.slashfilm.com/men-in-black-international-details/.

Antal, Nimród, dir. *Predators*. Twentieth Century Fox, 2010. Motion picture.

Argueta, Carla N. "Border Security: Immigration Enforcement between Ports of Entry." Congressional Research Service, April 19, 2016. https://fas.org/sgp/crs/homesec/R42138.pdf.

Autry, Gene, prod. *Death Valley Days*, seasons 13–15. Flying A Productions. Aired 1963–1965.

Barry, Tom. "El Paso: Where Homeland Security Meets National Security." Border Lines, TransBorder Project, Center for International Policy, September 10, 2009. http://borderlinesblog.blogspot.com/2009/09/el-paso-where-homeland-security-meets.html.

Bauman, Zygmunt. *Globalization: The Human Consequences*. New York: Columbia University Press, 1998.

Bay, Michael, dir. *Transformers: Dark of the Moon*. Paramount Pictures, 2011. Motion picture.

Bellamy, Richard. "Constitutive Citizenship versus Constitutional Rights: Republican Reflections on the EU Charter and the Human Rights Act." In *Sceptical Essays on Human Rights*, edited by Tom Campbell, Keith D. Ewing, and Adam Tomkins, 15–41. Oxford: Oxford University Press, 2015.

Berg, Charles Ramírez. *Latino Images in Film: Stereotypes, Subversion, and Resistance.* Austin: University of Texas Press, 2002.
Bergson, Henri. *Matter and Memory.* New York: Macmillan, 1911.
Berlatsky, Noah. "Why Sci-Fi Keeps Imagining the Subjugation of White People." *Atlantic,* April 25, 2014.
Berman, Bradley. "On Berkeley's Sidewalks, Bots with Burritos." *New York Times,* November 8, 2018.
Biesecker, Barbara A., and John Louis Lucaites, eds. *Rhetoric, Materiality, and Politics.* New York: Peter Lang, 2009.
Biesecker, Calvin. "CBP Awards Mistral $50 Million Contract for Mobile Border Surveillance Systems." *Defense Daily,* August 1, 2014. https://www.defensedaily.com/cbp-awards-mistral-50-million-contract-for-mobile-border-surveillance-systems/homeland-security/.
Black, Shane, dir. *The Predator.* Twentieth Century Fox, 2018. Motion picture.
Blecha, Peter. *Taboo Tunes: A History of Banned Bands and Censored Songs.* San Francisco: Backbeat Books, 2004.
Braidotti, Rosi. *Nomadic Subjects: Embodiment and Sexual Difference in Contemporary Feminist Theory.* New York: Columbia University Press, 1994.
Brandom, Russell. "New Homeland Security System Will Bring Facial Recognition to Land Borders This Summer." *The Verge,* June 5, 2018. https://www.theverge.com/2018/6/5/17427150/facial-recognition-vehicle-face-system-homeland-security-immigration-customs.
Brzenchek, Robert. "How Gangs Are Using Drones to Disrupt Law Enforcement." American Military University Edge, May 21, 2018. https://inpublicsafety.com/2018/05/how-gangs-are-using-drones-to-disrupt-law-enforcement/.
Buchanan, Ian. "Assemblage Theory and Its Discontents." *Deleuze Studies* 9, no. 3 (August 2015): 382–92.
Buchanan, Ian. "Assemblage Theory, or, the Future of an Illusion." *Deleuze Studies* 11, no. 3 (August 2017): 457–74.
Burton, Tim, dir. *Mars Attacks!* Warner Bros., 1996. Motion picture.
Cabral, Sam. "Covid 'Hate Crimes' against Asian Americans on Rise." BBC News, May 5, 2021.
Cagle, Susie. "'Protesters as Terrorists': Growing Number of States Turn Anti-Pipeline Activism into a Crime." *The Guardian,* July 8, 2019.
Caluya, Gilbert. "The Post-Panoptic Society? Reassessing Foucault in Surveillance Studies." *Social Identities* 16, no. 5 (2010): 621–33.
Cameron, James, dir. *Avatar.* Twentieth Century Fox, 2009. Motion picture.
Cantor, Paul A. *The Invisible Hand in Popular Culture: Liberty vs. Authority in American Film and TV.* Lexington: University Press of Kentucky, 2012.
Caputo, Anthony C. *Digital Video Surveillance and Security.* 2nd ed. Amsterdam: Elsevier, 2014.
Carpenter, John, dir. *The Thing.* Universal Pictures, 1982. Motion picture.
Center for Migration Studies of New York. "FY 2019 Budget Request: U.S. Customs and Border Protection." April 2018. http://cmsny.org/wp-content/uploads/2018/04/FY2019-POTUS-Budget-Request-CBPupdated.pdf.
Chávez, Karma R. "Embodied Translation: Dominant Discourse and Communication with Migrant Bodies-as-Text." *Howard Journal of Communications* 20, no. 1 (2009): 18–36.

Chow, Rey. "Postcolonial Visibilities: Questions Inspired by Deleuze's Method." In *Deleuze and the Postcolonial*, edited by Simone Bignall and Paul Patton, 62–77. Edinburgh: Edinburgh University Press, 2010.

Cisneros, Josue David. *The Border Crossed Us: Rhetorics of Borders, Citizenship, and Latina/o Identity*. Tuscaloosa: University of Alabama Press, 2014.

Cisneros, Josue David. "(Re)Bordering the Civic Imaginary: Rhetoric, Hybridity, and Citizenship in La Gran Marcha." *Quarterly Journal of Speech* 97, no. 1 (February 2011): 26–49.

Clinton, William J. "State of the Union 1995." Speech, Washington, DC, January 24, 1995.

Cohen, Deborah. *Braceros: Migrant Citizens and Transnational Subjects in the Postwar United States and Mexico*. Chapel Hill: University of North Carolina Press, 2011.

Connor, Roger. "The Predator, a Drone That Transformed Military Combat." Smithsonian National Air and Space Museum, March 9, 2018. https://airandspace.si.edu/stories/editorial/predator-drone-transformed-military-combat.

Corn-Revere, Robert. "Internet and First Amendment Overview." Freedom Forum Institute, First Amendment Center, November 20, 2002. https://www.freedomforuminstitute.org/first-amendment-center/topics/freedom-of-speech-2/internet-first-amendment/.

Coulier, Gilles, and Richard Clark, dirs. *War of the Worlds*, season 1. Written by Howard Overman. Fox/Canal, 2019. Aired October 29, 2019.

Crang, Mike. "Rethinking the Observer: Film, Mobility, and the Construction of the Subject." In *Engaging Film: Geographies of Mobility and Identity*, edited by Tim Cresswell and Deborah Dixon, 13–31. Lanham, MD: Rowman and Littlefield, 2002.

Cullen, Tara Tidwell. "ICE Released Its Most Comprehensive Immigration Data Yet. It's Alarming." National Immigrant Justice Center, March 13, 2018. https://immigrantjustice.org/staff/blog/ice-released-its-most-comprehensive-immigration-detention-data-yet.

Culp, Andrew. *Dark Deleuze*. Minneapolis: University of Minnesota Press, 2016.

da Silva, Denise Ferreira. *Toward a Global Idea of Race*. Minneapolis: University of Minnesota Press, 2007.

Davis, Ande. "Consumed by El Otro Lado: Alterations of the Neoliberal Self in *Sleep Dealer*." *Chiricú Journal* 4, no. 1 (Fall 2019): 38–55.

Davis, John, prod. *AVP-R: The Nightmare Returns; Creating the Aliens*. Twentieth Century Fox, 2008. Documentary picture.

Davis, John, prod. *The Making of Alien vs. Predator*. Twentieth Century Fox, 2004. Documentary picture.

DeChaine, D. Robert. "Bordering the Civic Imaginary: Alienization, Fence Logic, and the Minuteman Civil Defense Corps." *Quarterly Journal of Speech* 95, no. 1 (2009): 43–65.

De Giorgi, Alessandro. "Immigration Control, Post-Fordism, and Less Eligibility: A Materialist Critique of the Criminalization of Immigration across Europe." *Punishment and Society* 12, no. 2 (April 2010): 147–67.

DeLanda, Manuel. *Assemblage Theory*. Edinburgh: Edinburgh University Press, 2016.

DeLanda, Manuel. *Intensive Science and Virtual Philosophy*. London: Bloomsbury, 2002.

De León, Jason. *The Land of Open Graves: Living and Dying on the Migrant Trail*. Berkeley: University of California Press, 2015.

Deleuze, Gilles. *Cinema I: The Movement-Image*. Translated by Hugh Tomlinson and Barbara Habberjam. Minneapolis: University of Minnesota Press, 1997.

Deleuze, Gilles. *Foucault*. Minneapolis: University of Minnesota Press, 1988.

Deleuze, Gilles. *Negotiations, 1972–1990*. Translated by Martin Joughin. New York: Columbia University Press, 1995.

Deleuze, Gilles. "Nomadic Thought." In *Desert Islands and Other Texts (1953–1974)*, edited by David Lapoujade, translated by Michael Taormina, 252–62. Los Angeles: Semiotext(e), 2004.

Deleuze, Gilles. "Postscript on the Societies of Control." *October* 59 (Winter 1992): 3–7.

Deleuze, Gilles, and Félix Guattari. *A Thousand Plateaus: Capitalism and Schizophrenia*. Minneapolis: University of Minnesota Press, 1987.

Delgado, Rick. "From Edison to Internet: A History of Video Surveillance." Business 2 Community, August 14, 2013. http://www.business2community.com/tech-gadgets/from-edison-to-internet-a-history-of-video-surveillance-0578308#sDTpoCX8gK587DTK.99.

Derrickson, Scott, dir. *The Day the Earth Stood Still*. Twentieth Century Fox, 2008. Motion picture.

Dirks, Tim. "Greatest Visual and Special Effects (F/X): Milestones in Film." AMC Filmsite. www.filmsite.org/visualeffects.html.

Dixon, Chris. "The Opposite of Truth Is Forgetting: An Interview with Roxanne Dunbar-Ortiz." *Upping the Ante*, no. 6 (2008). https://uppingtheanti.org/journal/article/06-the-opposite-of-truth-is-forgetting.

Donaldson, Kate, and Aaron Donaldson, hosts. "*Mars Attacks!*" Alien Movie Project, episode 17 (podcast), July 17, 2018. https://www.alienmovieproject.com/blog/amp-episode-17-mars-attacks.

Dwan, Allan, dir. *Cattle Queen of Montana*. RKO Pictures, 1954. Motion picture.

Dwan, Allan, dir. *Tennessee's Partner*. RKO Pictures, 1955. Motion picture.

Ebert, Roger. Review of *Alien*. RogerEbert.com, October 26, 2003. https://www.rogerebert.com/reviews/great-movie-alien-1979.

Ellis, Lindsay. "Movies, Patriotism, and Cultural Amnesia: Tracing Pop Culture's Relationship to 9/11." *Vox*, September 11, 2017. https://www.vox.com/2016/9/9/12814898/pop-culture-response-to-9-11.

Emmerich, Roland, dir. *Independence Day*. Twentieth Century Fox, 1996. Motion picture.

Engler, Mark and John Feffer. "Science Fiction from Below: Alex Rivera, Director of the New Film *Sleep Dealer*, Imagines the Future of the Global South." *Foreign Policy in Focus*, May 13, 2009. https://fpif.org/science_fiction_from_below/.

Eriksson, Lindsay, and Melinda Taylor. "The Environmental Impacts of the Border Wall between Texas and Mexico." University of Texas School of Law, UT Working Group Human Rights Analysis, 2008. http://www.utexas.edu/law/centers/humanrights/borderwall/analysis/briefing-The-Environmental-Impacts-of-the-Border-Wall.pdf.

Felbab-Brown, Vanda, and Elisa Norio. "What Border Vigilantes Taught US Right-Wing Armed Groups." Brookings Institution, March 12, 2021. https://www.brookings.edu/articles/what-border-vigilantes-taught-us-right-wing-armed-groups/.

Feuer, Alan. "Oath Keeper Pleads Guilty and Will Cooperate in Jan. 6 Riot Inquiry." *New York Times*, April 16, 2021.

FLIR Systems. "FLIR Systems Awarded U.S. Customs and Border Protection Contract Valued at up to $101.9 Million to Support Mobile Surveillance Capabilities." GlobeNewswire, January 5, 2011. https://www.globenewswire.com/news-release/2011/01/06/1050101/0/en/FLIR-Systems-Awarded-U-S-Customs-and-Border-Protection-Contract-Valued-at-up-to-101-9-Million-to-Support-Mobile-Surveillance-Capabilities.html.

FLIR Systems. "FLIR Systems Receives Production Order Totaling $19.5 Million from U.S. Customs and Border Protection to Support Mobile Surveillance Capabilities." GlobeNewswire, July 7, 2015. https://www.globenewswire.com/news-release/2015/07/07/1049722/0/en/FLIR-Systems-Receives-Production-Order-Totaling-19-5-Million-From-U-S-Customs-and-Border-Protection-to-Support-Mobile-Surveillance-Capabilities.html.

Flores, Lisa A. "Constructing Rhetorical Borders: Peons, Illegal Aliens, and Competing Narratives of Immigration." *Critical Studies in Media Communication* 20, no. 4 (2003): 362–87.

Flores, Lisa. A. *Deportable and Disposable: Public Rhetoric and the Making of the "Illegal" Immigrant*. University Park: Pennsylvania State University Press, 2020.

Forbes, Cheryl. "Writing the Body: An Experiment in Material Rhetoric." *Rhetoric Review* 19, nos. 1–2 (Autumn 2000): 60–72.

Foucault, Michel. *Discipline and Punish: The Birth of the Prison*. Translated by Alan Sheridan. New York: Vintage Books, 1977.

Freedman, Carl. *Critical Theory and Science Fiction*. Middletown, CT: Wesleyan University Press, 2000.

Friedman, Jake S. *The Art of Blue Sky Studios*. San Rafael, CA: Insight Editions, 2014.

Fuchs, Hailey, Simon Romero, and Adam Goldman. "Prosecutors Unseal Chilling Accounts of Violence at the Capitol." *New York Times*, January 15, 2021.

García y Griego, Manuel. "The Importation of Mexican Contract Laborers to the United States, 1942–1964." In *Between Two Worlds: Mexican Immigrants in the United States*, edited by David G. Gutiérrez, 45–88. Lanham, MD: Rowman and Littlefield, 1996.

Gayomali, Chris. "A Brief History of the Real-Life Invisibility Cloak." *The Week*, January 9, 2015. http://theweek.com/articles/466216/brief-history-reallife-invisibility-cloak.

Geiger Bot. "Thermal Cameras." https://sites.google.com/site/geigerbot/tech-info/thermal-cameras.

Geraghty, Lincoln, *American Science Fiction Film and Television*. Oxford: Berg, 2009.

Glaude, Eddie S., Jr. *Democracy in Black: How Race Still Enslaves the American Soul*. New York: Broadway Books, 2016.

Gray, F. Gary, dir., *Men in Black: International*. Columbia Pictures, 2019. Motion picture.

Greene, Ronald. W. "Another Materialist Rhetoric." *Critical Studies in Mass Communication* 15, no. 1 (1998): 21–41.

Greene, Ronald W. "Rhetorical Materialism: The Rhetorical Subject and the General Intellect." In *Rhetoric, Materiality, and Politics*, edited by Barbara A. Biesecker and John Louis Lucaites, 43–65. New York: Peter Lang, 2009.

Gregg, Melissa, and Gregory J. Seigworth, eds. *The Affect Theory Reader*. Durham, NC: Duke University Press, 2010.

Gutiérrez, David G., ed. *Between Two Worlds: Mexican Immigrants in the United States.* Lanham, MD: Rowman and Littlefield, 1996.

Haberman, Maggie, and Charlie Savage. "Trump, Lacking Clear Authority, Says U.S. Will Declare Antifa a Terrorist Group." *New York Times*, May 31, 2020.

Haggerty, Kevin D., and Richard V. Ericson. "The Surveillant Assemblage." *British Journal of Sociology* 51, no. 4 (December 2000): 605–22.

Hallin, Daniel. "Whatever Happened to the News?" *Media and Values*, no. 50 (1990). http://www.medialit.org/reading-room/whatever-happened-news#bio.

Halperin, Terri Diane. *The Alien and Sedition Acts of 1798: Testing the Constitution.* Baltimore: Johns Hopkins University Press, 2016.

Hambling, David. "Invisibility Cloaks Are Almost a Reality with Fractal-Camouflage Clothing." *Wired*, May 8, 2012. http://www.wired.co.uk/magazine/archive/2012/06/start/hiding-in-plain-sight.

Harris, Malcolm. "Border Control." *The New Inquiry*, no. 6, July 2, 2012. https://thenewinquiry.com/border-control/.

Haufrect, Ian T., prod. *If It Bleeds We Can Kill It: The Making of "Predator."* Twentieth Century Fox, 2004. Documentary picture.

Homeland Security Act. Public Law no. 107-296, Statutes at Large 116 (2002), 2135–321.

Honan, Eileen. "Unplugging from the Goldberg Machine." In *Writing with Deleuze in the Academy: Creating Monsters*, edited by Stewart Riddle, David Bright, and Eileen Honan, 31–44. Singapore: Springer, 2018.

Hopkins, Stephen, dir. *Predator 2.* Twentieth Century Fox, 1990. Motion picture.

Hummel, Brady. "The Return of Law and Order in America: The Ghost of Conservativism Past Is Still Alive and with Us Today." *The Policy*, July 18, 2016. https://thepolicy.us/the-return-of-law-and-order-in-america-ac7c2b6ae7e6.

Hurwitz, Sam, dir. *Making a Scene*, season 4, episode 11, "Predators." Sam Hurwitz Productions. Aired September 1, 2010.

Illegal Immigration Reform and Immigrant Responsibility Act. Public Law no. 104-208, Statutes at Large 110 (1996), 3009–546.

Imai, Shiho. "Immigration Act of 1924." *Densho Encyclopedia.* http://encyclopedia.densho.org/Immigration%20Act%20of%201924/.

Immigration and Nationality Act of 1952. Public Law no. 82-414, Statutes at Large 66 (1952), 163–282.

Immigration and Nationality Act of 1965. Public Law no. 89-236, Statutes at Large 79 (1965), 911–22.

Immigration Reform and Control Act. Public Law no. 99-603, Statutes at Large 100 (1986), 3359–444.

Ingber, Sasha, and Riin Aljas. "Former Air Force Officer Fears Intelligence Collected on Protesters." *Newsy*, June 11, 2020. https://www.newsy.com/stories/surveillance-planes-above-floyd-protests/.

Internet Movie Database. "*Sleep Dealer* (2008)." https://www.imdb.com/title/tt0804529/.

Jacques, T. Carlos. "Whence Does the Critic Speak? A Study of Foucault's Genealogy." In *Michel Foucault: Critical Assessments*, vol. 3, edited by Barry Smart, 97–112. London: Routledge, 1994.

Jeffries, Fiona. "Cyborg Resistance on the Digital Assembly Line: Global Connectivity as a Terrain of Struggle for the Commons in Alex Rivera's *Sleep Dealer*." *Journal of Communication Inquiry* 39, no. 1 (January 2015): 21–37.

Jeunet, Jean-Pierre, dir. *Alien: Resurrection*. Twentieth Century Fox, 1997. Motion picture.

Johnson, Bryan, prod. *The Hunters and the Hunted: The Making of "Predator 2."* Twentieth Century Fox, 2004. Documentary picture.

Johnson, Travis. "'James Cameron's Story of Science Fiction' Names 'The War of the Worlds' the Greatest of All Time." Special Broadcasting Service (Sydney), September 9, 2020. https://www.sbs.com.au/guide/article/2020/09/07/james-camerons-story-science-fiction-names-war-worlds-greatest-all-time.

Johnston, Anna, and Alan Lawson. "Settler Colonies." In *A Companion to Postcolonial Studies*, edited by Henry Schwarz and Sangeeta Ray, 360–76. Malden, MA: Blackwell, 2000.

Juran, Nathan, dir. *Law and Order*. Universal Pictures, 1953. Motion picture.

Kanno-Youngs, Zolan. "U.S. Watched George Floyd Protests in 15 Cities Using Aerial Surveillance." *New York Times*, June 19, 2020.

Kephart, Janice. "10 Reasons Why Biometric Exit May Advance in 2014." Center for Immigration Studies, January 2014. http://cis.org/sites/cis.org/files/kephart-biometric.pdf.

Keremidchieva, Zornitsa. "The Congressional Debates on the 19th Amendment: Jurisdictional Rhetoric and the Assemblage of the US Body Politic." *Quarterly Journal of Speech* 99, no. 1 (2013): 51–73.

Klein, Paul. "War of the Worlds: Spielberg's Film Is Actually a Meditation on 9/11." No Majesty, April 23, 2020. https://nomajesty.com/war-of-the-worlds-spielbergs-film-meditation-on-9-11/.

Koebler, Jason, Joseph Cox, and Jordan Pearson. "Customs and Border Protection Is Flying a Predator Drone over Minneapolis." *Vice*, May 29, 2020. https://www.vice.com/en/article/5dzbe3/customs-and-border-protection-predator-drone-minneapolis-george-floyd.

Kolenc, Vik. "Border Tuner Will Open Communication between El Paso, Juarez Residents via Beams of Light." *El Paso Times*, October 18, 2019.

Konrad, Victor, and Heather N. Nicol. *Beyond Walls: Re-Inventing the Canada–United States Borderlands*. Abingdon, Oxon., England: Routledge, 2008.

Labor Appropriations Act of 1924. Public Law no. 68-153, Statutes at Large 43 (1924), 1110–30.

Langer, Jessica. *Postcolonialism and Science Fiction*. Basingstoke, Hants., England: Palgrave Macmillan, 2011.

La paperson. *A Third University Is Possible*. Minneapolis: University of Minnesota Press, 2017.

Lash, Scott. *Intensive Culture: Social Theory, Religion and Contemporary Capitalism*. London: SAGE Publications, 2010.

Latour, Bruno. "How to Talk about the Body? The Normative Dimension of Science Studies." *Body and Society* 10, nos. 2–3 (2004): 205–29.

Lawrence, Chase. "Questions Remain as to Ties Between Police, Border Militias and Trump Campaign in Southwest US." World Socialist Web Site, October 27, 2020. https://www.wsws.org/en/articles/2020/10/28/sout-o28.html.

Lechuga, Michael. "Battling Identity Warfare on the Imagined US/México Border: Performing Migrant Alien in *Independence Day* and *Battle: Los Angeles*." In *The Rhetorics of US Immigration: Identity, Community, Otherness*, edited by E. Johanna Hartelius, 240–66. University Park: Pennsylvania State University Press, 2015.

Lechuga, Michael. "A Minuteman in the White House: Performing Spectacle, Mobilizing Political Affect, and Gendering Vulnerability in the United States." *Women's Studies in Communication* 40, no. 4 (2017): 324–29.

Lechuga, Michael, and Sergio Fernando Juárez. "El Chamizal: Cementing National Identity with a Concrete Canal on the México/U.S. Border." In *Latina/o/x Communication Studies: Theories, Methods, and Practice*, edited by Leandra Hinojosa Hernández, Diana I. Bowen, Sarah De Los Santos Upton, and Amanda R. Martinez, 163–84. Lanham, MD: Lexington Books, 2019.

Lester, Richard, dir. *Superman II*. Columbia Pictures, 1980. Motion picture.

Levinson, Jonathan, and Conrad Wilson. "Federal Law Enforcement Use Unmarked Vehicles to Grab Protesters off Portland Streets." Oregon Public Broadcasting, July 17, 2020. https://www.opb.org/news/article/federal-law-enforcement-unmarked-vehicles-portland-protesters/.

Lichtblau, Eric, and John Markoff. "Accenture Is Awarded U.S. Contract for Borders." *New York Times*, June 2, 2004. https://www.nytimes.com/2004/06/02/business/accenture-is-awarded-us-contract-for-borders.html.

Livi-Bacci, Massimo. *A Short History of Migration*. Cambridge: Polity Press, 2012.

Lloyd, J. M. *Thermal Imaging Systems*. New York: Springer Science, 1975.

Lucas, George, dir. *Star Wars*. Twentieth Century Fox, 1977. Motion picture.

Machemer, Theresa. "Businesses Can Now Buy Spot, Boston Dynamics' Robotic 'Dog.'" *Smithsonian Magazine*, June 18, 2020.

Manning, Erin. *Relationscapes: Movement, Art, Philosophy*. Cambridge, MA: MIT Press, 2009.

Marback, Richard. "Detroit and the Closed Fist: Toward a Theory of Material Rhetoric." *Rhetoric Review* 17, no. 1 (Autumn 1998): 74–92.

Marciniak, Katarzyna. *Alienhood: Citizenship, Exile, and the Logic of Difference*. Minneapolis: University of Minnesota Press, 2006.

Massey, Douglas S., and Karen A. Pren. "Unintended Consequences of US Immigration Policy: Explaining the Post-1965 Surge from Latin America." *Population and Development Review* 38, no. 1 (March 2012): 1–29.

Massumi, Brian. "The Autonomy of Affect." *Cultural Critique*, no. 31 (Autumn 1995): 83–109.

Massumi, Brian. Foreword to *A Thousand Plateaus: Capitalism and Schizophrenia*, by Gilles Deleuze and Félix Guattari, ix–xv. Minneapolis: University of Minnesota Press, 1987.

Massumi, Brian. *Parables for the Virtual: Movement, Affect, Sensation*. Durham, NC: Duke University Press, 2002.

Massumi, Brian. *Politics of Affect*. Cambridge: Polity Press, 2015.

Mayer, Jane. "The Making of the Fox News White House." *New Yorker*, March 4, 2019.

McCosker, Anthony. *Intensive Media: Aversive Affect and Visual Culture*. Basingstoke, Hants., England: Palgrave Macmillan, 2013.

McTiernan, John, dir. *Predator*. Twentieth Century Fox, 1987. Motion picture.

Medel, China. "The Ghost in the Machine: The Biopolitics of Memory in Alex Rivera's *Sleep Dealer*." *Camera Obscura* 33, no. 1 (2018): 113–37.

Media Insight Project. "The Personal News Cycle: How Americans Choose to Get Their News." American Press Institute, March 17, 2014. http://www.americanpressinstitute.org/publications/reports/survey-research/personal-news-cycle/.

Meissner, Doris, and Donald M. Kerwin. "DHS and Immigration: Taking Stock and Correcting Course." Migration Policy Institute, February 2009. http://www.migrationpolicy.org/research/dhs-and-immigration-taking-stock-and-correcting-course.

Memmi, Albert. *The Colonizer and the Colonized*. Boston: Beacon Press, 1991.

Men in Black Wiki. "List of Men in Black Equipment." https://meninblack.fandom.com/wiki/List_of_Men_in_Black_equipment.

Merlino, John. "Beefing Up Border Security: Tips on Selling Advanced Surveillance Solutions to Protect U.S. Frontiers." *Security Today*, September 1, 2013. https://securitytoday.com/Articles/2013/09/01/Beefing-Up-Border-Security.aspx?Page=1.

Merlino, John. "Border Checkpoints Go High Tech: Science Fiction Is Quickly Becoming Science Fact." *Security Today*, March 1, 2015. https://securitytoday.com/Articles/2015/03/01/Border-Checkpoints-Go-High-Tech.aspx?Page=1.

Meyers, Deborah W. "U.S. Border Enforcement: From Horseback to High-Tech." Migration Policy Institute, November 2005. http://www.migrationpolicy.org/research/us-border-enforcement-horseback-high-tech.

Mider, Zachary R. "Tax Runaways Win Billions in U.S. Contracts Despite Bans." Bloomberg, July 8, 2014. http://www.bloomberg.com/news/articles/2014-07-08/tax-runaways-win-billions-in-u-s-contracts-despite-bans.

Mignolo, Walter D. "Delinking: The Rhetoric of Modernity, the Logic of Coloniality and the Grammar of De-Coloniality." *Cultural Studies* 21, nos. 2–3 (March–May 2007): 449–514.

Minkel, J. R. "The First Invisibility Shield." *Popular Science*, September 27, 2006. https://www.popsci.com/scitech/article/2006-09/first-invisibility-shield/.

Minkel, J. R. "Unveiling the First Invisibility Shield." *Popular Science*, November 5, 2008. https://issuu.com/yufei.chang/docs/popular_science_october2006/82.

Mintz, John. "Probe Faults System for Monitoring U.S. Borders." *Washington Post*, April 11, 2005. https://www.washingtonpost.com/archive/politics/2005/04/11/probe-faults-system-for-monitoring-us-borders/495248eb-2481-4938-abd8-7388842c4b3f/.

Morgan, Daniel, and William Krouse. "Biometric Identifiers and Border Security: 9/11 Commission Recommendations and Related Issues." Congressional Research Service, February 7, 2005. https://fas.org/sgp/crs/homesec/RS21916.pdf.

Muñoz, José Esteban. *Disidentifications: Queers of Color and the Performance of Politics*. Minneapolis: University of Minnesota Press, 1999.

Nail, Thomas. "The Crossroads of Power: Michel Foucault and the US/Mexico Border Wall." *Foucault Studies* 1, no. 15 (February 2013): 110–28.

Nail, Thomas. *The Figure of the Migrant*. Stanford, CA: Stanford University Press, 2015.

Nail, Thomas. "What Is an Assemblage?" *SubStance* 46, no. 1 (2017): 21–37.

National Commission on Terrorist Attacks upon the United States. *The 9/11 Commission Report: Final Report of the National Commission on Terrorist Attacks upon the United States*. New York: W. W. Norton, 2004.

National Immigration Project. "Who's Behind ICE? The Tech and Data Companies Fueling Deportations." August 23, 2018. https://www.nationalimmigrationproject.org/PDFs/community/2018_23Oct_whos-behind-ice.pdf.

Nevins, Joseph. "How US Policy in Honduras Set the Stage for Today's Migration." *The Conversation*, updated October 25, 2018. https://theconversation.com/how-us-policy-in-honduras-set-the-stage-for-todays-migration-65935.

Ngai, Mae M. *Impossible Subjects: Illegal Aliens and the Making of Modern America*. Princeton, NJ: Princeton University Press, 2014.
Nyby, Christian, dir. *The Thing from Another World*. RKO Pictures, 1951. Motion picture.
O'Brien, Matt. "Inside Boston Dynamics, the Secretive Lab Where Unnerving, High-Tech Robots Come to Life." *Spokesman-Review* (Spokane, WA), June 5, 2018.
O'Connor, Daniel. "Lines of (F)light: The Visual Apparatus in Foucault and Deleuze." *Space and Culture* 1, no. 1 (1997): 49–66.
Ore, Ersula J. *Lynching: Violence, Rhetoric, and American Identity*. Jackson: University Press of Mississippi, 2019.
Ortega, Bob. "Is Pricey Border Patrol Drone Program Worth the Cost?" *Arizona Republic*, updated June 21, 2015. http://www.azcentral.com/story/news/arizona/investigations/2015/06/21/border-patrol-drone-program/28999735/.
Parkes, Walter F., prod. *The Making of "Men in Black 3."* Sony Pictures Studios, 2012. Documentary picture.
Pike, John. "Integrated Surveillance Intelligence System (ISIS)." Global Security, July 13, 2011. http://www.globalsecurity.org/security/systems/isis.htm.
Predator, The, Wiki. https://avp.fandom.com/wiki/The_Predator_(film)#cite_ref-Twitator_24-0.
Pulaski, Alex. "$250 Million Deal Lights Up FLIR's Future." *The Oregonian* (Portland), July 12, 2006.
Reagan, Ronald. "National Security Decision Directive no. 221: Narcotics and National Security." April 8, 1986. http://fas.org/irp/offdocs/nsdd/nsdd-221.pdf.
Reagan, Ronald. "Remarks at the Annual Meeting of the International Association of Chiefs of Police in New Orleans, Louisiana." Speech, New Orleans, September 28, 1981.
Reagan, Ronald. "A Time for Choosing." Speech, Los Angeles, October 27, 1964.
Real ID Act of 2005. Public Law no. 109-13, Statutes at Large 119 (2005), 302–23.
Rieder, John. *Colonialism and the Emergence of Science Fiction*. Middletown, CT: Wesleyan University Press, 2008.
Rifkin, Mark. *Beyond Settler Time: Temporal Sovereignty and Indigenous Self-Determination*. Durham, NC: Duke University Press, 2017.
Rincon, Paul. "Stephen Hawking's Warnings: What He Predicted for the Future." BBC News, March 15, 2018.
Rivera, Alex, dir. *Before the Making of Sleep Dealer*. Maya Entertainment, 2009. Documentary picture.
Rivera, Alex, dir. *Sleep Dealer*. Maya Entertainment, 2008. Motion picture.
Rivera, Alex, dir. *Why Cybraceros?* Freewaves, 1997. Documentary picture.
Robley, Les Paul. "*Predator*: Special Visual Effects." *Cinefantastique* 18, no. 1 (December 1987): 34–42.
Robley, Les Paul. "Visible Invisibility for *Predator*." *American Cinematographer* 68, no. 12 (December 1987): 101–7.
Rodowick, David N. *Gilles Deleuze's Time Machine*. Durham, NC: Duke University Press, 1997.
Ronald Reagan Presidential Foundation and Institute. "Life and Times." https://www.reaganfoundation.org/ronald-reagan/reagans-life-times/.

Rose, Joel. "Immigration Agencies Ordered Not to Use Term 'Illegal Alien' under New Biden Policy." National Public Radio, April 19, 2021. https://www.npr.org/2021/04/19/988789487/immigration-agencies-ordered-not-to-use-term-illegal-alien-under-new-biden-polic.

Said, Carolyn. "Kiwibots Win Fans at UC Berkeley as They Deliver Fast Food at Slow Speeds." *San Francisco Chronicle*, May 26, 2019.

Savage, Charlie. "What Could a Domestic Terrorism Law Do?" *New York Times*, August 7, 2019.

Scott, Ridley, dir. *Alien*. Twentieth Century Fox, 1979. Motion picture.

Scott, Ridley, dir. *Blade Runner*. Warner Bros., 1982. Motion picture.

Sears, Fred. F., dir. *Earth vs. the Flying Saucers*. Columbia Pictures, 1956. Motion picture.

Seed, David. "The Course of Empire: A Survey of the Imperial Theme in Early Anglophone Science Fiction." *Science Fiction Studies* 37, no. 2 (July 2010): 230–52.

Seigworth, Gregory J., and Melissa Gregg. "An Inventory of Shimmers." In *The Affect Theory Reader*, edited by Melissa Gregg and Gregory J. Seigworth, 1–28. Durham, NC: Duke University Press, 2010.

Selzer, Jack, and Sharon Crowley, eds. *Rhetorical Bodies*. Madison: University of Wisconsin Press, 1999.

Shear, Michael D. "Border Officials Weighed Deploying Migrant 'Heat Ray' ahead of Midterms." *New York Times*, August 26, 2020.

Shull, Kristina K. "'Nobody Wants These People': Reagan's Immigration Crisis and America's First Private Prisons." PhD diss., University of California Irvine, 2014.

Silverberg, David. "Identity Verification on the Border: How Fast Can It Get?" Federal News Network, February 5, 2016. http://federalnewsradio.com/govtechworks-articles/2016/02/identity-verification-on-the-border-how-fast-can-it-get/.

Simon, Bart. "The Return of Panopticism: Supervision, Subjection and the New Surveillance." *Surveillance and Society* 3, no. 1 (January 2005): 1–20.

Skweres, Mary Ann. "'Alien vs. Predator': The Battle to Merge Practical Effects and CGI." Animation World Network, August 13, 2004. http://www.awn.com/vfxworld/alien-vs-predator-battle-merge-practical-effects-and-cgi.

Sonnenfeld, Barry, dir. *Men in Black*. Columbia Pictures, 1997. Motion picture.

Sonnenfeld, Barry, dir. *Men in Black II*. Columbia Pictures, 2002. Motion picture.

Sonnenfeld, Barry, dir. *Men in Black 3*. Columbia Pictures, 2012. Motion picture.

Spielberg, Steven, dir. *E.T. the Extraterrestrial*. Universal Pictures, 1982. Motion picture.

Spielberg, Steven, dir. *War of the Worlds*. Paramount Pictures, 2005. Motion picture.

StarsInTheCity1. "'Men in Black' Making Of (in Spanish)." YouTube, September 15, 2011. https://www.youtube.com/watch?v=Jh_KA8Xaf6o.

Sternstein, Aliya. "Homeland Security to Roll Out Biometrics along the Border this Summer." Defense One, January 28, 2015. http://www.defenseone.com/technology/2015/01/homeland-security-roll-out-biometrics-along-border-summer/103968/.

Straile-Costa, Paula. "Hacking the Border: Undocumented Migration and Technologies of Resistance in Alex Rivera's *Sleep Dealer* and Digital Media." *Theory in Action* 13, no. 2 (April 2020): 54–74.

Strause, Greg I., and Colin Strause, dirs. *Alien vs. Predator: Requiem*. Twentieth Century Fox, 2007. Motion picture.

Tangermann, Victor. "New Facial Recognition Tech at U.S. Borders Will Scan Your Face, Whether You Like It or Not: Making Every Border Crossing Experience Just a Little Bit More Dystopian." *Futurism*, June 6, 2018. https://futurism.com/facial-recognition-us-borders.

Taylor, Derrick Bryson. "George Floyd Protests: A Timeline." *New York Times*, November 5, 2021.

Thompson, Cadie. "Drug Traffickers Are Hacking US Surveillance Drones to Get Past Border Patrol." *Business Insider*, December 30, 2015. https://www.businessinsider.com/drug-traffickers-are-hacking-us-border-drones-2015-12.

Thompson, Krista. *Shine: The Visual Economy of Light in African Diasporic Aesthetic Practice*. Durham, NC: Duke University Press, 2015.

Timmons, Heather. "No One Really Knows What ICE Is Supposed to Be. Politicians Love That." *Quartz*, July 7, 2018. https://qz.com/1316098/what-is-ice-supposed-to-do-the-strange-history-of-us-immigration-and-customs-enforcement/.

Tlapoyawa, Kurly. "What 'Latinx' Doesn't Include." *Yes! Magazine*, November 22, 2019. https://www.yesmagazine.org/opinion/2019/11/22/latinx-indigenous-history-heritage.

Trachtenberg, Dan, dir. *Prey*. Twentieth Century Fox, 2022. Motion picture.

Trevithick, Joseph, and Tyler Rogoway. "Pocket Force of Stealthy Drones May Have Made Returning F-117s to Service Unnecessary." *The Drive*, December 1, 2019. https://www.thedrive.com/the-war-zone/26791/pocket-force-of-stealthy-avenger-drones-may-have-made-returning-f-117s-to-service-unnecessary.

Tucker, Patrick. "DHS: Drug Traffickers Are Spoofing Border Drones." Defense One, December 17, 2015. https://www.defenseone.com/technology/2015/12/DHS-Drug-Traffickers-Spoofing-Border-Drones/124613/.

Tussing, Bert. "New Requirements for a New Challenge: The Military's Role in Border Security." *Homeland Security Affairs* 4, no. 4 (October 2008): 1–22.

Urry, John. *Mobilities*. Cambridge: Polity Press, 2007.

US Congress, House of Representatives, Subcommittee of Management, Integration, and Oversight of the Committee on Homeland Security. "Mismanagement of the Border Surveillance System and Lessons for the New America's Shield Initiative, Part I, II, and III." 109th Cong., 1st sess., 2006, 16–19.

US Constitution, Amendment 1.

US Customs and Border Protection. *2012–2016 Border Patrol Strategic Plan*. Washington, DC: US Government Publishing Office, 2012. http://www.cbp.gov/sites/default/files/documents/bp_strategic_plan.pdf.

US Customs and Border Protection. *2020 Border Patrol Strategy*. September 23, 2019. https://www.cbp.gov/sites/default/files/assets/documents/2019-Sep/2020-USBP-Strategy.pdf.

US Customs and Border Protection. "Border Patrol History." July 1, 2020. https://www.cbp.gov/border-security/along-us-borders/history.

US Customs and Border Protection. "CBP to Begin Biometric Entry/Exit Testing at Otay Mesa Port of Entry." December 10, 2015. https://www.cbp.gov/newsroom/local-media-release/cbp-begin-biometric-entryexit-testing-otay-mesa-port-entry.

US Department of Homeland Security. "Creation of the Department of Homeland Security." September 15, 2015. http://www.dhs.gov/creation-department-homeland-security.

US Department of Homeland Security. *FY 2019 Budget in Brief.* Washington, DC: US Government Publishing Office, 2019. https://www.dhs.gov/sites/default/files/publications/DHS%20BIB%202019.pdf.

US Department of Homeland Security. "The Life Saving Missions of ICE." August 20, 2018. https://www.dhs.gov/news/2018/08/20/life-saving-missions-ice#:~:text=Bottom%20Line%3A%20U.S.%20Immigration%20and,national%20security%20and%20public%20safety.

US Department of Homeland Security. "Privacy Impact Assessment for the Automated Biometric Identification System (IDENT)." July 31, 2006. http://www.dhs.gov/xlibrary/assets/privacy/privacy_pia_usvisit_ident_final.pdf.

US Department of Homeland Security. *Report on the Assessment of the Secure Border Initiative-Network (SBInet) Program.* Washington, DC: US Government Publishing Office, 2010. https://www.globalsecurity.org/security/library/report/2011/sbi-net-assessment.pdf.

US Department of Homeland Security. *State of the Homeland Threat Assessment 2020.* Washington, DC: US Government Publishing Office, 2020.

US Department of Homeland Security, Office of Inspector General. *A Review of Remote Surveillance Technology along U.S. Land Borders.* Washington, DC: US Government Publishing Office, 2005. https://www.oig.dhs.gov/sites/default/files/assets/Mgmt/OIG_06-15_Dec05.pdf.

US Department of Homeland Security, Press Office. "Fiscal Year 2015 Six Month Border Security Update Statement by Secretary Johnson." April 24, 2015. http://www.dhs.gov/news/2015/04/24/fiscal-year-2015-six-month-border-security-update.

US Department of Justice. "Attorney General William P. Barr's Statement on Riots and Domestic Terrorism." Press Release no. 20-500, May 31, 2020. https://www.justice.gov/opa/pr/attorney-general-william-p-barrs-statement-riots-and-domestic-terrorism.

US Department of State, Office of the Historian. "The Immigration Act of 1924 (The Johnson-Reed Act)." April 8, 2018. https://history.state.gov/milestones/1921-1936/immigration-act.

US Government Accountability Office. *Border Patrol: Available Data on Interior Checkpoints Suggest Differences in Sector Performance.* Washington, DC: US Government Publishing Office, July 2005. http://www.gao.gov/assets/250/247179.pdf.

US Government Accountability Office. *Border Security: Additional Actions Needed to Strengthen Collection of Unmanned Aerial Systems and Aerostats Data.* Washington, DC: US Government Publishing Office, February 16, 2017. https://www.gao.gov/assets/690/682842.pdf.

US Government Accountability Office. *Border Security: Key Unresolved Issues Justify Reevaluation of Border Surveillance Technology Program.* Washington, DC: US Government Publishing Office, February 22, 2006. https://www.gao.gov/products/gao-06-295.

US Government Accountability Office. *Secure Border Initiative: DHS Needs to Strengthen Management and Oversight of Its Prime Contractor.* Washington, DC: US Government Publishing Office, 2010. http://www.gao.gov/new.items/d116.pdf.

US Government Accountability Office. *Secure Border Initiative: SBInet Expenditure Plan Needs to Better Support Oversight and Accountability.* Washington, DC: US Government Publishing Office, February 15, 2007. https://www.gao.gov/products/gao-07-309.

Van Heijningen, Matthijs, Jr., dir. *The Thing.* Universal Pictures, 2011. Motion picture.

Ventura, Jesse. *American Conspiracies: Lies, Lies, and More Dirty Lies That the Government Tells Us*. New York: Skyhorse Publishing, 2010.

Veracini, Lorenzo. "*District 9* and *Avatar*: Science Fiction and Settler Colonialism." *Journal of Intercultural Studies* 32, no. 4 (August 2011): 355–67.

Veracini, Lorenzo. "Review: On Settler Colonialism and Science Fiction (Again)." *Settler Colonial Studies* 2, no. 1 (2012): 268–72.

Veracini, Lorenzo. *Settler Colonialism: A Theoretical Overview*. Basingstoke, Hants., England: Palgrave Macmillan, 2010.

Veracini, Lorenzo. *The Settler Colonial Present*. Basingstoke, Hants., England: Palgrave Macmillan, 2015.

Verhoeven, Paul, dir. *Starship Troopers*. TriStar Pictures, 1997. Motion picture.

Viveiros, Craig, dir. *The War of the Worlds*, season 1. Written by Peter Harness. BBC, 2019. Aired November 17, 2019, AMC.

Voruz, Véronique. "The Status of the Gaze in Surveillance Societies." In *Re-Reading Foucault: On Law, Power and Rights*, edited by Ben Golder, 127–50. Abingdon, Oxon., England: Routledge, 2013.

Wells, H. G. *Anticipations of the Reaction of Mechanical and Scientific Progress upon Human Life and Thought*. London: Chapman and Hall, 1902.

Wells, H. G. *The Invisible Man: A Grotesque Romance*. New York: Random House, 1996. First published 1897.

Wells, H. G. *The War of the Worlds*. Vancouver: AD Classics, 2008. First published 1898.

White, Jack R. "Herschel and the Puzzle of Infrared." *American Scientist* 100, no. 3 (May–June 2012): 218–25.

Whitehead, Alfred North. *Adventures of Ideas*. New York: Free Press, 1967.

Wimmer, Bob. "Warming Up to Thermal Imaging: History of Thermal Imaging." *Security Sales and Integration*, July 1, 2011, 1–7.

Wise, Robert, dir. *The Day the Earth Stood Still*. Twentieth Century Fox, 1951. Motion picture.

Witney, William, dir. *Wagon Train*, season 7, episode 2, "The Fort Pierce Story." Written by John McGreevey. Universal Television, 1963. Aired September 23, 1963.

Wolfe, Patrick. "Settler Colonialism and the Elimination of the Native." *Journal of Genocide Research* 8, no. 4 (2006): 387–409.

Wolfe, Patrick. *Settler Colonialism and the Transformation of Anthropology: The Politics and Poetics of an Ethnographic Event*. London: Continuum, 1998.

Woodruff Swan, Betsy. "DHS Draft Document: White Supremacists Are Greatest Terror Threat." *Politico*, September 4, 2020. https://www.politico.com/news/2020/09/04/white-supremacists-terror-threat-dhs-409236.

Yang, Sarah. "Invisibility Shields One Step Closer with New Metamaterials that Bend Light Backwards." *UC Berkeley News*, August 11, 2008. https://www.berkeley.edu/news/media/releases/2008/08/11_light.shtml.

Yar, Majid. "Panoptic Power and the Pathologisation of Vision: Critical Reflections on the Foucauldian Thesis." *Surveillance and Society* 1, no. 3 (January 2003): 254–71.

Zaleski, Andrew. "The Biggest Hijacking Threat Americans Face Today." *CNBC, The Hacking Economy*, February 2, 2016. https://www.cnbc.com/2016/02/01/the-biggest-hijacking-threat-americans-face-today.html.

INDEX

Accenture, 94, 99
activism, 25, 103, 106, 108, 111–13, 122, 124, 126–28
Adams, John, 3
Africa, 12–14, 69, 75, 97
Ahmed, Sarah, 7
Air and Marine Operations (US), 42
Air Force (US), 41–42, 61, 66, 125
airports, 92–94, 100–101, 126
Alexander, Michelle, 149n8
Alien, 36–39
alien affects, 4, 7–8, 12, 16–21, 24–25, 28, 34–41, 50–69, 72–73, 79–82, 94–102, 108, 111, 115, 118, 124, 135, 141n37, 151n49; theory, 7, 134, 141nn35–37, 158n6
Alien and Sedition Acts, 3
Alien Movie Project (AMP), 161n6
Alien vs. Predator, 38, 49, 55–57, 71
Alien vs. Predator: Requiem, 38, 49, 55–57, 62
Alien Resurrection, 38
alienation, 7, 11–12, 17, 21, 116
alienhood, 6–11, 19–21, 28, 35–43, 45, 52, 58, 67, 74, 77, 92, 95, 101, 111, 122, 140n22, 147n36
alien-making, 17, 23, 28–46, 133–35. See also intensity; invasion
Amalgamated Dynamics, 40
America's Shield Initiative (ASI), 63, 89–90, 99
Anderson, Paul W. S., 55–57
Antal, Nimród, 57

antifa, 14, 44, 136, 147n42
antitypes: alien, 9, 14, 19–26, 44, 62–72, 75, 86–97, 102–3, 107–8; settler, 6, 13–15, 44–48, 58, 132–35
ArcNet, 84–85
Arizona, 63, 100
Army (US), 47, 57, 62, 65, 125
Arness, James, 36
art, 25, 104–7, 113, 122, 125–28
articulable expressions, 6, 11, 19, 28, 73, 115, 128
Asia, 67, 69, 75, 97–98, 134
assemblages: arrangements, 19, 22, 106, 109–10; citizenship control, 8, 17–20, 25, 28, 36–49, 58–73, 87–91, 96, 102–8, 118, 123, 135; nomadic, 25–26, 104–28, 136–37; political, 36, 112, 135; state, 41, 85, 106, 110–13; territorial, 41, 108, 124–25; theory, 18–20, 135, 143n66, 146n21
attacks: alien, 35, 37, 54, 64, 129–30; colonial, 34, 40; drone, 115; 9/11, 138n4, 148n56; nomadic, 127; on US Capitol (January 6, 2021), 26, 132–33
Automated Biometric Identification System (IDENT), 93
Autumn Light Entertainment, 40
Avatar, 40

Badejo, Bolaji, 37
Baker, Rick, 79
Barr, William, 43–44, 147n42
BBC, 29

becoming: theory of, 140n21; colonized, 9
Berg, Charles R., 140n22
Berkeley, California, 65, 126
Biden, Joseph, 133, 139n18
biometrics, 25, 29, 75–88, 91–102, 138n4
biopolitics, 13, 114, 159n31
Black, Shane, 58, 150n32
Black people, 7, 9, 15, 23, 27, 31, 43, 48, 66, 133, 136, 143n56, 149n8, 156n52
Blade Runner, 146n23
Blue Sky Studios, 38
Boeing, 90, 99–100
Border Patrol (US), 20, 59–71, 74, 77–81, 88–93, 98–100, 123, 150n34
borders: checkpoints, 20, 25, 88, 92; México/US, 5–9, 16, 42–43, 49, 63–75, 91, 97–100, 104–7, 115–25, 133, 148n58, 153n79, 161n17; militias, 133, 161n17; wall, 42, 96, 148n58; zone, 76, 89, 94
borderlands, 8, 25, 49, 63, 68, 89, 109, 143n65
Boston Dynamics, 30–31
Bova, Raoul, 55
Boyle, Lara Flynn, 81
Bracero Program, 68–69, 96, 114
Braga, Alice, 57
Braidotti, Rosi, 109
Britain, 32–33, 37, 60
Brody, Adrien, 57
Brolin, Josh, 84
Buchanan, Ian, 146n18
Burton, Tim, 160n4
Busey, Gary, 54
Bush, George H. W., 73
Bush, George W., 45, 62, 90

California, 47, 50, 65, 126
cameras: film techniques, 28, 35, 50–51, 106; thermal, 52, 57, 61–65, 89. *See also* Closed-Circuit Television
camouflage, 50–56, 63–65
Canada: military, 150n33, 152n65; and US border, 42, 68
Cantor, Paul, 131, 160n4
capitalism, 6, 19, 106–7, 124, 140n23

Capitol Building (US), 26, 129–34, 161n17; January 6, 2021, attack on, 26, 132–33
capture, as subjective, 20–22, 71–72, 104, 113, 128
Cattle Queen of Montana, 47
Central America, 4, 6, 10, 50, 54, 64, 70, 75, 98, 127
Central Intelligence Agency (CIA), 50
Chatwin, Justin, 3
Chinese Exclusion Act, 68–69
cinema effects, 35–40, 49–58, 79–84, 124
Cinovation, 79
Cisneros, David, 140–41n24
citizens: binary, 14, 17, 23, 45; constitutive, 6, 8, 12, 16–19, 25, 43, 72, 86, 94, 107–8, 122, 134, 139n15. *See also* assemblages; settler colonialism
Clement, Jemaine, 84
Clinton, Bill, 8, 74–76, 86, 97, 102–3
cloaking, 25, 49–57
Closed-Circuit Television (CCTV), 62, 87–88, 94–95, 117
Coast Guard (US), 93
coding citizen/noncitizen subjects, 21–22, 39–40, 66–71, 87–92, 106–13
Colombia, 127
colonialism: anxiety, 6–9, 13–15, 24, 28, 31, 41; binary, 13, 23, 142n44; culture of, 34; imperial, 12–13, 23–24, 28, 32–34, 108–9, 132; and invasion, 14, 64, 69; and logics, 8–10, 15–19, 24, 27, 33–34, 80, 86, 94, 131–35, 136; post-, 13; thought, 16, 108
color films, 36, 62
Columbia Pictures, 76
combat: with aliens, 55; and technology, 60–61, 64–65, 87, 99
communication: studies of, 6–7, 17–18, 134; and technology, 4, 20, 89, 104
computer-generated imagery (CGI), 3, 16, 28–29, 38–40, 56–57, 79–84, 95, 106, 114–18, 124, 147n36, 160n4
Congress (US), 45, 67, 69, 72, 75–76, 101, 129–33; appropriations, 70, 99, 101
Constitution (US): free zone, 76; First Amendment, 101

consumers, 30–31, 122, 124–25
contracts: government, 62–63, 71–72, 89, 94; settler, 132–33
COVID-19 pandemic, 108, 134
criminality, 11, 48, 102, 136; cross-border, 41
Cruise, Tom, 2–3, 31–32
Culp, Andrew, 19, 140n23, 143n68
Customs and Border Protection (CBP): agents, 59, 70, 77–78, 81, 88, 92–93; budget, 42, 71; history of, 68–71, 89, 99–100, 157n58; and technology, 41, 44, 59–66, 72–74, 88–93, 98–103, 123
Cybracero, 114

da Silva, Denise Ferreira, 145n1
databases, 76, 80, 92–93
Day the Earth Stood Still, The (1953 film), 35, 146n18
Day the Earth Stood Still, The (2008 film), 146n18
De León, Jason, 139n17
death lands, 132–33
Death Valley Days, 47
DeChaine, D. Robert, 153n79
Delanda, Manuel, 38, 143n66
Deleuze, Gilles, 19, 22, 109–10, 140n21, 141n35, 144n68, 146n21
democracy, 131–34
Department of Homeland Security (DHS), 9, 43–45, 62–66, 71, 75, 86–94, 99–100, 122–23, 148n56, 148n58
Department of Justice (US), 62, 147n42
deportation, 6–7, 69–70, 75–76, 90, 140n24
Derrickson, Scott, 146n18
desert, 77–78, 105
Digiscope, 40
disavowals, 14–15, 24, 28, 34, 41
discourse: discursive subject, 74–75, 102, 134; public, 9, 16, 19, 66, 101
DNA, 29–30, 92
Double Negative Studio, 56–57
drones: in films, 116–22; hacking, 122–26; and stealth technology, 65. *See also* MQ-9 Reaper

drugs: trafficking of, 48–49, 99, 123. *See also* War on Drugs
Dunbar-Ortiz, Roxanna, 16

Earth vs. the Flying Saucers, 131, 160n4
Ebert, Roger, 37
economy, extractive, 16, 70, 86, 108, 112, 114, 135–36, 149n8
Edgar-Jones, Daisy, 30
Edison, Thomas, 87
El Paso, Texas, 68, 71, 74, 88, 91, 104–5
Emmerich, Roland, 33
England, 29
entertainment industries, 16, 26, 125–26
environment, settler, 13–14, 51, 117
E.T. The Extraterrestrial, 39

facial recognition technology, 92–94, 100, 148n58
fingerprints, 92–93, 100
flashbulb narration, 77, 84, 86–87, 94–97, 101–2
FLIR Systems, 60–63, 71, 90. *See also* front-looking infrared
Flores, Lisa, 140n24
Floyd, George, 28, 41, 43
flying saucers, 33, 130–31
force multiplier, 59, 62, 72, 86, 92, 102
forgetting, 15, 22–23
Foucault, Michel, 11, 141n33, 141n35
Fox News, 101–2
Fox/Canal, 29–33
France, 3, 25
front-looking infrared (FLIR), 61–65, 71, 80, 151n49. *See also* FLIR Systems

Gbadamosi, Bayo, 30
General Dynamics, 63, 71, 90
genocide, 12, 27, 29–33
Glover, Danny, 54
Goldwater, Barry, 47, 131
ground sensors, 62, 88
Guatemala, 5
Guattari, Félix, 19, 110, 140n21, 143n66, 144n70

Haas, Lucas, 130–31
hacking, 116, 122–24, 136
Hall, Kevin Peter, 50, 53
Hamilton, Richard, 75
Hart-Celler Act, 69–70, 97–98
Hawking, Stephen, 32–33
HAZMED, 89
heat rays, 3, 44
Hemsworth, Chris, 85
Herschel, William, 60
Holbrook, Boyd, 57
Hollywood, 4, 8–10, 16, 21, 28, 34–41, 47, 58, 106, 122–25, 135, 140n22, 160n4
Honeywell, 60–61
Hopkins, Stephen, 53, 61
House of Representatives (US), 72, 100–101
human rights, 138n7, 139n15
Hunter/Gratzner Industries, 40
Hurt, John, 37
Hynek, Joel, 51–53

Illegal Immigration Reform and Immigrant Responsibility Act (IIRIRA), 75–76, 86, 102
imaging technologies, 6–7, 39, 134. *See also* thermal imaging
Immigrant Status Indicator Technology (US-VISIT), 100
Immigration and Customs Enforcement (ICE): agents, 41–44, 92–93, 102; budget, 42, 75; history of, 75–76, 82, 157n58; technology, 41, 87–94, 99, 123
Immigration and Nationality Act. *See* Hart-Celler Act
Immigration and Naturalization Service (INS), 62, 78, 88, 93
Immigration Reform and Control Act (Simpson-Mazzoli Act), 70
imperialism. *See* colonialism
Independence Day, 23, 33, 131, 161n10
Indigenous peoples, 12–16, 22–23, 27, 31–34, 42, 66, 109, 133, 142n49; erasing, 14–15, 23–24, 32, 142n49; and lands, 15, 23, 127; sovereignty of, 127, 134–36
individualism, 23, 47–48, 132

Industrial Light and Magic (ILM), 38, 40, 79, 82
infrared thermal cameras, 52, 57, 61–65, 89. *See also* front-looking infrared; FLIR systems
Integrated Microwave Corporation (IMC), 89
Integrated Surveillance Intelligence System (ISIS), 62–63, 87–90, 99
Intelligent Computer-Aided Detection (ICAD), 88–92, 99
intensity: affect as, 4; alien affects as, 7, 20, 29, 92, 109; movement, 53, 91, 94, 140n21
internet news, 95–96, 101
invasion: alien, 11, 29–41, 43–45, 48–55, 77–84, 95–96, 102–3, 107, 115, 129–32; extraterrestrial, 3, 6–9, 16, 23–28, 32, 39, 43, 76–79, 107
invisibility, 21, 37, 44, 50–52, 64–66, 77
iris scans, 92–93, 100. *See also* biometrics

Jeunet, Jean-Pierre, 38
Johnson-Reed Act, 67–69, 99
Joint Terrorism Task Forces, 147n44
Jones, Tommy Lee, 77, 80–81, 84
jungles, 50–53, 64
Jurassic Park, 50

Kiwi Bots, 126–27
knowledge: as power, 10–11; production, 10, 18, 149n14

labor: exploitation, 14–15, 66, 70, 79, 86, 101–2, 135, 143n49; migrant, 13, 68, 77, 96, 114–16, 119–27
Labor Appropriations Act of 1924, 68, 153n78
Lafayette Square (Washington, DC), 43–44
Lathan, Sanaa, 55–56
Latina/o/x, 134, 140n22, 140n24, 149n8
law: enforcement agencies, 6, 18, 40–45, 63, 92–94, 99–100, 122–23, 147n42; immigration, 67, 76, 86–87, 101; and order as political trope, 7, 44, 48
Law and Order (1953 film), 47

Led Zeppelin, 23, 144n79
lights, 10–12, 17–22, 28, 35–40, 50–57, 60–65, 80–87, 94–96, 104–6, 111, 134, 156–57n52
logics: colonial, 8–10, 15–19, 24, 33–34, 80, 86, 94, 131–35; organizing, 109–13, 136
Los Angeles, California, 42–43, 53, 64, 100
Lozano-Hemmer, Rafael, 104–5, 108
L-3 Communications, 89–90, 99
Lucas, George, 38–40, 80. See also Industrial Light and Magic; Star Wars
lynching, 133

maquiladora, 115–16
Marciniak, Katarzyna, 140n22
Markie, Biz, 83
Mars Attacks!, 26, 39–40, 129–32, 161n10
Massumi, Brian, 106, 141n35, 158n6
McCarran-Walter Act, 69–70, 97–98
McTiernan, John, 50–53, 61
media: popular, 16, 23–26, 87, 95–96, 101–2, 116, 133; studies of, 9–15, 134; technologies of, 9, 102, 114
memory: collective, 32; economy, 119–20; erasing, 76, 81–82
Men in Black (MiB) franchise, 8, 23, 33, 39, 115, 118, 124, 147n36; technologies, 9, 25, 74–102
Men in Black (1997 film), 76–81
Men in Black: International, 76, 85–86
Men in Black 3, 76, 84–85
Men in Black II, 76, 81–84
Mestiza/o/x people, 7, 22–23, 27, 31, 42, 66, 69, 124, 133–34
metamaterials, 65, 152n65
metropole, 47, 56–57, 132, 149n14
México: in film, 53, 55, 57, 115–22, 124; "Remain in Mexico" policy, 5. See also borders
microbolometer, 61
migration, 4, 7–18, 26, 45, 75–76, 88, 95–103, 134; quota, 67–69, 97. See also Hart-Celler Act
migrants: as aliens, 5–12, 16, 19–22, 71–72, 88–89; anti-, 8–9, 19, 44, 48, 69, 88, 96, 101, 124; apprehension of, 25, 70, 85, 133, 139n18; and asylum, 5, 70, 76–78; capture of, 49, 73, 97, 111; computerized tracking systems, 87, 89, 99–100; criminalizing, 4, 68, 73, 96, 104; detention of, 6–7, 21, 42, 45, 66, 75, 86, 90, 96, 102; entering the US without authorization, 6, 70, 76, 78; exclusion from US, 13, 67–70, 139n15, 153n78; exploitation of, 5, 7, 10, 20, 66, 102–8, 114, 119, 134, 145n1; expulsion of, 10, 20, 94, 97, 103, 105; identifying, 59, 75–76; from Mexico, 4–10, 68, 70–71, 75, 98, 114–15, 127; removal of, 4, 45, 69–70, 73–76, 80, 90–91, 103; status, 93. See also Chinese Exclusion Act; Immigrant Status Indicator Technology; National Defense Authorization Act of 1991
military intelligence, 59. See also Integrated Surveillance Intelligence System
militias, 133, 161n17
Minneapolis, Minnesota, 28, 41–43, 73, 102–3
mobile video surveillance system (MVSS), 90
mobility: global migration, 4–5; of settler citizenship, 39, 98, 132
MQ-9 Reaper (Predator B Drone), 42–43, 63–66, 71–73, 90, 102, 122

Nail, Thomas, 105, 112
narcotics. See drugs
National Commission on Terrorist Attacks upon the United States (9/11 Commission), 45, 100, 138n4, 148n56
National Defense Authorization Act of 1991, 49
National Guard (US), 49
nationalism, settler, 4, 6, 8, 24, 131–33
Natives. See Indigenous peoples
naturalization, 15, 67, 69. See also Immigration and Naturalization Services
Navy (US), 61, 125, 149n14
neoliberalism, 98, 118
neuralyzers, 25, 76, 80–85, 94
Nicholson, Jack, 129–30

nomad thought, 7, 25–26, 103, 104–28, 136, 158n6
Nyby, Christian, 36

Oath Keepers, 133, 161n17
Oaxaca, 115–22, 127
Obama, Barak, 71
occupation, settler, 7–8, 13, 15, 19, 66–67, 92, 97, 102, 117
Office of the Inspector General (OIG), 89
Operation Gatekeeper, 71, 74, 88, 91
Operation Hold the Line, 71, 74, 88, 91
optical machine, 21–22, 40
Ore, Ersula, 133
Otay Mesa Port of Entry, 94

panopticon, 11–12, 21, 28, 141n33, 141n35
Pentagon (US), 125
police brutality, 9, 41, 43, 73, 102
popular culture, 34, 7, 9, 28
Portland, Oregon, 44
Portman, Natalie, 130
ports of entry, 68, 74, 94, 98–101, 138n4
power: autoproduction of colonial, 10, 14–15, 25, 27, 50, 111, 140n23; cuts in flows of, 17, 106–7, 110–13, 158n6; diagram of, 11, 21, 141n35
Predator (1987 film), 49–53, 61, 63
Predator, The (2018 film), 49, 57–58
Predator B Drone. *See* MQ-9 Reaper
Predator franchise, 33, 49–73, 147n36; commandos in, 50–53. See also *Alien vs. Predator*; *Alien vs. Predator: Requiem*
Predator Technologies, 8, 25, 49–73, 74, 91, 98
Predator 2, 49, 53–55, 61, 63, 71
Predators (2010 film), 49, 57
Prey, 49
prisons, 5, 11, 21, 87, 136, 149n8
protests, 28, 41–45, 73, 102–3, 133, 147n42
puppets, 36–40, 79

queen: alien, 56; *Cattle Queen of Montana*, 47

race: alien, 33, 76, 130; and politics, 4, 13, 15, 27, 69, 76, 80, 86, 136, 139n15, 145n1

Raytheon, 60–61
Reagan, Ronald, 8, 47–50, 74, 97, 103, 149n8; directive no. 221, 49; speeches, 47–48, 66
REAL-ID Act, 45, 148, 56, 148n58
remote vehicle surveillance (RVS), 62–63, 89–91, 71–72
Reyes, Silvestre, 89
R/Greenberg, 51, 53
rhetoric, 9–21, 45, 133–35, 140–41n24, 143n68; materialist, 10, 17–20, 22, 50, 77, 103, 113, 127, 135
Rifkin, Mark, 142n69
Rivera, Alex, 106, 114–22, 124–28, 136
Robley, Les Paul, 51
robots, 36, 114–22, 124, 126–27
Rube Goldberg Machine, 36, 146n21

SAFE Act, 100
San Diego, California, 71, 74, 88, 91, 94, 119
San Francisco, California, 42, 126
Secure Borders Initiative (SBI), 63, 90; SBInet, 87, 90–91, 98–99
Schwarzenegger, Arnold, 50
Scott, Ridley, 37–38, 146n23
Seigworth, Gregory J., and Melissa Gregg, 141n37
seismic sensors, 49, 62, 88–89
self-defense, settler, 23, 40, 95, 117; claims of, 22; and land/sovereignty, 15, 26, 132
self-government, settler, 47, 131
Senate (US), 49, 72, 99–100
settler colonialism: ideology of, 7–8, 24–25, 34, 72, 96, 110; as imaginary, 24, 130; societies of, 5, 12, 19–21, 26, 34; theory of, 12–17, 27, 134–36; US, 6, 8, 12–17, 20, 86, 92, 95, 110
shimmers, 12, 22, 35–37, 49–50, 52, 141n37, 147n36
situational awareness, 41, 43, 59, 72, 91–92, 102
Sleep Dealer, 26, 104–28, 136, 160n54; Cybraceros in, 116, 119–21; and radios, 116, 123
Smith, Will, 80–84
social movements, 19, 118

societies: of control, 22, 71, 87, 95, 107, 109, 126, 141n35; discipline, 11–12, 21, 141n33, 141n35
sovereignty, settler, 12, 14–15, 23–26, 47–50, 56, 66, 107–8, 132–36. *See also* Indigenous peoples
Spielberg, Steven, 3, 31, 39, 80, 138n2
Stan Winston Studios, 50, 53
Star Trek, 33, 39, 64
Star Wars, 23–24, 33, 36–40
Starship Troopers, 39
Strause, Colin and Greg, 57
subalterns, 13–15, 23–24, 28, 35, 48, 56, 145n1
Superman II, 131
surveillance: aerial, 42–43, 60, 63, 116, 122; border, 49, 59–66, 70–72, 87–94, 99–101, 123, 127; equipment, 59, 88–89, 95, 100; technology, 34, 41–43, 87–88, 95, 99–101, 107, 123–24, 134

television, 23–24, 32–35, 41, 47, 58, 62–64, 87–88, 95–96, 101, 116, 129
terra nullius, 23–24, 132
terrorism: as antitype, 3, 11, 14, 45, 59, 73, 102, 116–17, 148n58; domestic, 42–45, 147n42; war on, 45, 138n4. *See also* National Commission on Terrorist Attacks upon the United States
Texas, 63, 100, 139n7
Texas Instruments, 60–61
thermal imaging, 49–66, 70–72, 88–89
Thing, The (1982 film), 146n18
Thing, The (2011 film), 146n18
Thing from Another World, The (1951 film), 35–36, 146n18
Thomas, Jim and John, 53, 150n23
Thompson, Krista, 156–57n52
Thompson, Tessa, 85
Tijuana, 118, 120
time loops, settler, 142n49
Transformers: Dark of the Moon, 131
Transformers: Revenge of the Fallen, 125
Transportation Security Administration (TSA), 93
tropes, 7–8, 39, 95, 132, 135

Troublemaker Studios, 150n31
Trump, Donald, 9, 28, 43–45, 72, 95, 101, 148n56, 148n58, 161n17
truth, 10–11, 15, 81. *See also* forgetting

United States of America: and Canadian border, 42, 68; constitutional rights in, 45, 67, 101–2, 108, 132; economy, 8, 79, 114, 119–22; elections, 44, 47, 73, 95–96, 133; entry of migrants into, 5, 49, 68, 88–90, 98–101, 148n56; exit from, 100–101; migrant exclusion from, 13, 67–70, 139n15, 153n78; migrants entering without authorization, 6, 70, 76, 78; 9/11 attacks, 138n4, 148n56; settler colonialism in, 6, 8, 12–17, 20, 86, 92, 95, 110
Unmanned Aircraft (UAVs), 59, 63, 65, 90–91, 122. *See also* drones; MQ-9 Reaper
Urry, John, 4
US Visitor and Immigrant Status Indicator Technology (US-VISIT), 100

Varela, Leonor, 118
Ventura, Jesse, 150n14
Veracini, Lorenzo, 14, 135, 142nn44–45
vigilantes, 133–34, 153n79, 161n19
virtual borders, 76–77, 84–91, 100, 102
virtual reality, 118
Vision Art Studios, 40

Wagon Train, 47
War of the Worlds (2005 film), 2–3, 31–33, 131, 138n2
War of the Worlds (2019 BBC Series), 29
War of the Worlds, The (1898 novel). *See* Wells, H. G.
War of the Worlds, The (2019 Fox/Canal), 29–31, 33
War of the Worlds franchise, 7, 24, 27–46
War on Drugs, 66, 97, 99, 149n8, 157n58
Washington, DC, 43, 100, 130–33
Wells, H. G.: *Anticipations of the Reaction of Mechanical and Scientific Progress upon Human Life and Thought*, 33;

The Invisible Man, 64; *The War of the Worlds*, 3, 24, 27–34, 39, 44, 64
whiteness, 13; and settler citizenship, 3, 16–18, 133–36, 139n18; and supremacy, 14, 19, 69
Wolfe, Patrick, 27
World Trade Center, 3
World War I, 29
World War II, 69, 87, 96

Xenomorph, 37–38, 49–58
X-rays, 57, 129

Yautja, 25, 49–58, 64

ABOUT THE AUTHOR

Credits: Photo by Anaís Lechuga

Professor **Michael Lechuga** researches and teaches cultural studies, settler colonialism, border studies, communication studies, rhetoric, and affect studies. He received his PhD from the University of Denver in 2016 and is currently an assistant professor of culture and communication at the University of New Mexico. He investigates the ways settler colonial logics and white nationalist ideologies persist in migrant control discourses, border security mechanisms, and the control technologies that subject migrant and Indigenous communities to violence, imprisonment, and death. Additionally, Professor Lechuga is interested in Indigenous/Xicanx futurism, surveillance studies, film studies, and mixed reality studies, which frame his work on how mainstream film, television, and gaming technologies circulate settler narratives to normalize colonial logics.

www.ingramcontent.com/pod-product-compliance
Lightning Source LLC
Chambersburg PA
CBHW030344240426
43661CB00052B/1739